# International Relations

## New Horizons and Changing Equations

# International Relations

## New Horizons and Changing Equations

Volume I

Biswaranjan Mohanty

ATLANTIC

PUBLISHERS & DISTRIBUTORS (P) LTD

Published by

**ATLANTIC**

**PUBLISHERS & DISTRIBUTORS (P) LTD**

7/22, Ansari Road, Darya Ganj, New Delhi-110002
Phones : +91-11-40775252, 40775214, 23273880, 23275880
Fax : +91-11-23285873
Web : www.atlanticbooks.com
E-mail : orders@atlanticbooks.com

**Branch Office: Chennai**
Phones : +91-44-48531784, 28291383
E-mail : chennai@atlanticbooks.com



Printed & bound in India by Atlantic Print Services

# Preface

The history of International Relations dates back to antiquity and remains one of the most vital disciplines in Political Science. Its purpose is to explore the everlasting questions of the origins of war and the maintenance of peace, the nature and exercise of power within an international system, and the changing character of the actors (both state and non-state) who participate in the various dimensions of international decision-making. The study of International Relations has traditionally focused on the competition for power among rival states. Today, the world has entered an era of multipolarization. So, the horizons of International Relations have become diversified in recent years with non-state and intergovernmental actors such as non-governmental organizations, multinational corporations, transnational diasporas, and organizations like the United Nations exerting a strong influence in international affairs. Furthermore, International Relations have become more complicated by an increase in the relative importance of international economic problems and by the fact that economic problems tend to become political issues with the intensification of interdependence among nations. The multiple dimensions of power go beyond the distribution of economic and military capabilities and include class, gender, culture, and discourse in contemporary international affairs.

I have tried to portray the expanding spheres of International Relations in this book with an understanding of leading approaches to the study of world politics. I have also attempted to describe the complexity of world politics and explain how new forces shaping the planet have changed our world. I hope this book will help to build deeper insights on the subject and develop an appreciation for the evolving relationships between the states. Besides, it will prove highly useful to the students and teachers of International Relations and researchers in this field.

In the preparation of the book, I have derived great help from the vast collection of literature on international issues in JNU library, Teen Murti library and Delhi University library. I am extremely thankful to Prof. S.D. Muni (JNU), Prof. C.P. Bhambri (JNU) and Prof. Ranganath Mishra (former Chief Justice of India and Chairman of NHRC) for extending their support for writing this book. I also express my deep gratitude to Prof. Ashwini Ray, Prof. Gurpreet Mahajan and Prof. Vidyut Chakravarty for being the source of encouragement in the preparation of the book. I thank Atlantic Publishers and Distributors (P) Ltd. for evincing interest in publishing this book. Last but not least, I thank my parents and family members for their strong moral support and standing by me through my thick and thin.

**Biswaranjan Mohanty**

# Contents

*Preface* *v*

**VOLUME 1**

1. Introduction 1
2. The Modern State 42
3. Theoretical Paradigm and Approaches in International Relations 63
4. Power Analysis and Balance of Power 137
5. National Interest 198
6. Development Discourse in International Relations 219
7. Cold War and Multipolarity 241
8. Determinants of Foreign Policy 267
9. Watershed Development of India's Foreign Policy 285

**VOLUME 2**

10. Ideology in International Relations 337
11. Third World in International Relations 353
12. Non-Alignment: Concept and Movement 364
13. Evolution of the International Economic System 398
14. Conflict and Cooperation in South Asia 437

15. Regional Organizations 476

16. International Organizations: UN and its Specialized Agencies 542

17. Contemporary Global Concerns in International Relations 600

*Bibliography* 634

# 1 Introduction

International relations is concerned with a systematic body of knowledge and understanding of government and society. The horizon of international relations is expanding day by day in the era of liberalization, privatization and globalization.[1] The study of international relations has traditionally focussed on the competition for power among rival states. Today, however, non-state and intergovernmental actors such as non-governmental organizations, multinational corporations, transnational diasporas, and organizations like the United Nations also exert important influence in international affairs. International relations is far behind other social sciences in the development of theories. It is quite natural as this discipline is of recent origin. Notwithstanding this limitation, some notable developments have already taken place in the sphere of theory building. The works of Hans J. Morgenthau, J. David Singer, Horace Harrison, James Rosenau, Morton Kaplan, J.W. Burton, William Fox, Stanley Hoffmann, Klaus Knorr, Sydney Verba, etc. have endeavoured to develop a theoretical perspective of this discipline. Efforts to propound a general theory of international relations are inspired by a number of factors. First of all, they are impressed and encouraged by the achievement of the natural sciences in precision and predictability.

A theory is very useful in bringing about an order in a mass of data. It may work as a guide to action in international life. It is a crucial tool for understanding that gives meaning to mass of phenomena. It would make international relations a real policy science that would be of great help to statesmen and decision-makers. It is also useful for further creative research. Thus, the significance of theoretical speculation and perspective in international relations cannot be ignored. International relations is considered wider in scope as it is the study of totality of relations of any people and groups in the world society.[2]

The interaction of people, ideas and institutions provide the basic understanding and the values of the society which are allocated and resources are distributed at many levels from the local through the sectoral, national, regional and global. Thus, it analyses of who gets what, when, how, why and where are central, and pertain to related questions of power, justice, order, conflict, legitimacy, accountability, obligation, sovereignty and decision-making. Politics encompasses philosophical, theoretical, institutional and issue-based concerns relating to governance.[3]

It covers all aspects of relations between countries and people, political or non-political, peaceful or war like, legal or cultural, economic or geographic, official or non-official. According to Harold and Margaret Sprout,[4] the term is used to designate all human behaviour on one side of a national boundary affecting the human behaviour on the other side of the boundary. The term relations has variety of meanings as contacts, connections and action and reaction, some scholars consider the international relations as an action on the part of a group—state or government directed towards another group which reacts to it.[5]

International relations is the study of the relations of states with each other and with international organizations and certain sub-national entities. International relations is treated as a branch of political science. It is concerned with the study of foreign policy objectives and conduct relations among states within the international system.[6] The parameters of international relations include the roles of civil society, states, intergovernmental organizations (IGOs), non-governmental organizations (NGOs), and multinational corporations (MNCs). So, to speak, the term international relations has a much wider connotation than international politics insofar as it embraces all sorts of relations among peoples and groups in the world society and these relations operate both at the official as well as non-official levels. But international politics includes only those aspects of international relations in which some conflict of purpose or interest is involved. As international relations is a study involving sovereign states, technically there could not be any international relations before the emergence of the nation states. But actually the principles and techniques of the international relations can be traced back, though in quite rudimentary form, to the ancient period of human history.

International relations shares the concerns of politics, but its focus is the regional and global arenas. Traditionally, preoccupied with anarchy (the absence of international or global government), the conflictual and co-operative engagement between states, international relations is increasingly concerned with engagement between states, intergovernmental organizations and non-state actors such as transnational corporations and transnational civil society groups. Aristotle said: "Man by nature and necessity is a social animal. A man who can live without other beings is either a God or a beast." In modern times, we can safely say that no nation or country can live in isolation. Co-existence of nations is the order of the day. No doubt, every nation is independent and sovereign, nevertheless it counts on other nations of the world in several respects. Cordial relations and understanding among nations have become an important phenomenon of modern life. International relations have thus assumed great pragmatic and academic significance in present times.

In simple term, it deals with world affairs and examines some of the critical issues of modern times such as:

- Changing nature of international cooperation and conflict
- The new character of warfare
- The impact of globalization upon the state and the societies
- The role of non-state actors
- The persistence of global problems such as war, poverty, migration and environment.

International relations explores the origins and evolution of the state system, and ideas of sovereignty, justice, democracy, legitimacy and order in an international context. It focuses on the changing nature of state power, the role of non-state actors, the spread of new norms and ideas, and the driving forces behind international cooperation and conflict.

It addresses the major issues of war and peace, but it goes beyond that. It investigates security and prosperity in the international system, including contending approaches to such questions as combating international terrorism and creating a fair international economic system. In addition, it touches on many regional and specialized topics such as international organizations, the Middle East, US foreign policy, European integration, and Africa, etc. in world politics.

Events in other parts of the world affect us as never before. 'Globalization' means that information and news are available virtually instantly, leading to a sense of connectedness that often brings new demands upon leaders of wealthy and powerful states. At the same time, the nature of international cooperation has become far more complex and technical, often removing decision-makers from the scrutiny of ordinary citizens.

How states manage these changes, and deal with competing and contradictory demands, is extremely important for the international system. This book will lead to a thorough understanding of the shifting nature of international cooperation and conflict, how ethical considerations might be incorporated into international relations, how new groups are making their voices heard, new ideas are being articulated, and new issues are rising up the agenda.

## INTERNATIONAL RELATIONS AND INTERNATIONAL LAW

The territorial sovereign and nation state emerged as a basic political unit and an effective actor in international relations. These sovereign states were very much aware of their independence yet they were also conscious about the reality of interdependence in the modern world. Modern international relations began to grow in the paradoxical situation of independence and interdependence, separateness, and closeness, individuality and mutality, nationalism, and internationalism. They continued to develop as a process of co-operation and conflict. In international law, sovereignty is the legitimate exercise of power by a state. *De jure* sovereignty is the legal right to do so; *de facto* sovereignty is the ability in fact to do so (which becomes of special concern upon the failure of the usual expectation that *de jure* and *de facto* sovereignty exist at the place and time of concern, and rest in the same organization). Foreign governments recognize the sovereignty of a state over a territory, or refuse to do so.

For instance, in theory, both the People's Republic of China and the Republic of China considered themselves sovereign governments over the whole territory of mainland China and Taiwan. Though some foreign governments recognize the Republic of China as the valid state, most now recognize the People's Republic of China. However, *de facto*, the People's Republic of China exercises sovereign power over mainland China but not Taiwan, while the Republic of China exercises its effective administration only over Taiwan and some outlying islands but not mainland China. Since ambassadors are only exchanged between sovereign high parties, the countries recognizing the People's Republic often entertain *de facto* but not *de jure* diplomatic relationships with Taiwan by maintaining 'offices of representation' such as the American Institute in Taiwan, rather than embassies there.

The autonomous province of Kosovo in Serbia provides a somewhat similar example, where the government of Serbia remains the *de jure* sovereign power but the United Nations has exercised *de facto* control since 1999. The province is still recognized as part of Serbia, though the Serbian government has no practical authority on the ground.

The same principle applies to internationally unrecognized separatist states such as Abkhazia in Georgia and Transnistria in Moldova. All are treated in international law as territory subject to the authority of the internationally recognized national government, even where that government has no *de facto* control of the territory.

Sovereignty may be recognized even when the sovereign body possesses no territory or its territory is under partial or total occupation by another power. The Holy See was in this position between the annexation in 1870 of the Papal States by

Italy and the signing of the Lateran Treaties in 1929, when it was recognized as sovereign by many (mostly Roman Catholic) states despite possessing no territory—a situation resolved when the Lateran Treaties granted the Holy See sovereignty over the Vatican City. The Sovereign Military Order of Malta is likewise a non-territorial body that claims to be a sovereign entity, though it is not universally recognized as such.[7]

Similarly, the governments-in-exile of many European states (for instance, Norway and the Netherlands) during the Second World War were regarded as sovereign despite their territories being under foreign occupation; their governance resumed as soon as the occupation had ended. The government of Kuwait was in a similar situation *vis-á-vis* the Iraqi occupation of its country during 1990-91.

## NATURE OF INTERNATIONAL RELATIONS

The term international relations is the totality of its dealings with the external environment. The nature of international relations can be easily assessed from its outside factors. It is the complex and dynamic political course that a nation follows in relation to other states. International relations contains three elements—goals or objectives, policy plans and actual actions undertaken by a state to regulate its external relations. Thus, it is a systematic statement of deliberately selected national interests, for achieving objectives in foreign relations by regulating the behaviour of other states. To define the meaning of and nature of international relations is a ticklish job. It has been a complex work owing to many reasons. First, the terms of international politics and international relations were and still used interchangeably and loosely. International relations perennially faces the question: What should the national goals be? The answer to this question we call foreign policy, and it is at once evident that not everything that could conceivably be desired is obtainable. In the days of the Congress of Vienna in 1815, small powers were actually referred to as 'powers with limited interests'.

The nature and scope of international relations are limited for great states as well as small states. No matter how much international relations is limited both absolutely and relatively. It is limited absolutely, for example, in terms of annual production of steel, coal, and oil. It is limited relatively in that the national appetite in foreign policy matters is always bigger than it can afford the power at its disposal. The list of wants is infinite, and each must be considered against every other. Consequently, the formulation of a realistic foreign policy must always being with an appraisal of the power reserve upon which it must rest. For many years, scholars remained confused over the contents of these terms.

The term international relations overdraws its bank account of power in courting, and often finds itself visited by, disaster. Yet even when a state attempts to keep its policy carefully equated with its power, it encounter at the outset several practical difficulties in following a rational policy. They were not clear as to what should be included in international politics and what in international relations. Second, world community is so dynamic and international environment changes so rapidly that what one studies few years ago with keen interest becomes obsolete today.[8] With this alters its approach and perspective. New developments at global level bring new actors to international stage. Third, many scholars put forward such definitions as explained the essence of the subject rather than its main areas of inquiry. This caused further disagreement and confusion among writers as no one could give with precision and authority the definition of a discipline whose scope is everchanging and growing. Fourth, newness of the subject also creates many difficulties in defining it. If definitions of old social disciplines like political science and economics are still in the melting pot then how can one take any definition of this young discipline as a last word.

The multiple dimensions of power go beyond the distribution of economic and military capabilities and include class, gender, culture, and discourse. The "international" in international relations is moreover inseparable from domestic concerns and is as much about co-operation and compromise among international actors as it is about competition and conflict.

The nature of international relations can be judged from the following perspectives:

### Size

The land area or size of a country influences the international relations of a country. Large states have more probabilities of becoming big power. In today's world, USA, China, Russia, India are bound to play effective role in the world politics in account of their vast size. Small states like Nepal, Bhutan, etc. can play an important role in moral politics. In the 19th and 20th century, Japan was an economic power and threatened not to overcome US in the economic sphere. Similarly, the oil-rich countries of the Middle East though small in size are playing significant role in international politics.

### Geography

India adopted Non-alignment as an international policy objective on account of geographical location. USA is also playing an effective role in geographical location on account of their geostrategic importance. US's isolationist policy could be a reference point in this regard.

### Culture/History

The culture and historical traditions of a country also deeply influences international policy of a country. Those countries which are culturally and historically fragmented cannot pursue an effective foreign policy.

### Economic Development

Industrially, advanced countries can pursue an independent international policy objectives whereas a backward nation is inclined to a dependent foreign policy. An industrial country can devote greater funds for external purpose. In recent years, the US has been able to pursue more vigorous foreign policy and secure national objectives on account of economic development.

### Technology

Advancement in technology which affects the military, industrial and communication capabilities of a state, also exercised profound influence. For example, USA, China, Russia, have the most specialized technologies of nuclear missiles.

### National and Military Capacity

It includes the military preparedness of a state. The economic development and enlightened political institutions are also associated with national capacity. National capacity determines as well as executes foreign policy effectively. If the state increases its national capacity, international relations undergoes radical transformation. For example, Britain after World War II considerably changed her foreign policy mainly due to decline in her national capacity. The US foreign policy is in progress due to military and economic group success.

### Social Structure

Homogenous society and national morale can pursue an effective international relations between the countries.

### Public Mood

In a democratic system based on political accountability, public opinion cannot be ignored as one of the determinants of international relations. Public opinion should be expressed in clear terms. It is well known that the US government was forced to withdraw the American forces from the South Vietnam and Krishna Menon had to resign in 1962 after the Chinese aggression due to the hostile public opinion in their respective countries.

### Leadership

Leadership determines the strength, and the direction of the working of international relations. In fact, policy decisions in external matters can never be separated from the psychological traits, intellectual strength, the personality or the predisposition of the leaders.

### Ideology

There has been a great debate on whether ideology *per se* acts as a parameter of international relations. Sometimes, a nation goes to a war not for national security, but only to compel others to subscribe to its ideology. Russian expansion after 1945 aimed at world revolution, establishment of Communism as much as her political domination.

### Domestic Instability

Sometimes, domestic instability also works as a basic parameter of international relations. It is a common saying that Pakistan has been continuously following a hostile attitude towards India and is popping up the Kashmir dispute as it has never been able to deal with numerous domestic issues challenging its existence. The Clinton administration took action against Iraq and Afghanistan in 1998 to divert the attention of the Americans from the Monica-Lewinsky affair.

## INTERNATIONAL RELATIONS AND EXTERNAL FACTORS

### 1. Power Structure (Global Strategic Environment)

- It affects the policy of a country
- Balance of power system
- Globalization trends and interdependence
- Partnership of power between government and market.

### 2. International Organizations

IMR, World Bank, WTO, NATO, ASEAN, EU, SAARC.

### 3. Reaction of Other States

Example—Pakistan's continuous support to cross-border terrorism.

### 4. Alliances

Operating directly and indirectly as important elements in the process through which foreign politics is formulated and implemented.

### 5. World Public Opinion

- It provides dynamism to external environment.
- It influences foreign policy only occasions.

### 6. Other Dynamic Factors

Human rights, drugs, currency, crisis, environmental pollutions, transfer of technology, AIDS, international terrorism have taken priority and are major factors responsible for transnationalization of international relations.

### 7. Geo-politics

The application of the knowledge of political geography to the problems of state-craft is commonly referred to as geo-politics. It is the study of geography. It stresses a state power and international conduct. It is an absolute determinant.

### 8. Geo-economics

It is the relationship between geography and the economic condition as behaviour of states. Geo-economics consists of the economic theory and related empirical data based on the premise that land is a distinct factor of production, the other two being labour and capital goods.

## ORIGIN AND GROWTH OF INTERNATIONAL RELATIONS

The history of international relations is often traced back to the Peace of Westphalia of 1648, where the modern state system was developed. Prior to this, the European medieval organization of political authority was based on a vaguely hierarchical religious order. Westphalia instituted the notion of sovereignty, which essentially meant that rulers, or sovereigns, would recognize no internal equals within a defined territory, and no external superiors. Classical Greek and Roman authority at times resembled the Westphalian system, but both lacked the notion of sovereignty.

Westphalia encouraged the rise of the nation-state and the institutionalization of diplomacy and armies. This particular European system was exported to the Americas, Africa, and Asia via colonialism and the "standards of civilization". The contemporary international system was finally established through decolonization during the Cold War. However, this is somewhat over-simplified. While the nation-state system is considered "modern", many states have not incorporated the system and are termed "pre-modern". Further, a handful of states have moved beyond the nation-state system and can be considered "post-modern". The ability of contemporary international relations discourse to explain the relations of these different types of states is disputed.[9]

It is related to a number of other academic disciplines, including political science, geography, history, economics, law, sociology, psychology, and philosophy. The field emerged at the beginning of the 20th century largely in the West and particularly in the US as that country grew in power and influence. The study of international relations has always been heavily influenced by normative considerations such as the goal of reducing armed conflict and increasing international cooperation. At the beginning of the 21st century, research focused on issues such as terrorism, religious and ethnic conflict, the emergence of sub-state and non-state entities, the spread of weapons of mass destruction and efforts to counter nuclear proliferation, and the development of international institutions. It is both an academic and public policy field, and can be either positive or normative as it both seeks to analyze as well as formulate foreign policy.

By the fifteenth century, writers, artists and architects in Italy were well aware of the transformations that were taking place and were using phrases like "modi antichi" (in the antique manner) or "alle romana et alla antica" (in the manner of the Romans and the ancients) to describe their work. As to the term "rebirth", it seems that Albrecht Dürer in 1523 was the first to use such a term when he used "Wiedererwachung" (German: rebirth) to describe Italian art. The term "la rinascita" first appeared, however, in its broad sense in Giorgio Vasari's *Vite de' più eccellenti architetti, pittori, et scultori Italiani* (*The Lives of the Artists*, 1550-68). Vasari divides the age into three phases: the first phase contains Cimabue, Giotto and Arnolfo di Cambio; the second phase contains Masaccio, Brunelleschi and Donatello; the third centres on Leonardo da Vinci, culminating with Michelangelo. It was not just the growing awareness of classical antiquity that drove this development, according to Vasari, but also the growing desire to study and imitate nature.

The development of the Italian Renaissance was intertwined with the intellectual movement known as Renaissance humanism and with the history of the fiercely independent and combative urban societies of the city-states of central and northern Italy in the 13th to 16th centuries. Florence, Italy can be considered the birthplace of the Renaissance for several reasons. International relations are shaped primarily by those states perceived to be Great Powers, countries whose interests and capabilities transcend their own self-defense or region. For some 200 years after the treaties of Utrecht and Nystad (1713-14, 1721), the roster of the Great Powers included the same five states: Great Britain, France, Prussia (and later Germany), the Habsburg monarchy (Austria), and Russia. A mere three decades after World War I, however, only one of these venerable powers, Britain, had not undergone two or more radical changes of government, and only one, Russia, was still a Great Power.[10] Between 1914 and 1945, the European system committed suicide, and two global superpowers rose to replace it. Five decades after 1945, the Soviet Union was no more, while the ability of the United States to control events was in turn challenged from many sources, giving rise to speculation that the world might be shifting back into a multipolar balance-of-power system.

## INDUSTRIAL REVOLUTIONS AND ITS IMPACT ON INTERNATIONAL RELATIONS

The Industrial Revolution was a major shift and has a positive as well as negative impact on international relations in world politics. The technological, socio-economic, and cultural conditions occurred in the late 18th century and early 19th century in some Western countries. It began in Britain and spread throughout the world, a process that continues as industrialization. The onset of the Industrial Revolution marked a major turning point in international history, comparable to the invention of farming or the rise of the first city-states; almost every aspect of daily life and human society is, eventually, in some way influenced.

### Demography and Economy

A demographic revolution took place in this period. Population grew very quickly due to a decreased death rate and increased fertility. Most of the people still lived in the countryside. Between 1750 and 1815, only 7 per cent of the European population lived in cities. Life in the villages changed, however. Agricultural production became more intensive and large scale (to produce raw materials for the rural industry) and as a result, the number of farmers without land grew. Towns with rural industry grew and provided much work. In other words, trade and industry grew. World trade and politics became more influential in the everyday life of the villagers. The group of proletarians grew quickly due to downwards social mobility and the fact that proletarians had more children than farmers.

In the 19th century, population continued to grow. In many countries, population doubled. Increasing scaling also continued and thus, the number of proletarians likewise continued to grow. The landless farmers did not have the security they had previously when working for a land-owning farmer. Modern farmers did not hire help for a whole year anymore, but only for the harvest season. Because they now only produced one or two crops, as the harvest season was very short. The economy needed teams of harvesters that went from town to town. Many people moved around in Western and also in Eastern Europe after the abolition of serfdom in 1861. By 1850, the countryside had become very overcrowded, partially because of the rural industry that was located there. Malthus developed a theory on the population growth. Too much population growth would lead to disaster and misery.

Between 1815 and 1914, an industrial revolution took place. The industries in the cities eventually won the competition with the rural industries. Because of the industrial revolution, urbanization started in the 19th century. Cities still needed many new people every now and again because of bad sanitary conditions and diseases. The cities however did not need a constant refill of people anymore. In 1800, there were only 23 cities with over 1,00,000 citizens. By 1900, there were 135 cities with over 1,00,000 citizens. Not everybody lived in the city permanently. There were several types of cities: cities with textile industry, cities with heavy industry and administrative/commercial cities. Industrial revolution also effected transportation. In the 19th century bicycles, steamships and trains made it easier for people to move further away. In the 20th century, the explosion motor further accelerated this process. An ever-growing part of world population became subdued to market economy.

**Politics**

The French revolution in 1789, opened an era of liberal revolution. Liberal revolution slowly established the right of every citizen to move whenever and wherever he liked. Religious tolerance grew. The idea of one nationality in one country started to develop and caused nationalism. Because of this and other ideologies a new group of refugees grew, the political refugees. Government policy had a large influence on people in Europe now. There were many wars going on in Europe, like the Seven-Year War (1756-63), the Austrian War of Succession.

In many countries, revolutions took place in the first half of the 19th century. Governments were afraid of social unrest and socialism. They tried to get rid of the surplus of proletarians, who were a potential source of unrest. European governments stimulated the migration of people towards colonies and former colonies. Across the ocean, a revolution had taken place also and had the result that an independent state came into existence there. Many labourers were wanted there after the abolition of slavery somewhat after 1833.

At the end of the 19th and the beginning of the 20th century, nationalism continued to grow. Large empires like the Austrian-Hungarian, the Ottoman and the Russian collapsed and were split up into separate states. Eastern Europe got its own share of nation-states after Western European concept. The idea of an own state for every nationality did not work out everywhere. In many countries, there lived a mixture of nationalities. This caused much movement of people towards their "own" country. Some groups however, like Jews and Gypsies, did not have their own country and were not welcome anywhere. From 1880 onwards, especially Jews in Eastern Europe were the victims of growing hostility.

## SCOPE OF INTERNATIONAL RELATIONS

International relations is the field concerning the theory and practice of politics and the description and analysis of international political systems and political behaviour of international objects. It is a study about the international society and the nation-state activities. It makes an enquiry into the origin of the international society and the state as well as political authority. In this sense, it is a historical investigations about the origin of the nation-state. The scope of international relations is multiplied day by day due to multiplicity of roles of international actors and non-actors. It can study the structure and functioning of the state government, inter-state organisations, etc. In this sense, it is an analytical study of what the state is. It also attempts to formulate principles of good government or in other words, it suggests what the international society is ought to be. It is sometimes alleged that international relations deals with the real while international politics deals with the ideal. The nature of international relations inquires into what international actors and non-actors actually do in an international hypothetical situation while international politics tries to determine what they ought to do in keeping with the ultimate good or purpose of human life. The scope of international relations are as enumerated below:

- A study of international civil society, state and government
- A study of international theory and international institutions
- A study of world developmental programme
- A study of international dynamics, process and leadership
- A study of adjustment of the individuals with the state in memorandum of understanding and cooperation, treaties and international protocol
- A study of international relations and international law
- A study of public policy perspectives.

The international relations primarily studies the problem of the state and government. The state is defined as a group of people organized for law within a definite territory. The state possesses four characterstics such as population, territory, government, and sovereignty.

International relations is a major branch of international politics. On the basis of the ideas or thoughts of international policy scientists, international relations formulates definitions or concepts like Civil Society, Human Rights, Democracy, Liberty,

Equality, etc. It can explain the rudimentary concepts of international relations. It also includes the study of international crisis management.

It deals with the nature of different international institutions including government explains their merits and demerits, their structure, and working and arrives at different conclusions on comparative basis.

The study of international relations has become significant in the 21st century. It means the current forces at work in international government and politics.[11] It covers a wide range and includes the study of political parties, public opinion, pressure groups the international context. A scientific study of the working of these international dynamics helps to explain the international behaviour of individuals and different groups.

The scope of international relations also includes a study of the nature of relationships between individuals and the state. It examines how man should adjust himself with the society. Man is the root of politics. The process of adjustment of men with the society is an important aspect of international relations. The international actors guarantee certain rights and liberties to its citizens and at the same time imposes certain reasonable restrictions on them.

The scope includes a study of international relations which has become significant since the first quarter of the 21st century. It covers a wide range of diplomacy, internatinal law, international organizations, like the UN, etc. Because of scientific inventions and discoveries, the cooperation and contact among the different nations of the world have become easier and the whole world turns to be a family.

The horizons and scope of international relations is increasing day by day and is touching upon various fields. These are outlined below:

- Realism
- Neo-realism
- Idealism
- Liberalism
- Neo-liberalism

- Marxism
- Dependency theory
- Functionalism
- Neo-functionalism
- Critical theory
- Constructivism

International relations theories can be divided into one of two epistemological camps: "positivist" and "post-positivist". Positivist theories aim to replicate the methods of the natural sciences by analysing the impact of material forces. They typically focus on features of international relations such as state interactions, size of military forces, balance of powers, etc. Post-positivist epistemology rejects the idea that the social world can be studied in an objective and value-free way. It rejects the central ideas of neo-realism/liberalism such as rational choice theory, on the grounds that the scientific method cannot be applied to the social world and that a 'science' of international relations is impossible. A key difference between the two positions is that while positivist theories such as neo-realism, offer causal explanations (such as why and how power is exercised), post-positivist theories focus instead on constitutive questions, for instance what is meant by 'power'; what makes it up, how it is experienced and how it is reproduced.[12] Often, post-positivist theories explicitly promote a normative approach to international relations, by considering ethics. This is something which has often been ignored under 'traditional' international relations as positivist theories make a distinction between 'facts' and normative judgments, or 'values'.

During the late 1980s/1990s, debate between positivists and post-positivists became dominant and has been described as constituting the Third "Great Debate" (Lapid, 1989).

Liberal international relations theory arose after World War I in response to the inability of states to control and limit war in their international relations. Early adherents include Woodrow Wilson and Norman Angell, who argued variously that states mutually gained from cooperation and that war was so destructive to be essentially futile. Liberalism was not recognized as a coherent theory as such until it was collectively and derisively termed idealism by E.H. Carr. A new version of "idealism", centered around human rights as basis of the legitimacy of international law, was advanced by Hans Köchler.

Realism was a response to liberalism that chiefly denies that states seek to cooperate. Early realists such as E.H. Carr, Daniel Bernhard and Hans Morgenthau argued that, for the purpose of increasing their security, states are self-interested, power-seeking rational actors. Any cooperation between states is explained as purely incidental. Realists saw World War II as the vindication of their theory. It should be noted that classical writers such as Thucydides, Machiavelli, and Hobbes are often cited as the "founding fathers" of realism by contemporary self-described realists. However, while their work may support realist doctrine, it is not likely that they would have classified themselves as realists (in this sense of the term).

Neo-realism is largely the work of Kenneth Waltz (who actually called his theory "Structural Realism"). While retaining the empirical observations of realism, that international relations are characterized by antagonistic inter-state relations, neo-realists point to the anarchic structure of the international system as the cause. They reject explanations that take account of states' domestic characteristics. States are compelled by relative gains and balance against concentration of power. Unlike realism, neo-realism seeks to be scientific and more positivist. What also distinguishes neo-realism from realism is that the former does not accept the latter's emphasis on the behavioural explanation of international relations.

Neo-liberalism seeks to update liberalism by accepting the neo-realist presumption that states are the key actors in international relations, but still maintains that non-state actors (NSAs) and intergovernmental organizations (IGOs) matter. Proponents such as Joseph Nye argue that states will cooperate irrespective of relative gains, and are thus concerned with absolute gains. The growing interdependence throughout the Cold War through international institutions means that neo-liberalism is also called liberal institutionalism.

Critical international relations theory is the application of "critical theory" to international relations. Proponents such as Andrew Linklater and Robert Cox focus on the need for human emancipation from states. Hence, it is "critical" of mainstream international relations theories that tend to be state-centric.

Social constructivism encompasses a broad range of theories that aim to address questions of ontology such as the structure and agency debate as well as questions of epistemology such as the "material/ideational" debate that concerns the relative role of material forces versus ideas. Constructivism is not a theory of international relations, for example in the manner of neo-realism, but instead, is a social theory.

Constructivism in international relations can be divided into what Hopf (1998) calls "conventional" and "critical" constructivism. Common to all varieties of constructivism is an interest in the role that ideational forces play. The most famous constructivist scholar, Alexander Wendt noted in an article in *International Organization* [later followed up by a book, *Social Theory of International Politics* (1999)], that "anarchy is what states make of it".

By this, he means that, the anarchical structure that neo-realists claim governs state interaction is in fact a phenomenon that is socially constructed and reproduced by states. For example, if the system is dominated by states that see anarchy as a life or death situation (what Wendt terms a "Hobbesian" anarchy) then the system will be characterised by warfare. If on the other hand anarchy is seen as restricted (a "Lockean" anarchy) then a more peaceful system will exist. Anarchy in this view is constituted by state interaction, rather than accepted as a natural and immutable feature of international life as viewed by neo-realist international relations scholars.

Critics, however, abound from both sides of the epistemological divide: post-positivists say the focus on the state at the expense of ethnicity/race/class/gender makes social constructivism yet another positivist theory. The use of implicit rational choice theory by Wendt has also raised criticisms from scholars such as Steven Smith. Positivist scholars of neo-liberalism/realism hold that the theory forgoes too many positivist assumptions for it to be considered positivist.

The study of international relations rests upon four basic principles:

- The search for a more comprehensive scope in international order
- The search for realism to study international relations
- The search for precision to study international crisis management
- The search for more intellectual order to study the developmental aspects of international relations.

The study of politics and international relations involves the description of political phenomena, which we try to explain using general theories and on which we reflect normatively. The study of international relations uses a series of research strategies and methods, the range employed varying according to purpose. These could include textual analysis, historical research, use of contemporary media sources, discourse analysis, elite interviews, mass surveys, statistical modelling, deductive modelling, and computer simulation techniques.

First, international relations composes our largest society. Since the age of colonization in the eighteenth century, international relations has encompassed the globe. There is:

- a worldwide system of communication regulated by international organizations (such as the Universal Postal Union, International Telecommunication Union, and Intergovernmental Copyright Committee), involving mail, telegrams, radio, television, newspapers, periodicals, and books;
- a global transportation system involving international shipping lines, and especially, the airlines regulated by the International Civil Aviation Organization;
- an extensive worldwide trade and division of labour, with states and multinational corporations specializing in extractive industries, forestry, fishing, food crops, or manufacturing;

- international social norms that frame the variety of interaction among states and international groups, some of which have the status of international law;
- a stratification system recognized by all and dividing states into those with wealth, power or prestige, and those without;
- a culture, of which the dominant language is English, with norms emphasizing the sovereignty, independence and equality of states, and valuing truth, education and knowledge, development, and government intervention, regulation, and planning; and opposing genocide, military aggression, colonialism, and racism.

As with the study of politics, the study of international relations encompasses philosophical, theoretical, institutional and issue-based concerns relating to governance, but at the regional and global levels.

Normative political theory or political philosophy concerns the normative study of the political values of society and the international order, investigated both historically and analytically. Positive political theory or explanatory political theory concerns the study of the general mechanisms and forces which steer the behaviour of individuals and institutions as they interact at domestic, regional and global levels to allocate values and resources. Political science or political analysis uses these theoretical perspectives to inform and assess the explanation of historical events, political behaviour, the workings of political institutions and actors, political processes and the policy outputs of governance and regulatory structures.

Politics and international relations also draw upon the knowledge bases of cognate disciplines. The study of international relations is both implicitly comparative and characterized by explicitly comparative investigations across time and space.

There are a number of approaches and areas of investigation in politics and international relations. These approaches cross-fertilize each other both methodologically and in subject matter; therefore certain topics may appear under more than one heading. Each has its own lines of debate and methodological disputes. Approaches may be competitive or complement each other. Debate within and between them has the effect of advancing knowledge and understanding. They may include:

- within normative political theory or political philosophy primarily but not exclusively: conceptual;
- analysis, historical textual analysis, rational choice and analytical political philosophy, liberalism;
- marxist and neo-Marxist approaches, environmentalism, human rights, feminism, multiculturalism;
- relativism, postmodernism, classical realism, neo-realism, conservatism, nationalism;
- within positive political theory or explanatory political theory primarily but not exclusively:
    - behaviouralism, comparative methods, game theory, institutionalism, political economy, political;
- sociology, postmodernism, rational or public choice, social choice theory, cultural theory, critical theory;
- pluralism;
- within political science or political analysis primarily but not exclusively: international organizations;
- regimes, legislatures, executives, party systems, electoral systems, voting behaviour, public policy;
- administration or public management, political communication, political development, urban politics;
- conflict analysis, peace research, human rights, foreign policy analysis, area studies, security studies;
- international law, international economic relations.

The study of the international relations and its government and civil society has always impacted upon human lives. At some point of time, international relations was considered a subsidiary part of international politics. From such a yoke, international relations has successfully evolved as an independent discipline. In the last century, there were certain trends in international relations—beginning from behaviouralism to post-behaviouralism to the present state of international situations.

International relations seeks to understand, explain and analyse the international foreign policy, phenomena and prescribe ways and means to rectify the shortcomings. It is a complex subject. This is because of the Western traditions. It is at least 2500 years old and has been attended to by philosophers, theologicians, kings, economists, sociologists and others. For the purpose of its utility, international relations is divided into distinct streams such as:

- classical,
- modern, and
- empirical.

The classical international relations was determined by philosophy and dealt with description, explanation, prescription, and evaluation of international phenomena. Empirical international relations claimed to be a science and has been primarily concerned with the description and explanation of international reality. Contemporary international relations has been tried to blend the theoretical and practical aspects crisis management of international relations.[13]

It is a network of concepts and generalisations about international life involving ideas, assumptions and statements about the nature, and key features of world government.[14]

The subject of international relations is concerned with describing and explaining the realities of foreign policy behaviour, generalizations on empirical evidence and role of power in the society. International relations is not only concerned about the behavioural study of the international phenomena from empirical point of view, but also prescribing the goals which states, government, societies and citizens ought to pursue.

International relations draws upon such diverse fields as economics, history, law, philosophy, geography, sociology, anthropology, psychology, and cultural studies. It involves a diverse range of issues, from globalization and its impacts on societies and state sovereignty to ecological sustainability, nuclear proliferation, nationalism, economic development, terrorism, organized crime, human security and human rights.

The other neo-emerging area of international relations include:

- Environmentalism,
- Ecology,
- Community,
- Issue concerning development,
- Communitarians,
- Subalternism,
- Globalisation,
- Liberalisation,
- Deregulation,
- New social movements, and
- Human rights.

The contemporary international system was finally established through decolonization during the Cold War. However, this is somewhat over-simplified. While the nation-state system is considered "modern", many states have not incorporated the system and are termed "pre-modern". A handful of states have moved beyond the nation-state system and can be considered "post-modern".[15] The ability of contemporary international relations discourse to explain the relations of these different types of states is disputed.

The increased attention has been paid in recent years to developing a more scientific understanding of the international system as a whole. Aspects of international relations have been studied. The use of capitalizations of the 'I' and 'R' in international relations aims to distinguish the academic discipline of international relations from the phenomena of international relations. Now post-positivist epistemology has stood the test of time. It rejects the idea that the social world can be studied in an objective and value-free way. It rejects the central ideas of neo-realism/liberalism such as rational choice theory, on the grounds that the scientific method cannot be applied to the social world and that a 'science' of international relations is impossible. In the twentieth century, in addition to contemporary theories of liberal internationalism, Marxism has been a durable foundation of international relations. Karl Marx, Engels, Lenin, Stalin, Rose Luxemburg, Gramsci, Luckas, Austro-Marxist, Frankfurt School, Herbert Marcuse are the Marxist theory. The theory puts more emphasis on liberation of mankind. The central theme of the theory is on class division, revolutions, etc. It has positive impact on international relations.[16]

International relations may be much more about exploring cultural differences or new technologies. So, they may in fact be more about relations between "nations" than about relations between "states" after all.

Apart from above-mentioned analysis, there are other parameters by which the study of international relations is gaining ground. These are discussed below:

- Power
- Polarity
- Hegemonic stability
- Balance of power
- Interdependence
- Negotiation
- Sanctions
- War
- Mobilization paradigm
- Psychological factors
- Bureaucratic politics
- Ethnic issues
- Poststructuralist theories
- Feminisms ("gendering" war)
- Post-colonialism

Bureaucratic politics looks at the role of the bureaucracy in decision-making, and sees decisions as a result of bureaucratic in-fighting, and as having been shaped by various constraints. Viewing these aspects of the sub-unit level has explanatory power with regards to ethnic conflicts, religious wars, and other actors do not consider themselves to fit with the defined state boundaries. This is particularly useful in the context of the pre-modern world of weak states.

Poststructuralist theories of international relations developed in the 1980s from postmodernist studies in political science. Poststructuralism explores the deconstruction of concepts traditionally not problematised in international relations such as 'power' and 'agency' and examines how the construction of these concepts shapes international relations. The examination of 'narratives' plays an important part in poststructuralist analysis, for example, feminist poststructuralist work has examined the role that 'women' play in global society and how they are constructed in war as 'innocent' and 'civilians'.

Examples of post-positivist research include:

- Feminisms ("gendering" war)
- Postcolonialism (challenges the euro-centrism)

## NEO-EMERGING SCOPE OF INTERNATIONAL RELATIONS

- Systemic level concepts
- International relations is often viewed in terms of levels of analysis, the systemic level concepts are those broad concepts that define and shape an international milieu, characterised by anarchy
- Unit-level concepts in international relations

As a level of analysis, the unit level is often referred to as the state level, as it locates its explanation at the level of the state, rather than the international system.

### Regime Type

It is considered that a state's regime type can dictate the way that a state interacts with others in the international system.

### Democratic Peace Theory

It is a theory that suggests the nature of democracy means that democratic countries will not go to war with each other. The justifications for this are that democracies externalise their norms and only go to war for just causes, and that democracy encourages mutual trust and respect.

### Communism

It justifies a world revolution, which similarly would lead to peaceful co-existence, based on a proletarian global society.

**World Body**

International institutions form a vital part of contemporary international relations. Much interaction at the system level is governed by them, and they outlaw some traditional institutions and practices of international relations such as the use of war (except in self-defence).

**United Nations**

The United Nations (UN) is an international organization that describes itself as a "global association of governments facilitating co-operation in international law, international security, economic development, and social equity". It is the most prominent international institution. Many of the legal institutions follow the same organizational structure as the UN.

**Economic Institutions**

- World Trade Organization
- World Bank
- International Monetary Fund
- Asian Development Bank

**International Legal Bodies**

***Human Rights***

- United Nations Human Rights Council
- Human Rights Committee
- European Court of Human Rights
- Inter-American Court of Human Rights
- International Criminal Tribunal for Rwanda
- International Criminal Court

***Regional Security Arrangements***

- NATO
- ASEAN
- Arab League
- CIS

## UNTOUCHED WORLD STATE OF AFFAIRS AND NEW BLUEPRINT OF INTERNATIONAL RELATIONS

Globalization is not a new phenomenon for international relations. Knowledge about governance with all its theories and practices has spread across the boundaries and frontiers of nations from time immemorial. They have in turn influenced the shaping of structures of governments and their functioning.[17] Today, no nation can claim to have a constitutional system which evolved exclusively from its native ethos without foreign influences. Mercantilism and colonial expansion led to new innovations in public administration in the lands which became laboratories for their colonial masters to try on new methods of governance. In Egypt, during the time of Mohamed Aly, young men were sent to Europe to study Public Administration and on their return, were absorbed in the government service. More recently, A.P. Sinker of Great Britain came to Egypt and after studying its administrative system recommended and helped create a Civil Service Commission in 1952 before the Revolution.

In the nineties, the progression of actions took such a rapid rotate that world circumstances bear no similitude with the world that existed in the post-World War II era. Just as international relations took a significant turn after the Second World War, likewise, a change of the same magnitude has taken place in the early nineties. In the wake of Perestroika and Glasnost, a wind of change swept the Soviet Union. It was followed by collapse of communism in all East European countries, crumbling of Soviet bloc and the eventual end of the Cold War. Gulf War (1991) rendered the USA as the only super-power in the world and a New World Order was claimed by it to be in the offing.[18] By the end of 1991, the world witnessed disintegration of the USSR and secessionist civil war in Yugoslavia. Contrarily, in Europe the process of integration is gaining momentum after EEC's decision to form single economic market by December 1992.

The pattern of international relations that was conspicuous in Cold War days has faded into oblivion. There has been a complete transformation of world scenario and a new pattern of international relations is emerging. It has in its womb some positive as well as negative developments giving rise to both hopes and fears. This pattern has its bearings on the developing nations of the Third World also. Amid the turmoil of the Persian Gulf War, President Bush began talking hopefully of a "new world order"—"a system of international understandings that could restore stability and prevent from conflicts from breaking out". After winning the Gulf War, President George Bush has reiterated his promise made in September 1990, to build a new world order which would be based on "cooperation" between the US and the Soviet Union, and which will allow the UN an important role. He aimed at building a new world order based on collective security and rule of law.

Another significant element of Bush's new world was nuclear non-proliferation. He did not want to miss the opportunity to "march forward". He wanted his countrymen to make maximum use of the opportunity provided by the Gulf War, to march forward on their proclaimed path of making the world better. For many Americans, the "Vietnam complex" was over and they were tempted to throw their new-found muscle power around to achieve their objectives. The spectacular success of Patriot missiles and other high-tech weapons seemed to have worked wonders for the US.

There is already rush of Third World countries for buying American arms. American arms industry that was facing slump after the end of the Cold War has suddenly regained its lost confidence. According to an estimate, Kuwait will spend $ 55 billion towards its reconstruction, and 70 per cent of 200 contracts that it signed with foreign companies during the last few days after the war was over have gone to the United States. Besides these sudden and unexpected gains, Washington may also utilise this "opportunity" to wrest vital concessions from others in regard to trade and business. It would try to dominate the Uruguay Round of talks and force the entry of its companies into Third World countries.

In mid-1990s, the nations of the South proposed a New International Economic Order (NIEO) intended to bridge the yawning gap between the rich and the poor worlds by instituting fairer international trading practices and increasing the order of magnitude of international assistance for rapid development. Now the US has adopted the slogan but the contents of the new concept are totally different from those of the previous exposition.

The main components of the previous concept of new economic world order demanded by Third World countries of the South were: new economic order, new information order, international peace, and democratization of international organizations including the UN. Some of their main demands are removal of poverty in the Third World, and reduction of gap between North and South, elimination of information imperialism practised by developed countries through multinationals, increasing the power of developing countries in UN, World Bank, IMF and GATT, checking the spread of nuclear weapons and gradually eliminating them, and removing war hysteria. None of these demands has been accepted by the rich countries of the North. The US has always used its dominance in different international bodies for thwarting efforts at fashioning a new economic order. The last decade of Reaganism and Thatcherism ridiculed the NIEO and put in its place new ideas such as "structural adjustments".[19]

The latest exposition of a new world order has come from President Bush. Ever since the Soviets went out of the Cold War business, he has been resorting to this catch phrase. Its scope is global, not national, as those of two former Presidents, Lyndon Johnson—"Great Society" and Kennedy—"New Frontier" were. All available evidence points to certain facts. The new world order will be dominated by the USA as the sole surviving superpower. The mighty dollar will be supreme again.

The US is likely to have a subservient UN at its disposal. New power alignments are being forged and a new world map of friends and enemies is being charted. After the end of the Gulf War, if one is to go by Bush's exposition the new world will not be the end of the old world order of guns and international power politics; it would mark according to critics, the beginning of a new world disorder. As a cynic has put it, the US will have the whip hand. Moreover, the disappearance of the Soviet Union as a rival and challenger to be reckoned with, the US is free to do as it pleases. The new world order is to be designed and run by the Group of 7 (G-7) with the USA as the star and others cast in supporting roles. This is a world to be run by the rich for the rich with reasonable pickings for the middle class. The poorer countries can fend for themselves.

### Emerging World Order

From time to time, we get used to the emergence of slogans and words which reign supreme until being replaced by new ones. The intelligentsia, the politicians, and then the media pick them up and spread across the boundaries of nations, languages and continents. Globalization and liberalization are terms which have acquired such currency within a short period. Today, the governments of such nations as well as their donor agencies exert considerable effort to convince less fortunate nations about the virtues of globalization. However, globalization literally is not new to many of these nations. Culturally, eagerness to acquire learning from other parts of the world was reflected in the global popularity of the ancient Alexandria library.

Today's talk about globalization however is more market-oriented and well entrenched in the network of narrow commercial nationalism, rational selfishness and corporate greed are paraded with a facade of universalism where protectionism is the privilege of mighty. Developing nations trying to build their infrastructure while at the same time struggling to have better fed, clothed, sheltered and more educated citizens are subjected to pressurise from international organizations to introduce policies to suit the agenda of globalization. Multinational corporations which are the principal sponsors of such globalization have been the beneficiaries as well as victims of criticism on that score. The main reason for such criticism is: because the globalization they seek is accomplished by a simultaneous process of liberalization of trade and economic policies thus advocating education in the role of the state in national economy. The search for a new world order has sustained, and in January 2007, it focused on an unusual summit meeting of the United Nations Security Council. The holding of this first ever summit meeting of the Security Council reflected the new realities of power in a world that is no longer dominated by the two superpowers of the Cold War. "It's symbolic of a world that isn't bipolar but it is also not a simple unipolar world run by the United States", said Professor Joseph S. Nye, Jr. of Harvard University. He further said, "It's symbolic of a world in which we are the biggest power, but we cannot do things alone—we need to leverage our power to get things done."

The emerging world order describes the world more or less as unipolar, at least clearly dominated by the sole superpower USA. After the end of the Cold War, the world is becoming unipolar where the US will most probably attempt to impose its political agenda on all regions. This extreme version claims that the US is a neo-imperial power wishing to force Third World countries into an exploitative global economic system. According to this viewpoint, after winning the Cold War, America is in the centre of world politics where its responsibility is to convert the American leadership into increasingly institutionalized forms. But American policymakers are realistic enough to assume, that the USA is hardly in a position to achieve this goal in an arbitrary manner. The military superiority alone provides only the frame for an envisaged system of domination through partnership.

It foresees an upward interdependence among the developed countries of the so-called north, based on shared values like democracy and free market economy and carried out through a concept of "partners in leadership" among the three major centres of power, the USA, the EC and Japan or in other words, in securing the wealth of the north. Thus, the world today is not unipolar, but global power relationship is in a flux because different centres of power have different kinds of power. In military affairs, the USA is pre-eminent. But in economic affairs, Germany and Japan are the centres of power and they do not recognize American economic leadership. Certain apprehensions were expressed throughout the world regarding Bush's concept of new world order. Many scholars criticized it to the extent of dubbing it as a new type of PaxAmericana. That is why Bush abruptly dropped the slogan as soon as the Gulf War was won. "People were trying to read too much into it", one of his aides complained. In its place of leadership by one or two superpowers, many scholars and government analysts predict the evolution of what some call "collegial power"—a loosely structured world in which leadership is shared among several key nations in different combinations depending on the nature of the issue.

**Global Power Scenario and Soviet Disintegration**

With the disintegration of the Soviet Union, the global power scenario has undergone a radical change as the Soviet Union was not just a nation but a superpower also. The emergence of a large number of independent nations that formed part of the former USSR within such a short span of time would no doubt go down as a momentous event in the history of international relations. Most of the newly independent republics have decided to form the Commonwealth of Independent States (CIS). After the independence of three Baltic states, the 12 independent nation states (republics) can be put into three categories. The first, the hardcore ones, comprises the three Slav republics, the Russian Federation, Ukraine and Byelorussia. The hardcore ones are the most powerful because of their common heritage and immense resources and military potential. The second consists of the central Asian states—Kazakhstan, Uzbekistan, Turkmenistan, Kyrgyzstan and Tajikistan. The third comprises such peripheral nation states as Georgia, Azerbaijan, Armenia and Moldavia which may be described as dissenters like the Baltic states. Newly independent republics are facing a number of problems—political, economic, military, social, cultural, ethnic, geographical, etc. Internal strife and sectarian tensions have now started surfacing in many republics with the disappearance of the central authority. Most of them have a diverse ethnic mix-up. In some republics like Georgia, Armenia, and Azerbaijan, ethnic relations have a troubled legacy. In the Central Asian Republics, the dominance of clannish political groups seem to prevail and the signs of any broad-based movement based on religious fundamentalism is yet to be discerned in a vast majority of these republics. Border disputes have been revived between neighbouring republics such as Armenia and Azerbaijan. Now it is to be seen how new CIS serves as a platform for settling emerging issues like border disputes and safeguards minorities in each republic. "Besides, the future of the new Commonwealth which has replaced the Soviet Union really hinges on the problem of control over the nuclear arsenal, the reorganisation of the Soviet Army and on their viable defence mechanism", observes Zafar Imam.

The top issue is the risk of the huge nuclear arsenal going out of control. The 27,000 warheads and more than three million troops and the "potentially explosive situation" within the CIS perturb the West most. In the Russian Republic, the new leadership is already struggling to control the growing discontent. The country is facing acute shortage of food and fuel and Russia is seeking the assistance of Western powers as part of the strategy to overcome the current pressing economic problems. As the main successor state of the USSR, the Russian Federation has all the characteristics of a powerful euro-centric state with an interest in Asia. But its euro-centricity will be conditioned by the degree of cooperation and coordination with Ukraine and Byelorussia. On the other hand, it is likely to maintain close cooperative relations with central Asian states, Kazakhstan in particular. There is also the likelihood of Russia emerging as leader of some form of pan-Slavic alliance that would include besides Ukraine and Belarus the neighbouring Slavic nations like Poland, Czechoslovakia and Bulgaria. Ukraine and Byelorussia are going to be truly euro-centric states with a marked regional interest in Poland and eastcentral Europe. In Central Asia, Uzbekistan and Tajikistan will perhaps act in conjunction, competing with potentially powerful Kazakhstan: The latter is very likely to act more European than Asian, perhaps a buffer state between Europe and Asia. These Central Asian Republics may also strive for closer links with Islamic nations like Turkey and Iran with which they have common cultural and religious bonds.

### International Relations and Global Implications

The 1990s have ushered in an entirely new era, both at the global and national levels. This era, popularly labelled as the era of globalization, has changed the outlook towards the problems of governance in a radical manner. The plural and liberal approaches point to the revolutions in technology and communication as facilitators of the process of globalization. They argue that states are no longer the central actors in a political system. They look towards supra-national integration and sub-national disintegration as sources of the erosion of the nation-state. The former includes the expanding scope of international law, globalization of markets resulting in borderless economies, advances in science and technology, terrorism, etc.[20] and the latter relates to the decline in the national consensus, growth of ethnic self-determination movements, and other issues. The emergence of a global economy, enormous technological changes, free flow of finance, capital and growth of foreign investments are some of the key features of the contemporary world order. At a cultural level, it has led to a kind of 'convergence', thus creating a global cosmopolitan (read western) culture. Attention has shifted to multicentricism, transnationalism and interdependency. Governments in the Third World need to address these changes.

International relations continues to tackle the unfinished agenda of development that it had sought to address through the framework comprising mainly three elements: (a) modernization of the economy; (b) self-reliance; and (c) socialist pattern of society with equity and social justice. The principal elements of this approach are so deeply rooted in our development process that they continue to constitute the basic tenets of our public policies. Historically, since independence, state intervention in the Indian economy was characterised by import-substitution industrialization, planned development, the creation of large-scale state enterprise, and the growth of a complex framework of regulation (licence-permit-quota raj) of private economic activity. Understanding contemporary administrative reform presupposes the understanding of the traditional model of governance. The parameters of acceptable public action through 'mixed economy welfare state' were that government could regulate the economy through taxing and spending and that it had sufficient economic resources to ameliorate socio-economic problems such as poverty, sickness and illiteracy. This envisaged an increased role for the public sector. Good governance in this context would involve promoting public sector transparency and accountability. The government of India has adopted the policies of globalization, liberalization and market economy in the wake of the economic crisis.

### Demise of the Socialist Superpower

The developing countries have in the past looked at the Soviet Union for success and moral support in times of need. The Third World is going to be excluded more and more from the benefits of integration in world market. Moreover, it is highly uncertain, whether a country like the USA is going to continue to float money without the slightest chance of returns to insignificant countries in the world anymore, as the need of aiding regimes in order to contain communism has become outdated.

### Beginning of New Era of Understanding and Peace (US and Russia as Allies)

There is no denying the fact that with the end of Cold War, the superpowers in their historic summit in Moscow (July, 1991) signed the Strategic Arms Reduction Treaty (START) that promised the beginning of new era of understanding and peace. After that, both the US and Russia have also twice made unilateral declarations for further cut in their nuclear and strategic weapons. In February 1992, Russian Federation President Boris Yeltsin made a formal declaration at the Camp David (USA) and proclaimed the beginning of a new era in US-Russian relations. New relations, US President Bush said, were "based on trust, based on a commitment to economic and political freedom". Yeltsin said: "There has been written and drawn a new line and crossed out all of the things that have been associated with the cold war...from now on, we do not consider ourselves to be potential enemies." Both the leaders hoped to unite the globe through their friendship and a new alliance of partners working against the common dangers that the world faces. Unlike the two Vietnams and two Germanys, where public opinion and practical wisdom overcame divisive forces and roaring rhetoric, and the dream of unification became a *fait accompli*, the governments and peoples of two Koreas may also go in for the much needed unification in the months or years to come. Notwithstanding the chronic hurling of charges and counter charges at each other, the two countries are more conciliatory and accommodating today than they were ever before. The day is not far off when this volatile and vulnerable region would become insulated against foreign intervention and interference. If there is disintegration in the Soviet Union simultaneously, there is a healthy trend of integration in Europe.[21] The European Community (EC) is about to take the most important step in its political history. The single European market came into being on December 31, 1992. The German Chancellor Helmut Kohl accepted an initiative of the French President Mitterand to move towards political as well as economic and monetary union. Intensive negotiations on this proposal have been taking place since the beginning of 1991. In the course of the negotiations, it has again become clear that very different views still exist on political union as well as on economic and monetary union. British Prime Minister John Major continues to be against political union if this entails a federation of European states. Paris envisages political union as close cooperation between individual national government. Germans argue for a considerable extension of the rights of the European Parliament.

New plan for monetary union is to achieve the goal of a single currency for the whole of Europe. The ECU is to become the means of exchange in all countries that are prepared to follow the strict rules necessary to maintain monetary stability. At present, Great Britain is not prepared to agree on this. The idea of giving up one's own national monetary policy is not yet acceptable in London. Paris is pushing for monetary union because it would like to cancel out the Deutschmark's dominant role in Europe, which currently gives Germany a position as the "anchor of the European Monetary System". However, it also sees the economic advantages that a common currency would bring. For the Federal Republic of Germany, the independence of a European Central Bank is an important factor, a view that is not shared in London or Paris. Despite this difference of approach, the single European market came into being in 1993 as planned, even if there were some compromises made with regard to its eventual form.

The problems which had been hanging fire for the last many years and so engaged the attention of the world are also likely to be resolved in the near future. The most significant gain of the Moscow Summit (July 1991) between big powers was an agreement to call a West Asia Peace Conference by October 1991.

The West Asia Peace Conference which began in Madrid on October 31, 1991 erupted into bitter polemics on November 1 and ended without agreement on where to hold face-to-face Arab-Israeli talks vital to ending bloodshed in the region. Though peace conference adjourned amidst bitter exchanges, it does not detract from the fact that history was made at Madrid when Israel and its Arab neighbours met face-to-face for the first time in 43 years. The question, however, arises is why the US has put in all the efforts when chances of success were so slim. First, President Bush has honoured his commitment to the Arabs made at the time of the Gulf War. Second, even if the talks collapse, the ice will have been broken and it will be possible if the sticks to its evenhanded stance. The present political scenario offers a unique opportunity to hammer out a solution which safeguards the rights of Palestinians as much as the security of Israel much will depend upon the outcome of the next rounds of peace conference.

**Relevance and Credibility of UN**

The UN stands at "a delicate point" in the search for a new international order of peace and justice that would promote human rights and eradicate poverty and other social plagues. This view was expressed by the then Secretary General Javier Perez de Cuellar in a message on the occasion of UN Day on October 24, 1991. He noted with gratification that the role of the organization is no longer questioned. It has proved both its relevance and credibility.

A new and enhanced role for the UN Security Council in continuing international peace in future was at the core of the declaration of the first summit of its 15 members. The entire exercise in convening the meeting at British initiative and involving the 15 heads of government is discussions, bilateral and otherwise, on crucial world issues seems to be a carefully designed postscript to the successful UN-authorized military action to put an end to Iraqi aggression against Kuwait in 1991. The Security Council has now sought to warn all potential aggressors in any part of the world driven by territorial ambitions that they, too will invite similar retribution. A clearer picture of how it will defuse potentially dangerous disputes in good time was expected to be available when the new UN Secretary-General, Boutros Ghali, submitted his report to the Council by July 1992, as he was asked to, on the best ways of strengthening the world to preserve peace in the post-Cold War era.

### Summing Up

International relations theory entails the development of conceptual frameworks and theories to facilitate the understanding and explanation of events and phenomena in world politics as well as the analysis and informing of associated policies and practices. The discipline of international relations was officially established after World War I with a view to avoiding future mass conflicts and ensuring peaceful change. This remains a worthy goal, but today the scope and complexities of world politics demand an understanding of a much wider range of issues.[22] Moreover, new conceptual frameworks and theories are required to improve our understanding and assist in the development of better policies and practices. International or 'external' influences of foreign policy include all activities occurring beyond a state's borders that structure the choices its officials make. Such factors as the content of international law, the number of military alliances, deterioration of the global environment, and the changing levels of international trade sometimes profoundly affect the choices of decision-makers.

## NOTES

1. Theodore A. Couloumbis and James H. Wolfe, "Introduction to International Relations", *Power and Justice* (New Delhi, 1986) 3rd edn., p. 25.
2. James N. Rosenau, ed., *International Politics and Foreign Policy* (New York: Free Press, 1969), 2nd edn. rev.

3. Rudolph Rummel, "Libertarianism and International Violence", *Journal of Conflict Resolution,* 27, I, March 1983, pp. 27-71.
4. Harold Sprout, "In Defence of Diplomacy", *World Politics,* 1 (April 1949), p. 407.
5. Morton A. Kaplan, System and Pr'JCess in "International Politics" (New York, 1957), p. 13.
6. Marie Jean Antoine Caritat Condorcet, Marquisde, tr., Jane Barraclough, *Sketch for a Historical Picture of the Progress of the Human Mind* (London, 1955).
7. J. David Singer and Melvin Small, "National Alliance Commitments and War Involvement 1818-1945" in *ibid.*, pp. 513-42.
8. Raymond Aron, "The Quest for a Philosophy of Foreign Affairs" in Hoffmann, ed., n. 25, p. 88.
9. Kenneth N. Waltz, "Review: Dilemmas of Politics", *American Political Science Review,* 53 (June 1956), pp. 529-32.
10. Morton A. Kaplan, "Balance of Power, Bipolarity and Other Models of International System" in James Rosenau, ed., p. 22.
11. Benno Wasserman, "The Scientific Pretensions of Professor Morgenthau's Theory of Power Politics", *Australian Outlook* (Melbourne), 13 (March, 1959), p. 67.
12. Harold Sprout, "In Defence of Diplomacy", *op. cit.*
13. Rudolph J. Rummel, "Libertarianism and International Violence", *Journal of Conflict Resolution,* 27, I, March 1983, pp. 27-71.
14. Quincy Wright, "Realism and Idealism in International Politics", *World Politics* (October, 1952), p. 133.
15. Mahendra Kumar, "Theoretical Aspects of International Politics" (Agra, 1972), 2nd revised edn., p. 37.
16. Wolfram F. Hanrieder, "The International System: Bipolar or Multiblock?", *The Journal of Conflict Resolution,* IX (September 1965), p. 209.
17. Vandana Shiva, "Democracy in the Age of Globalization", *Link*, Hong Kong, Vol. 16 (1998), p. 18.
18. M.A. Oommen, "An Examination of Some Issues of Globalization", *Link*, Hong Kong, Vol. 16 (1998), p. 23.
19. Ashini Sharma, "Globalization, Liberalization, and Health Policy in India", *Link*, Hong Kong, Vol. 16 (1998), p. 7.
20. Arthur Schtesinger, Jr., *A Thousand Days: John F. Kennedy in the White House* (Boston, 1965), p. 406.
21. Thomas C. Schelling, *That Strategy of Conflict* (New York, 1963), pp. 15-16.
22. Karl W. Deutsch *et. al., Political Community and the North Atlantic Area* (Princeton, Princeton University Press, 1957).

# The Modern State

2

The entire world is today divided into territories known as modern states or nation-states. The nation-state is the dominant political formation of our times. It is relatively a recent development in human history. It is also a dominant feature of the international relations. The scholars traced the origin of the state system from the year 1648.[1] The Peace of Westphalia paved the way for the emergence of the nation-state system. Only two hundred years ago, there were less than twenty states which could be called nation-state; today there are more than one hundred and ninety-three. Generally speaking, nation-state is understood by certain characteristics such as nation consciousness, unified territory, common ancestry, common language, history and culture.

## STATES

States are vital actors in international relations. These are considered as the basic entities in international system and world politics. States are regarded as sovereign in the territories under their jurisdiction, which means that the state, or rather its government controls what goes on within its borders. There is no overriding body in the world which rules over the states and their governments. Legally speaking, there is nothing anyone can do in the area of a state without the implicit consent of that state (the state's government). Formally, in the state system, all states are fully sovereign in that no authority takes precedence over them in their territories, which is otherwise known as the realist approach.

The primary concern of the traditional view of international relations was the behaviour of the states and their interactions with each other, i.e. the study of politics. We can say, there was a very little role played by the non-state actors in the traditional view. But in the post-Second World War era, with the development of the behavioural approach, the non-state actors started playing a greater role in the changing equation of world politics and international relations. Despite the emergence of the non-state actors, states still retained a leading and dominant, although not exclusive role. Reasons behind, this can be pertained to the following facts, first, the non-state actors lack the basic salient features of the states, i.e. sovereignty and territoriality. Second, they are behaviourally less important, and lastly, their interaction is still not known.

States and nations are often confused. Both play an important part in international relations as the very name of the discipline suggests. A few more careful definitions are needed in order to talk precisely about international relations. First let us consider states. A state consists of an area of territory which is under the single rule of a government. Broadly, the people who live in that territory are citizens of the state, something which confers both obligations and benefits. Citizens pay taxes. However, if they are lucky and the state works reasonably efficiently, they will receive benefits such as roads, and schools, internal security. They are expected to comply with the laws and their compliance can be enforced. In principle, at least, the laws are for the benefit of the citizens of a state as a whole and as law against. Only one government controls the area of the state at a time. Supposedly governments have the monopoly of violence in that state but clearly but that is not always the case in practice.[2] The lack of an overriding world government, or a government of governments, is held by many to be the distinctive characteristic of international relations and the source of the problems of the international system.

## WHAT IS MODERN STATE?

We can define a modern state as a particular type of state, characteristic of post-medieval and modern times, in which a government has sovereign power within a defined territorial area, and the mass of the population are citizens who know themselves to be part of a single nation. Nation-states are closely associated with the rise of nationalism, although nationalist loyalties do not always conform to the boundaries of specific states that exist today. Nation-states developed as part of an emerging nation-state system, originating in Europe, but in current times spanning the whole globe.

## CONCEPT OF THE MODERN STATE

In his survey of the foundations of Modern Political Thought, Quentum Skinner observed that by the beginning of the seventeenth century, the concept of the state—its nature, its powers, its right to command obedience—had come to be recorded as the most important analysis in European thought. He added: "We may be said to enter the modern world; the modern theory of the state remains to be constructed, but its foundations are complete." 'What' concepts of the state led Skinner to argue that? Briefly they are as follows.[3]

The first element is the notion of 'the powers' of the state—its right to command obedience. Of course, states have duties towards their citizens, too—e.g. to protect their lives and property or defend them against external attack. And citizens usually have 'rights', too—thought these vary greatly from one type of state of another. But Hobbes' emphasis is the prior one. The state is itself a power—the central and supreme power—in the land. And it exercises the power by imposing its rule over us and commanding obedience. The state has many other functions; but fundamentally the state is about rule.

Rule may take many forms—monarchy, democracy, dictatorship, etc. but wherever the state is sovereign—the supreme power—it involves the subjection of its subjects to the power of the state, its domination over them. Even in modern democracies, where the 'will of the people' is supposed to be sovereign, the government, once formed and in charge of the machinery of the state, nevertheless does constitute a power 'up there', separate from 'the people' who helped to form it. The concept of the modern state, therefore, always entails a notion of power.

The powers of the state include the power to employ force to oblige conformity to its rules, laws and regulations. The issue of legitimacy covers the whole spectrum of what might be called sanctioned domination of which physical force is only an extreme special case. If the state regulates, directs, legislates and compels 'legitimacy', it is because it can lay claim to the authority to do so. Authority is power which the state is licenced or 'authorized' to exercise.

The question of the modern state is closely tied up with the notion of sovereignty means that the state is the supreme power, subject to the rule neither of some external power nor of a rival power within its own boundaries. Other centers of power within a state must be subordinated to it; or, power must be developed to them by the states as the central state delegates certain powers to local authorities; or the state must licence or, by its lack of legislation, permit them to exist and function.

Another of the 'distinctive modern ideas of the state is of the state as a public power, separate from both the ruler and the ruled...'. Under Absolutism, ruler and state—person and pubic —were often indistinguishable.

The above description of the development of the modern state establishes a salient historical sequence. It explains the different states of the evaluation of the modern state and suggests why the question of the state has become the principal point of contribution in political theory.

## EVOLUTION OF THE MODERN STATE

The modern nation-state is a highly complex occurrence. It is the result of a long historical evolution. This evolution has not been uniform and continuous. Historically, it is difficult to find out as to when and how the state came into being. But we have sufficient evidence to trace the development of modern nation-state from the primitive times till date. Following have been the forms of evolution of the modern nation-state:

- The tribal formations
- Early empire in the orient
- The Greek city-state

- The Roman empire
- The feudal state
- The modern nation-state

The development of the modern state in the West typically begins with the dissolution of the western Roman empire. This led to the fragmentation of the imperial state into the hands of private lords whose political, judicial, and military roles corresponded to the organization of economic production. In these conditions, according to Marxists, economic unit of society—was the state.

Historically, nationalism is the product of rise of nation-state in Europe. During its earlier phase it was identified with the absolute monarchies of Europe. In the 18th and 19th centuries, it acquired an imperialist form in the struggle of or colonies in Asia, Africa, in the 19th century, it associated itself with liberalism, democracy, constitutionalism and civil liberties. In the 19th and 20th centuries, it played an important part in the reorganization of Europe, unification of Italy, Germany, etc. After the First World War, it acquired an aggressive and racial form in the garb of Fascism and Nazism. During the 20th century, it brought a new awakening in the Asian and African countries through the national liberation movements. After the Second World War, in spite of the challenges posed by Marxism and Internationalism, it still remains the dominant political force in the world politics.

## FACTORS FOR THE RISE OF NATION-STATE

The modern nation-state emerged out of the womb of medieval period and was the product of many forces and struggles. The principal factors responsible for the rise of nation-state are:

1. The individualistic climate of opinion that characterized Renaissance and Reformation.
2. The collapse of universal authority of the Church.
3. The desire of the rising commercial classes for uniform trade regulations, etc.

4. Changes on account of the rise of representative government.
5. Industrial revolution.
6. Growth of international law.
7. Development of diplomacy.
8. Growing interdependence of states.

The major landmarks and factors contributing towards the development of sovereign state system are briefly touched upon as under:

- The development of the nation-state system was characterized by four historic events running from 17th to 20th centuries. These are:
  - (i) The 1648 Treaty of Westphalia (Germany)
  - (ii) The 1713 Treaty of Utrecht (Holland)
  - (iii) The 1815 Vienna Congress (Austria)
  - (iv) The 1918 Treaty of Versailles (France).
- The disintegration of the religious and political empires and the institution of feudalism.
- The birth of nation-states on the basis of territory, population, sovereignty and the law besides common heritage, culture, aspirations, language, literature, etc.
- The state system through a world wide phenomenon in consequence, was essentially a European development with all western characteristics.
- The increase in number of the nations joining the system and the gradual widening of the system so as to embrace —besides Europe where the system was originated—the continents of America, Australia, Asia and Africa.
- The theoretical or intellectual contribution of thinkers like Machiavelli, Bodin, Grotious, Hobbes, Althusius, Luther, Calvin and others laid the foundations of an independent secular nation-state.
- The progressive assumption and practice by the nation-states of the feature like territoriality, sovereignty,

nationalism, national power, diplomacy, balance of power, collective security, etc.

- The invention of new military techniques was also responsible for the rise of the modern state. Besides, the development of modern techniques of administration which has given to the governments the ability to have greater control over their people.
- Development of the means of transport and communication has given states a greater unity and has also facilitated the consolidation of central power. Economic progress has provided more national wealth and resources at the disposal of governments.
- Finally, the nationalism has helped the state in getting more loyalty and devotion from its people thus making it more strong and powerful. With the rise of nationalism citizens became more deeply involved in the affairs of their state. It was no more feasible for the statesmen to trade territories on the basis of ancient titles or strategic considerations. Now the ethnic or linguistic affinity or common aspirations were regarded as the legitimate basis for the organization of the state.

## GROWTH OF NATION-STATE

The growth of nation-states has not been uniform and has followed different patterns in different regions. These are:

1. Growth of nation-state in Western, Southern and Eastern Europe
2. Nation-state in America
3. Nation-state in Asia and Africa
4. Marxism and the question of nationality.

Nation-state was the product of combined influence of reformation renaissance and commercial revolution. The decline in the authority of the Church raised the question of loyalty of the individuals. The authority of the Church over the Peasantry began to decline and the authority of the feudal lords began to be consolidated in the hands of the powerful kings. The period was also characterized by a new development, i.e. colonialism.

It spread both in Eastern and Western directions—Asia and America. The industrial revolution gave birth to a new economy and a new class—the capitalist class—whose interests clashed with those of absolute monarchy.[4]

The French revolution in the 18th century was a turning point in the rise and growth of nation-state. In 1792, Napoleon began national revolutionary struggles, rational consciousness of the German state. Fichte, Hegel, etc. stood for nation-state. The formation of national in Eastern Europe did not take place under a centralized authority. The theory of self-determination was welcomed. Nation-state in America was something different. Their first slogan was 'no taxation without representation'. This slogan subsequently changed into full war in independence. This resulted in the formation of new states and national identities.

The Second World War was another important landmark in the rise and growth of nation-state. It destroyed Fascism and Nazism. It involved in the process of liberation movement in Asia and Africa. New nations like China, India, Pakistan, Egypt, etc. grew on the world scene which gave a new meaning of nation-state. A new form of nationalism and a new meaning of concept was born in countries like India, China and Arab lands.

The idea of nationalism and the nation-state has a different connotation in Marxism. Marx was of the opinion that the societies were divided not on nationalities but on class basis. Extreme nationalism is an ideological means which helps in the class domination. Marx and Engels gave the idea of abolition of nationalities. Marx supported the national liberation movement in Poland because it was a part of Russia. Engels introduced the concept of 'new historical nations'. Lenin also understood clearly the dialectical relationships between internationalism and the right of self-determination of nationalities. Stalin's solution of the problem was realistic but far away from the Marxist tradition. Stalin gave autonomy to different nationality within the south state.[5]

## ELEMENTS OF MODERN NATION-STATE

There are three elements of modern nation-state. These elements are:

1. Sovereignty
2. Territorial integrity
3. Legal equality.

Sovereignty implies that the government is the supreme law making authorities in its respective territories. This principle was first established by the Treaty of Westphalia.

The second important feature of a nation-state system is territorial integrity. The states may influence behaviour of each other through established diplomatic channels and must respect each other's territorial integrity.

All the nation-states irrespective of their size, population, military capabilities, economic resources, etc. are equal members of the international community.

## DEVELOPMENTS IN THE 90'S

Since 1945, three developments have affected the nation-state in different directions.

1. Consolidation
2. Disintegration
3. Globalization.

Firstly, there has been dramatic consolidation of the trend. The domination of thc nation-statc as the most powerful of political organization has been extended the virtual end of colonial empires. The power of the national government has been consolidated in the 1970s and 1980s, particularly in the Third World countries like Zaire, Nigeria, Malaysia and Pakistan.

The second development relates to ethnic resurgence. There has been revival of minority nationalist movements and such trends have increased since 1970s. For example, Quebecois nationalists wanted independence from Canada. More recently, India and Sri Lanka also faced the problem of Kashmir and Tamil nationalists respectively leading to certain amount of bloodshed in both cases. After the disintegration of Soviet Union and East European Communists blocs, the ethnic resurgence has spread like an infection. The creation of small states was more because of the forces of dichotomization, revolution, or intervention by outside powers.

The third development relates to the process of globalization. During the last two decades, the world has become highly interdependent. Today, the nation-state has to operate in an interdependent world. Information, money, weapons, technology pollution, values, radiation, food, computers, drugs, diseases, data all flow rapidly around the globe. The role of international and super national organizations such as UNO, World Bank, IMF, GATT (WTO) and NGOs is increasing by leaps and bounds. Numerous academicians and politicians have drawn attention to the development of global interdependence.

## SETBACK TO THE NATION-STATE SYSTEM

In the post-World War II, the nation-state system suffered a setback. These are:

1. Growing interdependence compelled the states to have greater international interaction and enhanced their dependence on each other.
2. The rise of nuclear weapons has also greatly weakened the nation-state system.
3. The growing role of public opinion in recent years has also affected the character of the nation-state system.
4. The growing role of MNCs in post-Second World War period has weakened the nation-state system.

It may be concluded according to the critics, the nation-state has become obsolete. In simple words, the nation-state is still a leading actor in international relations and citizen of a state.

## BASIC FEATURES OF THE MODERN NATION-STATE

There are four features of the modern nation-state:

- The consolidation of policy-making, or centralization of political authority;
- The expansion of nation-state's tasks and purposes from defence to social security;
- The creation and expansion of state bureaucracy, i.e. a large civil service; and
- The expansion of citizen's role in public affairs—citizen's participation.

## THE CONSTRUCTION OF THE MODERN NATION-STATE

There are different aspects to the construction of the state: nation-building (i.e. the political aspects to modernity and modernization); economic development (i.e. the economic aspects of modernization), and urbanization and migration (i.e. the social aspects of modernity).

There are four key factors in establishing the modern-state:

### Nationalism

To sustain a common set of symbols (e.g. flag, currency, anthem and myths) is the very heart of nation-building. Nation-building is a process of forging and constructing a set of common beliefs. For example, in the US, liberal ethos (i.e. freedom and equality of all individuals) are central and all-pervasive. At the beginning, Protestantism contributed to the formation and maintenance of liberal ethos.

Most often, beliefs are distinct and in reaction to previous nations, England was the first modern nation-state. Its defining features were:

- the individual as the seat of authority
- equality of all individuals under God and
- the importance of science, especially experimental science.

France, in reaction to England, fashioned its own special identity. The idea of the nation was not based on the sovereign and the people (as in England), but took a highly abstract character, one that was reified and materialized in the notion of l'etat' [state].

Germany, distinct from England and France, focused on 'peoplehood' (or 'brotherhood'), emphasising 'blood of the people' as the basis of its collective identity. This was translated into ethnic nationalism. On obtaining its independence from England, the US adopted the English ideal features of individualism and equality. In fact, more so than in England.

Emerging nations (such as Islamic states of Iran and Indonesia) are creating their own features in reaction to (or, rather, in antagonism to) Western values and beliefs. Islam has become the central defining feature. Interestingly, most post-socialist countries have adopted the Western features (such as individualism and free market principles) in defining their nation. Though they also possess their own cultural history upon which to draw on in recreating their collective identity after the legacy of the Soviet rule.

**Political Legitimacy**

Legitimacy of rule and of the rulers are critical in nation-building, though inevitably, considerable conflicts occur to achieve nationhood. In absence of social and moral bonds and norms, wide and common consensus, based on dialogue and communication, is required. As already noted, when examining Tocqueville, political legitimacy and stability require political institutions (i.e. political parties, trade unions and voluntary associations) to be durable and strong. In other words, civil order, social trust and participant political culture precede and provide firm grounds for legitimacy.

**Citizenship**

Creating a new nation is a construction of a sense of citizenship and identity. T.H. Marshall claims that citizenship is a status bestowed upon those who are full members of a community, making them equal with respect to the rights and duties with which the status is endowed and possessed.

In the UK, citizenship has evolved over several centuries:

- Civil rights—equal rights under the law
- Economic rights—free to engage in work and
- Social rights—welfare rights provided by the state.

These rights temper and limit the inequalities of harsh capitalism, and provide citizens with universal rights, regardless of who they are. In effect, creating an equality of opportunity for all.

Yet citizenship cannot only be understood from the point of view of the citizens, but also of the nation-states, seeking to preserve their integrity of the state by policing the national borders. Twentieth and Twenty-first centuries have seen widespread migration—economic workers, political refugees, ethnic expulsions and forced migration. Nations vary in their granting of citizenship. For example, Germany stresses the importance of people's ethnicity and 'blood' as the basis of their citizenship, whereas France emphasises political and economic rights (such as voting and paying taxes) for people's inclusion into the French citizenry, and the UK points to the place of birth for people's identity. Consequently, nation-states have strict or flexible approaches to citizenship.[6]

Some social scientists have argued that a post-national form of citizenship has emerged. It suggested that human rights are, or ought to be, attached to all people regardless of their origins. For example, people from the EU have similar rights irrespective of their national citizenship.

Some scholars have suggested that citizenship has been constantly re-defined and re-constructed. This has become especially significant as nation-states attempt to maintain their productive economies by inviting and granting citizenship to people from outside. For instance, the US grants green cards and then bestows US passports on economic workers required for its industrial sectors.

**Economic Development**

There are several features to the economic development that accompany the emergence of modern nation-states:

- a change in agricultural techniques and the emergence of market organization of economic practices and relations
- the emergence of an economic elite (e.g. the bourgeois class) to direct investment and innovation and
- the role of the state to boost economic growth via monetary and fiscal policies.

What kind of a state is required to get an emerging nation to take off and develop? A democratic state like the UK and the US, or an authoritarian state like Taiwan, Hong Kong, Japan and South Korea. However, this distinction fails to capture the complexity of the state-society relationship. Instead, Peter Evans offers another distinction:

- a predatory state—profits and revenues are appropriated by leaders, their family and clients and

- a development state—a delicate balance is achieved where the state provides capital and leadership, yet loosen its reign over industries' strategies.

The latter is conducive to economic growth. The nature of such a structural situation can be referred to as embedded autonomy. The development state is autonomous of other institutions, grounded in its own meritocratic standards of performance, and not shaped by nepotism and other such webs of social ties and relationships. At the same time, the development state and its leaders are embedded in that they share important relationships with new entrepreneurs and corporate leaders. Such relationships are built upon a sense of shared trust and purpose, rather than a sense of opposing loyalties and conflicts.

## ACTORS IN THE CONSTRUCTION OF THE NATION-STATE

There are three key social actors involved in constructing the modern nation:

### Intellectuals

Individuals are responsible both for creating and for articulating symbolic themes that play a crucial part in the creation of the nation-state. Intellectuals occupied a special role in nation-building efforts in Asia and Africa, in part, because no other groups were available for that task. The merchants had no special reason or desire for sever ties with colonial nations, and other social groups were insufficiently organized.

Twentieth century intellectuals voiced the theme of nationalism (ideas of national independence and unity) that seemed to reconcile the tension between the appeal of the urban life in the order nation-states and the parochial tugs of family and friends in the colonial country. This theme was associated with two other sets of ideas. Populism provided a means of articulating the feeling of loyalty to home as well as a device to arouse the mass required for nation-building. Socialism came to be attractive to intellectuals as they felt it seemed to demonstrate practical political success of accommodating nationalism and populism in the face of imperialism and capitalism.

Whether intellectuals in emerging and developing nations will continue to play a dominate role depends on their ability to commensurate their skills with expanding economic opportunities that come with economic development.

**Military**

Like the intellectuals, the military has often been propelled to the forefront of organized efforts to change simply because there are no other groups that could assume that part. It possess the training, organizational skills and resources for an active role.

It is a force for innovation and for conservatism depending on the stage of nation-building. It begins with being an agent of transformation and change, shifting from traditional to transitional political orders, having the will and ability to challenge the existing political regime. In these early stages of political modernization, the military plays a highly modernizing and progressive role, promoting social and economic reforms.[7]

With the transformation of a nation-state from oligarchic to radical praetorianism, the military becomes the conservative guardian, suppressing forces aimed at overthrowing the government and securing the reign of representatives of the middle class. In the future, the military in the developing nations will become ultimately subordinate to that of the civilian rule, as in developed countries.

**Peasants**

They are the foot soldiers, and willed by the intellectuals and the military. Yet peasant wars and revolts testify to their ability to engage in political protest, as they become aroused due to the changes towards a market society.

Peasants are naturally disinclined to engage in rebellions or revolutions, because they work alone and value their own individual efforts. They view themselves as competitors, rather than collaborators. In addition, they lack organizational skills, and possess parochial and local interests related to farming.

Hence, peasants become active only when they are led by outside agents, and usually middle and landless peasants are most engaged as the former are most likely to be affected by the transition towards urban capitalism, and the latter least to be subjected to the power of landowners.

As societies become complex and industrialized, the peasant rebellions will become narrower in scope and less intensive, as the peasants lose their significance in the economy and society.

## PATHWAYS TO NATIONHOOD

There are certain events that are more likely to result in a democratic rather than an authoritarian regime.

### Seeds of Democracy

Lipset argues that economic development and material abundance are more likely to result in democratic rather than authoritarian governments:

- values of material growth (e.g. enterprise, self-responsibility, and infrastructural social development) are associated with a set of democratic ideas and values (e.g. free expression and association, and equality) and
- economic growth provides the conditions for equality of opportunity and greater citizen political participation: the social mobility of the working class means economic security and better education, and; the tendency of the middle class to engage with moderate and democratic parties, and to penalise extremist parties.

Yet Lipset fails to demonstrate the transmission mechanisms from economic development to democracy. His analysis is suggestive, and a product of associational thinking.

### Democracy and Oligarchy

Barrington Moore argues that there are several conditions that promoted the growth of democracy in states such as England and France:

- the emergence of a balance of power between the principal social groups that reduced the power of the royal authority and the landed upper class
- the development of commercial agriculture promoted the growth of a class of capitalists, whose power counteracted

the urban manufacturing groups and displaced the peasants from the land, so undercutting the seeds of peasant revolution and

- the absence of a coalition between the landed aristocracy and the capitalist class.

Nation-states (e.g. Germany and Japan) that produced fascism had landed elites who were sufficiently adopt to manipulate the growth of industrialism, and in doing so prevented the emergence of a balance of power. Nation-states (such as Russia and China) that would turn to communism still comprised a large and significant force of peasants, and such societies were either compelled to repress them, or to enlist their support for fundamental political change.

Yet Moore fails to examine how bureaucratic administrations play a decisive role in nation-building. In addition, he neglects the position of the nation-state in a larger international setting; e.g. substantial losses in war precede the revolution as in the case of Russia.

**Capitalism and Democracy**

Rueschemeyer, Stephens and Stephens offer a clear, though conventional definition of democracy. Democratic governments consist of:

- regular, free and fair elections in a system of universal suffrage
- responsibility of the state to the parliament and
- basic citizen rights such as freedom of expression and association.

Authoritarian governments are those that lack the first two elements, whereas totalitarian regimes lack all three.

Rueschemeyer, Stephens and Stephens reach two important conclusions:

- large landlords were the most anti-democratic force of all the forces
- working class, and not the middle class, was most crucial to the emergence of democratic governments.

They argue that capitalist development weakened the landed upper class, and strengthened the working class. Democracy was the outcome of the contradictory nature of capitalist development, which of necessity, created subordinate classes with the capacity for self-organization, so strengthening the civil society.

## SUCCESS AND FAILURE OF NATION-BUILDING

Some societies achieve great success in creating a modern nation-state, whereas others accomplish next to nothing. A successful outcome of nation-building is a nation-state in which policy-making has become consolidated and routine, there is some regular means of renewing political leadership, the interests of the citizens regularly receive recognition from political leaders, and there exists a complex and active machinery of the state. Failure, thus, means the absence of at least one of these conditions.

The principal obstacle to success lies in a system of economic interdependence among advanced and developing nation-states. The world system is one in which some countries are dominant over others. It is a system whose foundations lie in a world economy that had its origins in capitalist agriculture but has changed into industrial domination.[8]

The world economy is responsible for the expansion of the world system. As technology expands, the boundaries and the content of the economy incorporate more and more territories into the system. First, imperialism, and then colonialism insisted on the economic and political character of subordination respectively. For instance, the efforts of the US to secure economic dominance over other nations have major political repercussions; the efforts severely reduce the likelihood that the subordinate nations can develop a viable and successful state machinery. Yet this account neglects that subordinate nations are not necessarily victims of this process, and can and do make some significant difference to how trade is conducted.

### Globalism

The issues of immigration and citizenship become more pressing as old boundaries and barriers between nations seem to be disappearing. It becomes even more important for transnational bodies to begin to re-think the matter of citizenship. The global economy has now become an even more competitive market. Yet emerging nations are unlikely to be able to compete given the lack of capital to create productive domestic markets. International organizations (such as the IMF and the World Bank) are unlikely to facilitate a change in the economic competitiveness of nations. In addition, in the light of social problems of AIDS, poverty and violence, emerging nation-states will struggle to become productive societies.

The contemporary trends in the advanced industrial countries and the Third World:

- The Third World political process operates largely without benefits of political 'brokers'.
- Political parties or groups are not oriented to a distinct political arena or particular political principles.
- The political process is characterized by a prevalence of cliques.
- Political loyalty is governed more by a sense of identification with the concrete group than by identification with the professed policy goals of the group, and leadership has a high degree of freedom in determining matters of strategies and tactics.
- Since the leadership and the ruling party are committed to a total change in society or fundamental questions about its destiny or the interest of the whole nation.
- The political process is fragmented and is characterized by a lack of integration among the participants on account of the absence of a communications system in society. This limits the types of political issues that can arise in such societies.
- In non-Western societies, the political sphere is not sharply differentiated from the social and personal spheres, but follows from the latter. Power, prestige, and influence are based largely on social status. The fundamental framework of politics is communal, and national politics is dominated by an educated urban and upper-class elite.

- The political process is characterized by a high rate of recruitment of new elements into political roles. There is a constant increase in the number of participants and type of organization involves in the political process.
- The political process is characterized by sharp differences in the political orientation of the generations. The younger generations who are the aspiring elite, put pressure on the current leaders who took part in the revolutionary movement, for inclusion in the circle of national politics but are thwarted by them. This results in a clash of view and consequent tensions.
- There is little consensus regarding the legitimate ends and means of political action. Since the urban elite and the village peasant live in different worlds and have different attitudes, outlook and orientation, they can rarely exhibit a common approach towards political activity.
- There is wide divergence between the level of information and knowledge through discussion of the masses and their actual participation in political decision-making.
- There is a high degree of interchange of roles which are not clearly differentiated but are functionally diffuse. There are no sharply defined divisions of labour in any sphere of life.
- The national leaderships have to appeal to an undifferentiated public and have no means for calculating the relative distribution of values and attitudes throughout society. They have few guides to how the public opinion is divided over particular issues.
- The unstructured character of the Third World political process encourages leaders to adopt more clearly defined positions in international issues than on domestic issues. They seek a role in world politics that is out of proportion to their national's power.
- The affective or expressive aspect of politics tends to override its problem-solving or public policy aspect.

Charismatic leaders tend to provial in Third World politics because societies experiencing cultural change are characterized by a confusion over values providing an ideal setting for such leaders. The problem of political communication further reinforces the position of the charismatic leader.

## NOTES

1. Kenneth N. Waltz, "Review: Dilemmas of Politics", *American Political Science Review,* 53 (June 1956), pp. 529-32.
2. Couloumbis and Wolfe, n. 4, p. 28.
3. James Rosenau, "The Functioning of International Systems", *Background,* VII, (November, 1963).
4. Robert W. Tucker, "Professor Morgenthau's Theory of Political Realism", *American Political Science Review,* 46 (March 1952), pp. 214-24.
5. Wolfram F. Hanrieder, "The International System: Bipolar or Multiblock?", *The Journal of Conflict Resolution,* IX (September 1965), p. 302.
6. Raymond Aron, "The Quest for a Philosophy of Foreign Affairs" in Hoffmann, ed., n. 25, p. 88.
7. Wolfram F. Hanrieder, "The International System: Bipolar or Multiblock?"
8. Stanley Hoffmann, "International Systems and International Law", *World Politics,* XIV (October 1961), p. 207.

# Theoretical Paradigm and Approaches in International Relations

3

Theories in international politics are a logical deductive and inductive system of concepts, definitions, and propositions which states a relationship between two or more selected aspects of phenomena from which testable hypothesis can be derived.[1] International theory building is a creative achievement and involves a qualitative jump beyond evidence. It is provisional in character and always open to revision depending upon new insights and evidences. It is neither necessary nor desirable for a international theory to be a final formulation. Many international theories have been developed in 20th century to study state behaviour. International theory in international relations means different things to different people. Alexander George and Juliette George[2] are scientifically oriented scholars, have given a brief definition. To them, theory is "a body of internally consistent empirical generalizations of descriptive, predictive, and explanatory power". For them, these generalizations should best be expressed in the form of hypotheses and propositions that are testable, verifiable, falsifiable and quantifiable.

Theories in international politics are conceptual models upon which international relations get analyzed. Each theory is reductive and essentialist to different degrees, relying on different sets of assumptions respectively. As Oli Holsti describes them, international relations theories act as a pair of coloured sunglasses, allowing the wearer to see only the salient events relevant to the theory. An adherent of realism may completely disregard an event that a constructivist might pounce upon as crucial, and *vice versa*.[3]

The number and character of the assumptions made by an international relations theory also determine its usefulness. Realism, a parsimonious and very essentialist theory is useful in accounting for historical actions (for instance why did X invade Y) but limited in both explaining systemic change (such as the end of the Cold War) and predicting future events. Liberalism, which examines a very wide number of conditions, is less useful in making predictions, but can be very insightful in analyzing past events. Traditional theories may have little to say about the behaviour of former colonies, but postcolonial theory may have greater insight into that specific area, where it fails in other situations.

Particularly, international theory is a symbolic construction and does not share the ineluctability of fact. It is a much abused term in popular speech, philosophical discourse and scientific treatise alike. The proponents of every theory has its own definitions of what constitutes a theory. In short, the traditionalists have presented some general propositions about international politics that serve to explain and, to a limited degree, predict the responses of foreign policy elites in crisis situations. Traditionalists generally regard international relations to be a sub-field of political science and philosophy, but a sub-field with characteristics that give it a separate status. Unlike political science which they believe is mainly the study of the governance of established political communities, traditionalists regard international relations as the study of the nearly anarchic relations existent among sovereign political enities. In this way, whereas traditionalists view entities as the analysis of "order" in the distribution of political goods in relatively stabilized and advanced political systems, they treat international relations as the study of 'disorder' in a nearly primitive and inegalitarian international system. International relations theories can be divided into "positivist/rationalist" theories which focus on a principally state-level analysis, and "postpositivist/reflectivist" ones which incorporate expanded meanings of security, ranging from class, to gender, to postcolonial security. Many often conflicting ways of thinking exist in international relations theory, including Constructivism, Institutionalism, Marxism,

Neo-Gramscianism, and others. However, two positivist schools of thought are most prevalent: Realism and Liberalism; though increasingly, Social-Constructivism is becoming mainstream and postpositivist theories are increasingly popular, particularly outside the United States.

## WHY DO WE NEED THEORIES?

A theory tries to pose and hopefully answer the 'why' questions which link different cases to each other and not just the 'what' questions. The scholars try to find patterns in the international system. If all events are *sui generis* (i.e. things on their own which cannot be categorised together with any other events) then we just get into a muddle. If there is no pattern to behaviour, then truly the outlook is grim. Only by exploiting the patterns we detect can we seek to alter them. Theory may help us to develop a better understanding of world events, and devise better solutions to problems of world order. Theory is not simply an abstraction. Nor does it exist in isolation from the policy realm.[4]

Theory-building closely follows the course of world politics. It often reflects our desire not only to explain change, but also to provide better solutions to problems of world order. Second, theory reflects the accumulated wisdom of a discipline by building on comparisons between actors, events and outcomes in many different parts the world. As such, theory can help us learn from the experience of others, and overcome the parochialism that often characterises the policymaker's mental universe. Third, theory provides us with alternative lenses for explaining events and responding to them. Finally, theory can help us anticipate, if not always predict accurately, the course of events in world politics. For example, neo-realist theory tells us that multipolar international systems are likely to prove less stable than bipolar ones. The more the number of major actors, the greater the room for uncertainty, misperception and miscalculation.

In developing the theories we need to make sense of the world, we formulate concepts such as 'state' or 'power' or 'globalization'. We categorise things together with the aim of making the world comprehensible. We say what will happen in various circumstances. We assume that there is some consistency to behaviour so we can go to a little further rather than talking of patterns, causes and consequences.

**Way Out**

The idealists presented the following meaningful remedies for solving international problems. Moral actions should act according to moral principles in their international behaviour, eschew all kinds of traditional power politics, and follow policies of non-partisanship. Secondly, attempts should be made to create supranational institutions to replace the competitive and war-prone system of territorial states. Setting up of the League of Nations and an insistence on international cooperation in social matters as approaches to peace were symptomatic of idealists' institutional solutions to the problem of war. Many idealists went further in suggesting that power politics could only be abolished by instituting a world government. Thus in the ultimate analysis this theory aspires for the ideal of world federation or one world. Thirdly, the legal control of war was also suggested. It called for new transnational norms to check the initiation of war and, should the war occur, its destructiveness. The Kellogg-Briand Pact of 1928, which outlawed war as an instrument of national policy, represent the high point of legal approach. They also advocated more faithful adherence to international law. Another way suggested by idealists was to eliminate weapons. The attempts towards global disarmament and arms control were symbolic of this path to peace. Fifthly, the efforts should be made to see that the totalitarian forces cease to exist, as the idealists believe that the struggles so far have been between democratic and totalitarian states. Totalitarianism is one of the main causes of war and it must be eliminated. Lastly, some idealists saw the way to peace and welfare in the restructuring of the international monetary system and in the elimination of barriers of international trade. Still others saw in the principle of self-determination the possibility to redraw the world's political map under the conviction that a world so arranged would be a peaceful world.

**Realism**

Realism makes several key assumptions. Primarily, it assumes that mankind is not inherently benevolent and kind but self-centred and competitive, in contrast to other theories of international relations such as liberalism. It also fundamentally assumes that the international system is anarchic, in the sense that there is no authority above states capable of regulating their interactions; states must arrive at relations with other states on their own, rather than it being dictated to them by some higher controlling entity (i.e., no true authoritative world government exists). It also assumes that sovereign states, rather than international institutions, non-governmental organizations, or multinational corporations, are the primary actors in international affairs. According to realism, each state is a rational actor that always acts towards its own self-interest, and the primary goal of each state is to ensure its own security. Realism holds that in pursuit of that security, states will attempt to amass resources, and that relations between states are determined by their relative level of power. That, level of power is in turn determined by the state's capabilities, both military and economic.

Moreover, realists believe that states are inherently aggressive (offensive realism) and/or obsessed with security (defensive realism); and that, territorial expansion is only constrained by opposing power(s). This aggressive build-up, however, leads to a security dilemma where increasing one's own security can bring along greater instability as the opponent(s) builds up its own arms. Thus, security is a zero-sum game where only relative gains can be made.

There is a distinction between structural realism and liberal realism (also known as "Neoliberal Institutionalism"): The former emphasizes the permanent condition of conflict. Thus, to ensure state security, states must be on constant preparation for conflict through economic and military build-up. The latter holds that while the system is anarchical, through diplomacy, international law and society, order can be promoted (English School). This gives credence to establish IGOs such as the United Nations.

### Six Principles of Realism by Morgenthau

Political realism contains not only a theoretical but also a normative element. It knows that political reality is replete with contingencies and systemic irrationalities and points to the typical influences they exert upon foreign policy. Yet it shares with all social theory the need, for the sake of theoretical understanding, to stress the rational elements of political reality; for it is these rational elements that make reality intelligible for theory. Political realism presents the theoretical construct of a rational foreign policy which experience can never completely achieve.

At the same time, political realism considers a rational foreign policy to be good foreign policy; for only a rational foreign policy minimizes risks and maximizes benefits and, hence, complies both with the moral precept of prudence and the political requirement of success. Political realism wants the photographic picture of the political world to resemble as much as possible its painted portrait. Aware of the inevitable gap between good, i.e. rational, foreign policy and foreign policy as it actually is, political realism maintains not only that theory must focus upon the rational elements of political reality, but also that foreign policy ought to be rational in view of its own moral and practical purposes.

Morgenthau in his famous book *Politics Among Nations* has developed realist theory in the form of six principles of political realism. Principles are explained in brief as under:

#### *Focus on Human Nature*

Political realism believes that politics is governed by the objective laws that have their roots in human nature. In order to improve society, it is first necessary to understand the laws by which society lives. The operation of these laws being impervious to our preferences, men will challenge them only at the risk of failure. Realism, believing as it does in the objectivity of the laws of politics, must also believe in the possibility of developing a rational theory that reflects, however imperfectly and one-sidedly, these objective laws. Human nature, in which the laws of politics have their roots, has not changed since the classical philosophies of China, India, and Greece endeavoured to discover these laws. Hence, novelty is not necessarily a virtue in political theory, nor is old age a defect. The fact that a theory of politics, if there be such a theory, has never been heard of before tends to create a presumption against, rather than in favour of its soundness. Conversely, the fact that a theory of politics was developed hundreds or even thousands of years age was the theory of the balance of power does not create a presumption that it must be outmoded and obsolete. A theory of politics must be subjected to the dual test of reason and experience. The laws by which man moves in social world are eternal. He cannot get rid of those laws because they are eternal and permanent. Man is a mixture of good and bad, selfishness and altruism, loving and quarrelsome, traits and possessive and sacrificial qualities. His is the story of struggle for survival. Human nature has not changed, and it explains constancy and repetitious nature of political conduct. The complexity of international politics can best be understood only with the help of these objective laws. If one desires to appraise the nature of foreign policy, it can be done only when one examines the activities of the statesmen, who always act in a manner that safeguard their country's interests. For realism, theory consists in ascertaining facts and giving them meaning through reason. It assumes that the character of a foreign policy can be ascertained only through the examination of the political acts performed and of the foreseeable consequences of these acts.

### *Focus on Interest in Terms of Power*

National interests are the motivating force of a state's activity in the sphere of international politics. The state meets these interests with the help of power. That is why every nation wants to acquire more and more power. In this way, international politics is a struggle for power. The theory of realism does not bother about what is desirable or immoral. It cares only for the national interests which are desirable under the concrete circumstances, time and place. In other words, this theory preaches that states should not be led by ideologies; ethics or motives, as they do not govern the field of international politics.

In short, the main function of a state and its statesman is to protect national interests with the help of power.

Concept of interest is defined in terms of power. This concept provides the link between reason trying to understand international politics and the facts to be understood. It sets politics as an autonomous sphere of action and understanding apart from other spheres such as economics (understood in terms of interest defined as wealth), ethics, aesthetics, or religion. Without such a concept a theory of politics, international or domestic, would be altogether impossible, for without it we could not distinguish between political and non-political facts, nor could we bring at least a measure of systematic order to the political sphere. The main signpost that helps political realism to find its way through the landscape of international politics is the concept of interest defined in terms of power. We assume that statesmen think and act in terms of interest defined as power, and the evidence of history bears that assumption out. That assumption allows us to retrace and anticipate, as it were, the steps a statesman—past, present or future—has taken or will take on the political scene. We look over his shoulder when he writes his dispatches; we listen in on his conversation with other statesmen; we read and anticipate his very thoughts. Thinking in terms of interest defined as power, we think as he does, and as disinterested observers, we understand his thoughts and actions perhaps better than he, the actor on the political scene, does himself. The concept of interest defined as power imposes intellectual discipline upon the observer, infuses rational order into the subject matter of politics, and thus makes the theoretical understanding of politics possible. On the side of the actor, it provides for rational discipline in action and creates that astounding continuity in foreign policy which makes American, British, or Russian foreign policy appear as an intelligible, rational continuum, by and large consistent within itself, regardless of the different motives, preferences, and intellectual and moral qualities of successive statesmen. A realist theory of international politics, then, will guard against two popular fallacies; the concern with motives and the concern with ideological preferences. To search for the clue to foreign policy exclusively in the motives of statesmen is both futile and deceptive. It is futile because motives are the most illusive of psychological data, distorted as they are, frequently beyond recognition, by the interests and emotions of actor and observer alike. Do we really know what our own motives are? And what do we know of the motives of others?

Yet even if we had access to the real motives of statesmen, that knowledge would help us little in understanding foreign policies, and might well lead us astray. It is true that the knowledge of the statesman's motives may give us one among many clues as to what the direction of his foreign policy might be. It cannot give us, however, the one clue by which to predict his foreign policies. History shows no exact and necessary correlation between the quality of motives and the quality of foreign policy. This is true in both moral and political terms. We cannot conclude from the good intentions of a statesman that his foreign policies will be either morally praiseworthy or politically successful. Judging his motives, we can say that he will not intentionally pursue policies that are morally wrong, but we can say nothing about the probability of their success. If we want to know the moral and political qualities of his actions, we must know them, not his motives.

***Interests are Dynamic***

The meaning attached to interest and power is not static and fixed once for all. National interests are changed and shaped by the circumstances. If the circumstances make the state a powerful one, its national interests become different from what they had been when the state was a weaker one. Not only interests are dynamic, but the power position of most countries also varies with time.

***Universal Moral Principles Inapplicable***

Political realism is aware of the moral significance of political action. It is also aware of the ineluctable tension between the moral command and the requirements of successful political action. And it is unwilling to gloss over and obliterate that tension and thus to obfuscate both the moral and the political issue by making it appear as though the stark facts of politics were morally more satisfying than they actually are, and the moral law less exacting than it actually is. It cannot be applied to the actions of states in their abstract universal formulations. They must be filtered through the concrete circumstances of time and place. Prudence is the supreme virtue in politics and political ethics judges action ultimately by its political consequences. An individual may sacrifice his interests to safeguard the abstract or moral value but the state cannot and should not sacrifice its interests. On the contrary, the states generally sacrifice the abstract or moral laws for the sake of national interest. Realism maintains that universal moral principles cannot be applied to the actions of states in their abstract universal formulation, but that they must be filtered through the concrete circumstances of time and place.

### *Moral Aspirations of the Nations*

Political realism refuses to identify the moral aspirations of a particular nation with the moral laws that govern the universe. As it distinguishes between truth and opinion, so it distinguishes between truth and idolatry. All nations are tempted—and few have been able to resist the temptation for long—to clothe their own particular aspirations and actions in the moral purposes of the universe. To know that nations are subject to the moral law is one thing, while to pretend to know with certainty what is good and evil in the relations among nations is quite another. There is a world of difference between the belief that all nations stand under the judgement of God, inscrutable to the human mind, and the blasphemous conviction that God is always on one's side and that what one wills oneself cannot fail to be willed by God also.

Political realism considers the nations as actors of international relations which strive to pursue and achieve their national interest with the help of power. The actions of the states can only be interpreted with this principle. The moral laws that govern the universe do not apply to states. Realism seeks to distinguish between truth and idolatry. Each state is tempted to identify its particular aspirations and actions in terms of universal moral principles.

### *Autonomy of Political Sphere*

Realism declares the autonomy in political sphere. The difference between political realism and other schools of thought is real and profound. A political realist thinks in terms of interest defined as power, as an economist thinks in terms of utility, a lawyer in terms of conformity of conduct with legal rules and a moralist of such conformity with moral principles. He is exclusively concerned about the relevance of a particular policy to the national power. Although this theory is aware of thoughts which are other than political, it regards and puts them subordinate to political science.

### *Decisive Assessment*

In spite of its wide acceptability, the realist theory suffers from many weaknesses and limitations. It has been criticized by many scholars on the ground that it is an incomplete theory. The realist theory neglects all factors that influence the quality and quantity of power used by the state. The domestic compulsion that affect national power, the nature of regime, the structure of power beliefs and values which account a great deal for nation's goal are either left out or ignored.

Morgenthau equates politics with power, but politics should deal with all other variables of social sciences. Morgenthau places too much emphasis on the aspect of interests and power. A 'power monism' does not account for all politics even in world affairs. Participation and community also play a role. The realist did not explain the forces behind the new institutions beginning to be constructed in Western Europe in 1950s and 1960s, where the cooperative pursuit of mutual advantage rather than narrow self-interests appeared to dominate. Finally, to say that international behaviour comes out of human nature does not mean anything. International behaviour is often indeterminate-defies all these laws. It forgets that same facts or realities may mean different things to different people.

Despite the shortcomings of realism, much of the world continues to think about international politics in its terms. World War II, the onset of rivalry between the United States and Soviet Union, the expansion of Cold War into a global struggle between the East and the West, the stockpiling of nuclear weapons, bloody wars in former Yugoslavia in the 1990s rekindled enthusiasm for realpolitik. The continuing relevance of realism finds expression in its "new" reformulation, known as "neo-realism" or "structural realism". To neo-realist, the structure of the system dictates national leaders' foreign policy. Thus, realist theory is a pioneer toward the development of international theory.

The most interesting conceptual development within the realist paradigm has been the emerging split between the "defensive" and "offensive" strands of thought. Defensive realists such as Waltz, Van Evera, and Jack Snyder assumed that states had little intrinsic interest in military conquest and argued that the costs of expansion generally outweighed the benefits. Accordingly, they maintained that great power wars occurred largely because domestic groups fostered exaggerated perceptions of threat and an excessive faith in the efficacy of military force.

Realism claims a long pedigree. Thucydides, in the fifth century before Christ, is often portrayed as the founder of the school. His analysis of the Peloponnesian War was an exposition of realist concepts. For Thucydides, "the real reason...[for the war]...was the growth of Athenian power and the fear this caused in Sparta". Yet Thucydides founded a school of thought that (at least in Europe) went into recession. The notion of independent states were supplanted firstly by the Roman Empire and then by Christendom. A sort of "civilized unity" existed in Europe until at least 1500 and in a modified form until about 1800. It was not until the early 1500s that a political philosopher of the realist tradition could share the status of Thucydides. Machiavelli was widely condemned at the time for his cynical and amoral advice on the way government should be conducted. Nevertheless, what he captured in his writings became the essence of what we know today as realism.

Many have dreamed up republics and principalities which have never in truth been known to exist; the gulf between how one should live and how one does live is so wide that a man who neglects what is actually done for what should be done learns the way to self-destruction rather than self-preservation. The fact is that a man who wants to act virtuously in every way necessarily comes to grief among so many who are not virtuous. Therefore, if a prince wants to maintain his rule, he must learn how not to be virtuous, and make use of this or not according to need.

In the sphere of diplomacy, realism was introduced through the policies of the French minister Cardinal de Richelieu. He led France into the bitter Thirty Years War to ensure that the various states controlled by the Habsburgs did not dominate Europe. That war ended in the Treaty of Westphalia (1648) which is widely credited with establishing the modern system of states. From that time, there were sporadic writings promoting realism. The philosopher Thomas Hobbes and the military theorist Carl von Clausewitz were among the best known.

First World War presented a major challenge to realism. Realist practices were increasingly challenged, particularly in the United States whose national experience to date differed markedly from the European states. US President, Woodrow Wilson framed his Fourteen Points as the basis for the subsequent peace. These points included banning secret treaties, freedom of navigation and trade (aimed at increasing interdependence), arms reductions, self-determination and the formation of what became the League of Nations. The allies largely acquiesced. The post-war era was one of optimism and pacifism. The "war to end all wars" had been fought, and the Kellogg-Briand Pact had outlawed war. The discipline of international relations was founded in a climate that saw a responsibility of academia being to contribute a further nail in the coffin of armed conflict.[5]

### Neo-realism

Neo-realism explains international relations in terms of the structural properties of the international system, especially the distribution of power. Unlike classical realism, it does not see human nature as an important variable in war and peace. Neither does it pay much attention to domestic politics, which is central to Liberal theory's explanations of international relations. Neo-realists take a dark view of international relations. Conflict and war are unavoidable because the international system is anarchic, i.e. having no higher authority above the state. In anarchy, states seek security through self-help, either by increasing their own military and economic capabilities, and/or through alliance with stronger powers. But security can only be achieved in a limited way, because of the operation of the "security dilemma", whereby attempts by any state to improve its security by acquiring the means of power provokes other states to follow suit, thereby rendering the initiating state as insecure as before. Neo-realists dismiss the role of international institutions in regulating state behaviour and promoting peace. Institutions are creatures of self-interested great powers.[6] They simply reflect, rather than shape, the prevailing distribution of power. In terms of international stability, institutions matter only in the margins. What really matters is the balance of power. All self-help systems tend to be governed by a balance of power dynamic maintained by the great powers. States tend to balance their rivals domestically, by acquiring greater military and economic power, or by building alliances with stronger powers.

## System Theory

### *System Theory in General*

System analysis came to Political Science via other sister disciplines, particularly, Anthropology and Sociology, Social Anthropologists such as Emile Durkheim, A.R. Radcliffe-Brown and Malinowski, and Sociologists such as Talcott Parsons, Robert K. Morton and Marion Levy Jr. have significantly contributed to the growth of systems analysis in social science. The three political scientists who have pioneered systems analysis in Political Science are David Easton, Gabriel Almond and Morton Kaplan. While Easton and Almond have applied it to national politics, Kaplan has applied it in his study of international politics. The key concept in systems analysis is 'systems'. Ludwig von Bertalanffy defines system as "a set of elements standing in interaction". According to Gabriel Almond, "a system implies interdependence of parts and a boundary of some kind between it and its environment."[7]

System analysis is another milestone on the path of the modernization of Political Science. System analysis is considered to be the pioneering model of political analysis. David Easton was the first major political scientist to develop a systematic framework on the basis of the system—analysis approaches for the study of politics.

System analysis conceives politics in terms of the political system. Easton has selected the political system as the basic unit of analysis and concentrated on the intra-system behaviour of various systems. He says that outside the political system, there are other systems—physical, biological, social and psychological for instance political system is distinguished from the other systems by the authoritative allocation of values made by the former which broadly constitutes the political process.

It has encouraged interdisciplinary study of political phenomena, particularly of large ones. System analysis was first developed by a biologist named Ludwig von Bertalanffy in the 1920s. Physical theorists and engineers also contributed to its development. It then entered Social Sciences such as Anthropology, Sociology, Psychology and Political Science.

David Apter observes:

1. Systems have boundaries within which there are functional relationships mainly based on some of the communications.
2. Systems are divided into sub-systems, with exchanges existing between the sub-systems.
3. Systems have a capacity for coding that is they take inputs; they are able to learn from inputs, and translate inputs into some kind of output.

Morton A. Kaplan observes that system analysis is "the study of a set of interrelated variables, as distinguished from the environment of the set, and of the ways in which this set is maintained under the impact of environmental disturbances".

These definitions point to the following characteristics of a system.

1. A system consists of parts or elements
2. These parts or elements interact with each other
3. Through their interactions, they influence each other

4. The system exists within a boundary
5. It is open to influences from the environment
6. It translates inputs into outputs.

David Easton defines political system as "that system of interaction in any society through which binding and authoritative allocation of values are made and implemented". Gabriel A. Almond and James S. Coleman have observed that "political system of interaction is found in all independent societies which perform the functions of integration and adaptation (both internally and vis-à-vis other societies) by means of employment, or threat of employment, of more or less legitimate physical compulsion".[8]

The political system is a set of interactions through which authoritative decisions are made. It consists of several sub-systems which, through their interactions, influence each other and also affect the behaviour of the political system.[9]

The political system, like other systems, has its boundary which divides it from other systems. Any claim on the use of 'public authority' passes the boundary and enters the political system as an act of 'interest articulation'. There is constant interaction, and interchange between the political system and its environment. The political system, which is exposed to demands flowing from the environment, has its own regulatory mechanisms to cope with them.

According to Gabriel A. Almond, political systems can be compared with one another in respect of four characteristics. Firstly, all political systems comprise political structures which can be compared with one another in terms of the degree and form of structural specialization. Secondly, all political systems perform same functions. Thirdly, political structures are multifunctional. Lastly, political systems are 'mixed' systems in respect of culture. They are neither all-modern, nor all-primitive.[10]

Political system tend to persist and survive. Their persistence and survival depend on the fulfillment of the following conditions. Firstly, the system should be good at effecting conflict resolution. Persistence of conflicts, resulting from clash of demands and expectations, is a threat to the maintenance of the system. These conflicts need to be resolved. Secondly, the political system should be able to generate sufficient support for it. Without such support, its survival may be endangered. Thirdly, it should be accorded legitimacy. The people must accept it as legitimate and obey its decisions without any fear or coercion. Fourthly, it should have regulatory mechanisms to regulate the flow of demands coming from the environment. It should have the capacity to manage stresses and crises.

David Easton, who has pioneered systems analysis in Political Science stands for a unified theory of politics a theory which can explain political behaviour in both national politics and international politics. He is interested in the persistence and growth of political systems. He is critical of the equilibrium model which is static and oriented towards status quo. Easton takes a dynamic view of system's behaviour. He has tried to explain how political systems persist not only in a stable environment but also in a changing world. The most important part of Easton's systems theory is input-output analysis. The system has the capacity to convert inputs into outputs. While inputs consist of demands and support, outputs comprise laws, rules, regulations, decisions, etc. The quality of outputs is relayed back to the system. As a result of this, there may take place changes in the nature of inputs in succeeding rounds. This process is known as 'feedback loop'.

Systems analysis is an exercise in studying the inter-relationship and inter-connectedness of politics with the other parameters. As a method, it marks a shift from analysis to synthesis. Classical science tried to isolate the elements of the observed universe in order to understand them separately. Systems analysis, in contrast, lays special emphasis on the interrelationship between one element and another in the belief that a part can be understood only as a part of the whole, and not as a part in itself. Systems analysis takes a full view of the picture and recognizes the interrelations within and beyond.

**Uses and Advantages**

Systems analysis is hailed as a scientific method of studying politics. It has introduced interdisciplinary orientation in Political Science and developed some useful concepts and tools.

1. Systems analysis presents an orderly scheme which can be utilized for dealing with the complex political problems in a broad social context.

2. The general systems theory has developed a number of concepts which have opened up new questions and new dimensions. Political scientists can make use of them for studying and explaining political realities.

3. Systems analysis is of great help in studying the system's change and breakdown. It may suggest ways for saving a system from collapse or disintegration.

4. Kaplan claims that systems analysis has suggestive value as it is a heuristic method of gaining knowledge and interpreting the real world.

5. It facilitates the integration of variables that do not belong to a single discipline. It is possible to generate hypotheses on the basis of structural similarities between the political system and other systems.

6. The interdisciplinary approach, employed in systems, analysis, is highly successful in explaining political behaviour.

### *System Approach in International Politics*

The system approach in international politics has been undertaken by Morton Kaplan, Karl Deutsch, Raymond Aron and McClelland. Their assumption is that there is a system in international relations. The systems theory is the result of the behavioural revolution in social sciences. System connotes relationship between units. The nations (states) being its parts involved in the process of interaction as each nation (a unit) is in constant contact with 'the whole' or the international environment.

The theory assumes the existence of an international system at the global level. Aron explains, there "has never been an international system including the whole of the planet", but the post-war period, when "for the first time humanity is living one and the same history", has witnessed the emergence of a kind of global system. But at the same time it must be admitted that such a system suffers from great heterogeneity and is perhaps too loose to be properly designated a system. An international system, in the words of Hoffmann, "is a pattern of relations between the basic units of world politics, which is characterized by the scope of the objectives pursued by these units and of the tasks performed among them, as well as by the means used in order to achieve those goals and perform those tasks".

This theory also assumes that a theory of international politics normally cannot be expected to predict individual actions because the interaction problem is too complex and because there are too many free variables. It can be expected, however, "to predict characteristic or model behaviour within a particular kind of international system". Thus, this theory analyses international behaviour of a state from an empirical investigation of political facts, classified and arranged in appropriate categories.

**Nature of System Theory in International Politics**

McClelland[11] first expounded the system theory in 1955 but the theory was accessible in a most organized manner by Morton Kaplan who affirmed that the systems approach provided the only possible methods which can make certain the development of scientific politics. Morton Kaplan is of the opinion that there is some rationality, reliability and order in international relations. International relations implies two things: International system, and nation-state system.

Kaplan defines a system of action as a set of variables so related in contradistinction to its environment, that desirable behavioural regularities characterize the internal relationship of the variables to each other and the external relationship of the set of individual variables to combinations of external variables.

According to him, nation-states acquire political systems but the international system itself lacks one as is often characterized as an unacceptable political system. In international affairs, it is nothing else but the national interest which governs the behaviour of nation states:[12]

- Firstly, the system is described an arrangement of international actors in which interactions are identifiable.

- The second usage relates to a particular arrangement in which the nature of arrangement itself is considered the most important variable in explaining the behaviour of states.
- The third view is that system is the application of special types of approaches (methods) to the study of international politics.

The United Nations is the only universal actor. Nation-states are the main actors in international politics and the roles of the states change with the change of international system.

***Six Models of Systems Theory***

According to Kaplan, international system can be divided into six models on the basis of functions and stability. Kaplan (1957) in his *System and Process in International Politics* presents six models of international system.

- The balance of power system
- The loose bipolar system
- The tight bipolar system
- The universal system
- Hierarchical system and
- The unit veto system.

The balance of power means even distribution of power between various nations to prevent any particular nation from imposing its will upon others. Balance of power is an over-used concept in international politics. It means many things to different people. As has been said by Claude,[13] it is an "ambiguous concept" and it has got many meanings. Sometimes it is used as a policy. It is also used as a symbol. It is also used at times as a propaganda ploy. If in the 19th century the theory of balance of power took strong roots, in 1970s it gained immense popularity due to the effort of Henry Kissinger, the "star" of the foreign policy establishment of the US in the first half of 1970s. Kissinger, who has all along been a keen student of the balance of power, went on theorizing on it even after he joined the Nixon administration. His attachment to Metternich and Bismarck whom he studied extensively did not diminish with the passage of time.[14] On the other hand, his faith in balance of power and his admiration for these original protagonists of this theory were reinforced by his active association with "real politics" of the world.

To understand balance of power, we may take the analogy of a balancer with a pair of scales. If the weights in the two scales are equal, there is balance. The same analogy may be extended to international politics. The two states or two coalitions of states are in balance if they are equally powerful. Morgenthau rightly says that the balance of power is "an actual state of affairs in which power is distributed among several nations with approximate equality". Balance of power refers to "equilibrium" in international politics. In a normal human body, there is equilibrium. When an individual suffers from a serious disease, this equilibrium is disturbed. But different organs of the body would automatically react to prevent such disturbance. Further, an external input like medicine is injected into the body to maintain equilibrium at the original level or at a different level. Thus, the maintenance of equilibrium in the body in the face of external attack requires automatic internal reactions and at times, external intervention duly planned and executed. Similarly, the equilibrium in the international system is not an automatic process only. It involves human choice and decision planned and implemented. It has been described as "diplomatic contrivance".[15]

Loose bipolar system is characterized by two bloc actors (USA and USSR) surrounded by a group of smaller powers, non-member bloc actors (non-aligned states) and universal actor (the UN).

This model places both the superpowers in the category of nuclear giants and calls for long-term institutional alliances based on interests that are perceived as permanent and couched in ideological terms. In a tight bipolar system, non-aligned states will disappear and the system, will operate only around the two super blocs (the NATO and Warsaw Bloc).

The universal international system grows when the universal actor (UN) is sufficiently powerful to prevent war among national actors but national actors retain their individuality and yet jockey for more and more power. In such a system, the universal actor becomes powerful enough to prevent war among nations, but national actors retain their individuality.

In the hierarchical international system, the universal actors becomes too powerful and the international community becomes a sort of world-state and states would be territorial sub-divisions of world system rather than independent political units.

In the unit veto system, all states would have equal potentialities to destroy each other and when all the actors are prepared to resist threats and retaliate in case of an attack. It comes into existence in the post-nuclear proliferation era. Due to the changes in the international situations, Kaplan incorporated some additional 'mixed empirical models' to his original scheme. These four models are Very Loose Bipolar System, Détente System, Unstable Bloc System and Incomplete Nuclear-diffusion System. Kaplan's projections about the progression of the international system has been belied. The bloc system today has disappeared and trends point towards either a unipolar or multipolar system.

The end of Cold War has ushered in a new international system. Prof. Robert E. Harkavy deduces seven distinct images, models or paradigms regarding international system. These seven models are:

- The Uni-polar Dominance Model
- Zones of Peace of Turmoil
- The Global Village
- The Three-bloc Neo-Mercantilist Models
- The Revitalized Balance of Power Model
- The Clash of Civilization Model
- The Bipolar Redux Model

### *Criticism of Systems Theory*

The systems theory is severely criticized and is regarded as too general and abstract and too remote from reality. System model is considered as an exclusively closed system and is ill-equipped to analyze the world reality which is open and subject to continuous change. It did not explain the forces or issues that determine the behaviour of states.

The system theory does not predict what will actually happen, but it only forecasts what would happen if certain conditions develop, which rarely develop exactly as envisaged. Too much discussion on methodology and building of models are activities in futility. These models serve as useful framework for the classification and analysis of regularities of international behaviour pattern of states in proper levels in order to formulate a coherent body of timeless propositions.

But in spite of these difficulties, the systems approach has obtained a set of structures which describe the international system and explain the behaviour of individual states and explain the particular configuration of relationships which can be found in the international relations. The trend towards integration is growing and with the growth the importance of the systems approach. Its relevance to international system is related to this trend which seems the prime need of our time.

### *Decision-making Theory*

Decisions on foreign policy are made not on the basis of reality as such, but on the basis of perception of reality. It is dependent upon how an actor defines a situation. Two inputs would significantly affect his "definition of the situation". First is transformation which reaches him. Second is his values, orientations and pre-dispositions which would, to some extent, determine the way he would read that information and give meaning to it. It is pertinent to mention that due to several reasons a foreign policy actor is normally not able to have access to all relevant information. First, those who are responsible for collecting information often fail in their duty. They generally succeed in getting less than what they want. Secondly, they do not send all information at their disposal to policymakers. In their perceived interests, they suppress or destroy some information and send the rest which, they hope, will lead to making a policy that they favour. Sometimes, they manufacture certain information that do not have any basis in reality. Manipulation and distortion of information is a common thing in policy-making process. It has now been revealed that army officers on the field often sent false data to Washington to prove their assertion that the US was winning the war in Vietnam.

The policymaker may not use all information that manages to reach him. He may feel that it would not help him in making a policy he favours. Hence, at his level, he may indulge in the same things which have already taken place at the level of information gathering agencies. He would be inclined to distort and manipulate information so that a policy, that he advocates, can be formulated. Further, his interpretation of facts would be significantly coloured by his predispositions and biases resulting from his socialization and other sources like his own interests. Thus, a foreign policy actor takes a decision on the basis of his perception of reality. In other words, he sees the facts the way these are presented to him or the way he wants to see them. But his perception of the situation does not change the situation as it really exists. It is thus irrespective of in whatever form it is fed into the policy-making machine. The real conditions are called the "operational environment" while the information on which planning and policy-making defines the "psychological environment". Perception would define the situation and form the basis of a decision taken. But the consequences of this decision that the policymakers would face one day or the other would result not from this perception, but from the reality itself. As has been pertinently pointed out with respect to policy-making and the content of policy decisions, our position is that what matters is how the policymaker imagines the milieu to be, not how it actually is. With respect to the operational results of decisions, what matters is how things are, not how the policymaker imagines them to be.

Another scholar has used the phrase, "strategic image" to connote definition of the situation. Strategic image has two components, viz. cognitive and affective. The cognitive component refers to the policymaker's view and definition of the central features of the international environment (his perception); the affective (the emotional and volitional) component refers to the valuational dimension of the image structure, the way he assigns his likes and dislikes, his approval and disapproval of these conditions. To some extent, says Frankel, the affective component overlaps the cognitive one as it acts as, a sort of a "filter" in determining our evaluation of the importance and relevance of the things observed; thus in a way, it also determines what we actually perceive because it fits into our image and what we ignore because it does not.

One of the important principles of decision-making is rationality. A policymaker aims at making rational choice. While taking a decision, he is faced with several possibilities and uncertainties. He thinks of several alternative courses of action. But all courses are not of equal nature nor are they of equal potential. One alternative may have higher potential than the other. In other words, one may be more paying than others. It is always the nature of man to go for that alternative which would fetch him maximum gain and minimum loss. He calculates the profit and loss of each possible alternatives and chooses that one which would ensure the maximum net gain. That choice, based upon the cost-benefit analysis, is known as rational choice.[16]

The principle of making this choice is called maxi-mini-principle. It has been argued that rationality in decision-making is a theoretical concept without much practical relevance. Often, it is not possible for a decision-maker to go through the whole process of making the rational choice. He has several limitations for doing it. First, many situations demand quick decisions. Specially in crisis situations he has got only a little "decision time". In other words, he is required to decide his policy within a short time. Even in normal times, he may not get enough time to calculate the pros and cons of all possible alternative courses of action. Secondly, the rationality of the actor is limited. He is not a computer. Like a chess player, he may calculate the possible consequences of a limited number of alternatives. But it is almost impossible for him to calculate the cost and benefit of all possible alternative strategies.[17] In addition to skill, he also lacks in having access to all relevant information. However, hard he may try, he is not likely to have all information he wants. As Herbert Simon has pointed out, there are "practical limits to rationality". Individual human beings are "limited in knowledge, foresight, skill and time". Therefore, in general, the actor, instead of looking for the best move,—stops, in his search, the moment he finds a "good enough move". Simon says: "The key to an effective solution appears to lie in substituting the goal of satisfying, of finding a good enough move, for the goal of miximizing, of finding the best move." Thus, "satisfying" not maximizing is, by and large, the criterion for selecting one of the several alternatives while taking a decision.

In a crisis, many normal procedures are bypassed/short-circuited while formulating appropriate responses to it. A crisis is a sudden and unexpected development and involves quick rise in tension, and unless managed in a short time, it would lead to war with catastrophic consequences. So, the time for decision-taking is very short. It is not possible to complete all procedures and formalities for taking a decision at such an hour. Many relevant actors are just ignored. The policy-making is confined only to a few, all of whom are not necessarily the formal members of the policy-making process. If the chief executive so likes, he can include in this body some outsiders in whom he has sufficient confidence. The most famous example is the way the Kennedy government acted to deal with the Cuban missile crisis. Snyder, Bruck and Sapin first pioneered decision-making approach in the field of international politics and foreign policy in 1954. The decision-making approach inquires on actors called decision-makers and the state defined as decisional units. This approach offers a 'state centric' or 'state as actor' model of international relations. This approach viewed that actions in international relations can be defined as a set of decisions made by recognizable units and tries to prove that decision-makers "tend to fit incoming information into their existing theories and images".[18]

***Models of Policy-making***

The American response to the Middle East War of 1973 was formulated by only a few persons who were close to President Nixon. It was mainly Nixon and Kissinger, his National Security Adviser, who took the very controversial "alert" decision to alert the nuclear force of the US to deal with any eventuality.

The following are the characteristics of crisis decision-making.

First, the decision-makers are small in number and they are close to the Chief Executive. Second, many normal time procedures which are to be followed to arrive at a rational choice are either ignored or short-circuited. Effort is made to reach quick decisions. Third, the compulsion for taking quick decisions forces the policymakers to underplay or even suppress their perceived organizational and personal interests and keep at the centre the perceived interests of the nation. In crisis times, bureaucratic politics is reduced to the minimum. Further, there is little chance for public opinion to significantly influence the crisis decisions.[19] Because of paucity of time, political parties, legislatures, and pressure groups which articulate and aggregate the interests of people are not able to mobilize themselves. Further, because of national interests at stake and seriousness involved, they would not deem it proper to hinder the crisis response by the Chief Executive. All other tasks would accord precedence to the urgency of effectively tackling a crisis by the government.[20]

Writers dealing with the theoretical question of decision-making on foreign policy may broadly be divided into two groups. One group treats the state as the sole actor and accords little importance internal variables. For it, foreign policy-making is mainly determined by internal dynamics.[21] This group is again divided into two sub-groups. While one of them emphasizes the role of organizations, the other lays exclusive emphasis upon the interaction among governmental actors in this regard.

Accordingly, we discuss below the three models of foreign policy-making.

1. *Black-box Model*

The main protagonists of this model are Hans Morgenthau, Arnold Wolfers, Thomas Schelling and Hennan Kahn. Apart from these scholars, the revisionist historians of the US also believe in this approach to the study of foreign policy. All of them are American scholars. Many foreign policy scholars of other countries are also believers of this approach. All of them, with varying degree of emphasis, assume that the state is the sole actor and it is the lone voice deciding its foreign policy. It thus implies that whichever political party or individual is in power, the policies and actions of the state would be geared towards the realization of this end-defence and promotion of its vital interests. The revisionists American historians like William Appleman William and Gabriel Kolko hold that the foreign policy of the US has, as its main objective, the promotion of capitalism both within and outside it and whoever may be the ruling elites in Washington, they would act to gain this paramount objective of the US. In trying to serve its interests best, the state tends to select rational strategy; it would choose that alternative which would fetch the maximum benefit with minimum cost. Because of its emphasis upon rationality in decision-making, this approach is known as the Rational Actor Model.

2. *Organizational Model*

This model is based on the assumption that happenings are the outcomes of organizational processes. The way information moves inside an organization and the way it reaches a decision-maker will have some bearing on his decisions. Another assumption of this model is that the rules and habits that grow up within an organization will affect the way the decisions are made within that organization.

Organization means the system of activities and the structure of relationships. The activities and relationships will primarily be the outputs of formal rules governing the allocation of power and responsibility, and the flow of information in the organization. An actor tends to take a decision on the basis of his "definition of the situation", which, in its turn, would be influenced by the nature and amount of information that would reach him.[22]

3. *Governmental Policy-making Model*

The purpose of the framework is to make explicit the nature of nation-state functioning in international politics. The basic idea is to understand international politics in the context of interaction of foreign policies and foreign policy decisions. The partial relevance of the decision-making approach cannot be underestimated and its importance lies only in its usefulness as a tool for foreign policy. This model conceives state action as resultant from the way in which identifiable decision-makers define the situation of action. The emphasis is on identifiable official actors working in a very complex organizational setting. It analyses the 'why' and 'how' of a decision and why a particular decision has been taken than some other. They attempted a speculative examination of the activities of actors in international relations along with the factors that shape and influence such actions. The "Black Box" model is criticized on the ground that it does not take into consideration what takes place inside the box. Once the box is opened, we may see that the process (of foreign policy-making) is very complex. The output is the resultant of many stresses and strains interacting inside the box. The advocates of Governmental Politics Model (GPM) state that the body entrusted with the task of making foreign policy is not homogeneous in its composition and nature. It consists of several units and sub-units which tend to perceive issues more from the point of view of their parochial interests than that of the national interest. Halperin and Kanter say: The bureaucratic perspective implies (1) that change in the international environment is only one of several stimuli to which participants in the foreign policy process are responding (it is possibly among the weakest and least important); and (2) that events involving the actions of two or more nations can be best explained and predicted in terms of the actions of two or more national bureaucracies whose actions affect the domestic interests and objectives of the other bureaucracies involved.

The decision-making approach laid emphasis on the questions as to how and why a nation acts in international politics. The primary assumption in that if sufficient number of factual propositions concerning the behaviour and activities of known actors can be established, it can lay the foundation for an explanation of a decision. The official decision-makers take action in the name of the state. The approach insists that behaviour should be understood and to analyze and understand the social world in the view of the decision-makers. The best way to understand international politics lies in knowing the process in which the official decision-maker makes his final choice of a policy out of a series of alternatives. Snyder[23] defines decision-making as "a process which results in the selection from a socially defined, limited number of problematical alternative projects, of one project intend to bring about the particular future state of affairs envisaged by the decision-makers".

The setting in which the foreign policy decisions are made is the one which is perceived by the decision-makers. The setting consists of internal and external parts. The internal setting is made up of two components—the total social structure and the total governmental institutional structure. The role of public opinion, interest groups, socio-economic conditions, personalities, roles, organizations in the decisional unit, the physical and technological conditions, demographic factors, the basic values and other influences in service in society from part of internal setting. The external setting includes all the relevant factors in the total situation of the international system existing at a given time. It includes situations beyond territorial boundaries of state in the form of actions, reactions, counteractions of other states emanating from the decisions of men in authority.

This theory successfully analyses deeper roots of behaviour pattern of states and try to investigate the relationship between personality traits, situational variables and behaviour and empirically tracing the role of domestic variables as sources of foreign policy behaviour. Foreign policy is understood to be the outputs of large organizations each with a substantial life of its own.

The actions of decision-makers can be described in terms of three basic determinants:

- sphere of competence
- communication and information
- and motivation.

Hillsman scheme centres on a model of consensus and conflict. Since both decision-making and decision-makers are a process, Lasswell has identified seven stages in this process. Intelligence, stage of recommendations, stage of prescription, stage of innovation, application stage, appraisal stage, and termination stage. Harold Sprout and Margret Sprout[24] give emphasis on environmental factor which mean how the environments influence the decision-making. They follow the same approach but place more emphasis on the 'environmental factor' defining environment in terms of a milieu which has a physiological as well as operational aspects laying down limits on what can be achieved by these decision-makers within those limits. They adopt decision-making as a tool in the context of environment as defined by them. Alexander George and Juliete George have articulated another line of approach. They study decisions in the light of the personality of decision-makers. It is based on the fact that all foreign policy decisions require an analysis of the personality factor of decision-makers.

Bernard Cohen postulates five elements at the centre of any theory of foreign policy-making:

- Political interest groups
- The media of mass communication
- Specific agents in the executive branch
- General climate of public opinion
- Specific committees of the legislature.

Burton believes decision-making to be a process. Burton identifies three factors which determine a decision:

- Perception
- Expectations
- Information.

**Game Theory**

Game theory is functional to political science to present a experimental and quantifiable analysis of the phenomena such as elections, voting behaviour, process of negotiation, military movements and coalition formulation. Kaplan, Schilling and Riker tried to apply this theory in the field of international politics. Kaplan describes game analysis as "the best tools available for the analysis of problems of strategy and, if properly used, it is likely to increase the exploitation of success in policy". But he fails to deal effectively with the problems of application and only ends up in technical discussions. Schilling has enriched the theory by the introduction of complex human experience into the procedures of decision-making. Thus, he has introduced new concepts like 'bargaining games', 'making threats', 'giving promises', 'relinquishing the initiative', 'identifying the friends and enemies' and 'delegating authorities'. Riker, similarly, used game theory in international politics to find out the principle, that governs the formation of coalitions and applied three major principles.

Game theory is defined as "a body of thought dealing with rational decision strategies in situations of conflict and competition, when each participant or player seeks to maximise gains and minimise losses".[25] The models of game theory were first developed in mathematics. The theory that should be studied as an exercise in political simulations to study international politics is the game theory. This theory applies mathematical models to the study of political science. Emil Borel originally developed it in the 1920s.[26] Martin Shubik, Oskar Morgenstern and Karl Deutsch were among the first to recognise the importance of the game theory in international relations. As S.P. Varma says, "Game theory owes its origin to parlour games like chess, chicken poker or bridge, with obvious elements of conflict, decision-making and cooperation, played between two or more players, where the decisions of each player are contingent upon the decisions of others and the central point is the interdependence among the decisions of different players in the game."[27] In a situation of this kind, where each player is interested in 'winning' the game and two or more individuals have to make choices, it is necessary that they have some knowledge of the choices available to, and made by, each other and of the preferences the other players have in their choice: whatever choice he makes depends inextricably on the choice or the choices made by the other players.

The theory of game has certain concepts and assumptions which are distinguished below:

- There are the rules of the game that each player has to observe. The rules refer to the distribution of resources and the strategic possibilities open to each player for his employment.

- There are the players or the decision-makers; they may be individuals or institutions.
- There are certain situations that may be described as outcomes in a game. The players are supposed to be engaged in choosing alternatives for the sake of winning, or at least not losing the game.
- The full range of possible outcomes is called the prospects. The inventor of the game generally design a very small range of prospects, limited in number and possible combinations.
- The reward of the game is called pay-off. The best pay-off is victory; draw is the second best.
- Strategy is the most important concept that informs the player to act in a way that his purpose is served. The norm of rationality is, for this reason, sufficiently diluted.

There are basically four types of games:

- Zero-sum two persons games
- Non-zero-sum two persons games
- Zero-sum n-persons games and
- Non-zero-sum n-persons games.

In the first type of game, there are only two players and the gains of one are always equal to the loss of the other, the sum of outcomes for the two players being zero. In the second and third types, involving two or more persons in the contest, the players may share the division of the awards in some way, and the gain of one need not be equal to the loss of the other. In such a situation, the pay-off is divisible and some principle of distribution is applied. In the fourth type, where there are three or more players the game situation develops a large number of features and it becomes possible for two or more of the players to cooperate against the others by pooling their resources and making collective decisions during the play. The players may 'gang up' to form their 'proto-coalitions' reducing the number of their adversaries.

Game theory has certain weaknesses. In the first place, it cannot be applied successfully to an empirical investigation as it is deductive in nature. Secondly, it assumes that decision-makers are perfectly rational which is not true in every case. Thirdly, it is interested only in situation ethics, rather than the ethics of man. Finally, there is the difficulty of identifying the field to which the theory is related.

**Liberal Economies and Globalization**

Closely related to the arguments about the spread of ideas are those about material well-being. Wealth presents some contradictions as it provides the wherewithal for military action. Yet many commentators see wealth as a path both to democracy and civilized behaviour. As states become wealthier, they are more satisfied and less attracted by the risks of military adventure. Where the wealthy state did use its military strength, it was for good. Power, democracy and benevolence had seemingly merged in the new era.

Some, like Fukuyama, saw that the fact that increased wealth was being generated through "liberal economics". He argued that, just as liberal democracy was the end-state of political development, only capitalist culture, market forces and competition could generate wealth.... "No other path towards full economic modernity has proven to be viable."

The inter-relationship between political choice and the free market is not immediately apparent, but Fukuyama argued that the "desire for recognition, then, can provide the missing link between liberal economics and liberal politics...." In his formulation, economic growth plus recognition led to liberal democracy. At the same time, irrational expressions of recognition such as imperialism were eliminated.

Yet the evidence for such forces is slim. Fukuyama is forced to turn to the attractiveness of consumerism as an element of western culture. He thus argues that the "ultimate victory of the VCR" is that it forced the adoption of economic liberalism. Despite this, he is not alone in arguing that the success of the West will serve as a beacon for others to follow.

**Realism and Pessimism on a Back Foot**

Throughout the Cold War, it was the realist school of international relations that held sway. The Cold War was dominated by a confrontation of force and it appeared that the cold, rational calculations of the school must be the logical course. Even Fukuyama agreed "The twentieth century, it is safe to say, has made all of us into deep historical pessimists."

The post-Cold War world saw numerous pessimistic interpretations of the future. Samuel Huntington postulated new power blocs based on race and religion replacing the old ones based on ideology. John Mearsheimer anticipated a multitude of small states competing with each other. While, Martin Van Creveld predicted nuclear weapons proliferation eliminating war between states and at the same time sub-national violence increasing with greater access to conventional weaponry.

However, in the new era, pessimism went onto the back foot. Three issues were important in making the old theories of the past unpopular.

Firstly, the way the Soviet Union broke up was a challenge to the underlying assumptions of realism. Seemingly, one day the world faced a hulking superpower and the next day it was gone. According to realists, survival was the prime objective of the state. They assumed the fate of major powers would be decided by interaction with other powers—and inevitably that would involve conflict and loss of life. Meanwhile, they paid little attention to the internal workings of the state. Realism failed to explain how internal factors within the state could lead to such major changes by themselves—as happened to the Soviet Union.

Secondly, the new era was one of optimisms. It was clear to the casual observer that things were getting better and not worse. Realism took war and conflict to be facts of life, often based on an assumption that man was greedy and selfish. The psychology had changed. The old pessimism of realism seemed inappropriate to the new era.

Finally, the pessimists could not agree on the future shape of the world. In the past, they could make simple extrapolations of the consequences of Soviet power. Now, while the liberal internationalists could not agree on the mechanisms to achieve a more peaceful world, they at least agreed that this was the way things were going. For the pessimists, there was no such agreement. At one extreme, there was fragmentation and anarchy—a return to the middle ages. At the other there were new power blocs constructed on cultural or economic bases. Without a common theme, the pessimists remained divided.

Despite all these arguments, liberal internationalists agreed that war would continue for some time. According to Fukuyama, it was history that would end and not violence. Peace would still take some time to establish in the developing world. Mueller also acknowledged that war would persist in the developing world. Singer and Wildavsky's zones of peace, wealth and democracy contained only 15 per cent of the world's population —the rest live in zones of turmoil. Is the liberal ideal at best a 15 per cent solution?

The United Nations only briefly looked like the solution to warfare. In the end, its effectiveness was determined by the extent of support of the United States. The Gulf War, like the Korean War before it, was conducted by the United States and its allies with only a UN label.[28] The effectiveness of the UN depended as much as ever on the active involvement of the US and its funding. Realists acted unsurprised—having argued that such institutions reflected the self-interest of member states rather than being able to act as an independent restraint on violence.

While authors on all sides of the debate seem content to place liberal democracy on a pedestal as the superior form of government—this often reflects a personal preference. Some attempt had been made at analytical observation, but scope still exists for argument. Relatively few democracies have existed until recent times, and room exists to debate whether some of the older ones were truly democratic until they had adopted universal suffrage and human rights. Over the last 50 years, it could be argued that the Cold War, with the superpowers maintaining discipline in their camps, prevented such conflicts arising (such as between Greece and Turkey). Nor does the spread of democracy say anything about the wars caused to achieve it, or the likelihood of violence between and with non-democratic states.

Even if liberals win their argument that liberal democracy is a more peaceful form of government, notwithstanding the problems of transition and interaction with non-democratic governments, there is little to support the inevitability of liberal democracy spreading quickly. Certainly, it has made enormous progress over the past decade, but who is to say whether this will continue or simply prove to be a short-lived spurt? Just as Communism was collapsing in Europe, China veered strongly towards authoritarianism—signalling their resolve with the Tiananmen Square massacre. Many cases exist in the past of other states being dragged back from democratic government. Fukuyama claims that that the progress towards democracy is an inevitable one, but he rests his case on the shoulders of Hegel. Hegel had dated the end of history at 1806—and Fukuyama is loathed to contradict the master—but since that time there has been two world wars, an unprecedented Cold War, and more loss of life than ever before in history.

The strength of the economic arguments is also subject to challenge. Some question whether viable economic models—between the command economy and pure market forces might also lead to wealth. With the recent collapse of several Asian currencies, what appeared to be a viable alternative—the market with strong government protection and guidance—also fell by the wayside. Others question the theoretical link between liberal politics (premised on man's humanity) and liberal economics (premised on man's greed). The power of the restraint imposed by international contact has also been the subject of debate.

### Marxist Theory

The starting point of Marxism is the Hegelian dialectics. Marx was very much impressed by the Hegelian way of explaining social evolution. According to Hegel, human evolution has not been in a straight line. It has moved in a zig-zag way. It consists of contrast, negations and contradictions. Every stage in history gives birth to its opposite, the antithesis; and out of the conflict between the thesis and antithesis results the synthesis which reconciles the opposite tendencies present in the earlier system on a new higher level. According to Hegel, "contradiction is the moving principle of the world". It became one of the basic principles of his philosophy.

Marx was impressed by Hegel, but he felt Hegel had made the dialectic stand on its head. He, therefore, rejected Hegel's philosophic idealism, whereas Hegel had regarded the 'spirit' to the ultimate reality, Marx regarded matter as the ultimate reality. For Hegel, the inevitable goal of social evolution was the idea fully conscious of itself; for Marx the inevitable goal was the establishment of a classless society. The Marxian dialectics hold that contrary forces are present in every stage of society and constitute the moving force of history. The present capitalistic stage is also faced with its antithesis—the proletariat. The capitalists and the workers are in conflict with each other. The outcome of this class-struggle will be the establishment of a society where there shall be no classes and, therefore no class struggle. Marx thus accepted only the 'rational kernel' from Hegel and not its kernel or idealistic shell. It may be pointed out that dialectic is a process of nature and form of thinking, which is capable of being put to the service of both materialism and idealism. Stalin indicated the following essentials of dialectical materialism: (i) all phenomena are organically connected with, dependent on, and limited by each other; (ii) all phenomena should be considered from the standpoint of their movement, change, and development; (iii) the changes that occur are not merely quantitative; at certain stages, and development accumulation of gradual, quantitative changes lead to qualitative changes; (iv) internal contradictions are inherent in things away and something which is still developing.[29] The struggle between the opportunities, the process of development, and also leads to the transformation of merely quantitative changes into qualitative.

Starting with the Hegelian dialectic, Marx developed three important doctrines:

(1) the materialist conception of history,

(2) the doctrine of surplus value, and

(3) the doctrine of class war.

Communism of Marx is an ideology that seeks to establish a classless, stateless society on the basis of egalitarian order. Communism is known as "scientific socialism". Communism as a systematic and consistent political doctrine is as old as Karl Marx. Marx was one of the first to have attempted a scientific analysis of the evolution of society through history. His scientific work was in the first place of a new historiography. His historiography also became historical sociology. He saw himself as a historian, not as a philosopher of history. His main criticism against Hegel and Young Hegelians was that they were philosophers of history and not historians. Karl Marx (1818-83) is popularly called the the father of Communism. He is a scientific philosopher of the ages. According to Marx, social organization is based on common ownership of the means of production. It can be considered a branch of the broader socialist movement. It is an eloquent protest against the system of capitalism. The phrase "scientific socialism" was used by him in order to distinguish his idea from that of the Utopian Socialism. C.E.M. Joad rightly said, "Karl Marx, is in a very real sense, the father of socialism."

Karl Marx observed, "Philosophers have sought to interpret the world: what matters, however, is to change it." When this standard is applied, argues Wayper, Marx must be regarded as one of the most important, because most influential, political philosophers who have ever lived. The detractors of Marx are many, but his followers and admirers are equally large in number. Many sharply disagree with what Marx has said, but few would deny the strength and widespread expanse of the impact of his ideas. He criticized those who believed in a 'supra-historical' theory which could be imposed upon all peoples irrespective of the historical circumstances in which they are placed. He was of the view that analysis of society should take into account real historical circumstances.

Karl Marx was born in the Rhenish City of Trier of Germany on 5 May 1818. His parents, Heinrich and Henrietta

Marx, belonged to a middle class family. His father, being a prosperous lawyer, gave him good education. He did Law at the University of Berlin in 1836, and got doctorate in Philosophy from the University of Jena in 1841. Being a member of the 'Young Hegelians', he shared radical ideas. But, because of that, he could not get a teaching job at the University of Berlin. In the pre-Marxian period, there were traces of communistic thought in the writings of Plato, Thomas More, St. Simon, Robert Owen and Charles Fourier. But Marx had dismissed their ideas as "utopian socialism" and claimed to have established the first scientific doctrine of socialism. Hence, our study of communism should begin with Marx. Communism as a political goal is generally a conjectured form of future social organization, although Marxists have described early forms of human social organization as "primitive communism".

Self-identified communists hold a variety of views, including Marxism, Leninism, Trotskyism, council communism, Luxemburgism, anarchist communism, Christian communism, and various currents of left communism, which are generally the more widespread varieties. Saint Simon, Robert Owen, Charles Fourier, Proudhon, Lousis Blanc, John Gray, etc. are the leading socialist thinkers in the pre-Marxian period. They are criticized on the ground that they were more theoretical in their approach. Karl Marx made socialism scientific and pragmatic or practical. Socialism before Marx was merely a protest and aspiration but Marx made it practical and militant. Marx, therefore, is considered to be the greatest socialist of the world. His scientific socialism is otherwise known as Marxism. However, various offshoots of the Soviet (what critics call the "Stalinist", and supporters call Marxist-Leninist) and Maoist interpretations of Marxism comprise a particular branch of communism that has the distinction of having been the primary driving force for communism in world politics during most of the 20th century. The competing branch of Trotskyism has not had such a distinction.[30]

### Life and Works

Karl Marx held that society could not be transformed from the capitalist mode of production to the advanced communist mode of production. Marx described the revolutionary dictatorship of the proletariat is the first stage of communism. Marx envisioned the communist society which is emerging from the spirit of capitalism. Marx, in fact, commented very little on what communist society would actually look like. However, the term "Communism", especially when it is capitalized, is often used to refer to the political and economic regimes under communist parties that claimed to embody the dictatorship of the proletariat. Before one examines the ideas of Karl Marx on socialism, one should know a little about his life and works. He was born in 1818 in Germany and educated at Bonn, Berlin and Jena. He was a brilliant student. He planned for a career in teaching after obtaining his doctorate degree from the University of Jena. But owing to some difficulties, he had to go for journalism. He was expelled from Germany and France because of his radical views. Soon he came to England where he met Engels, and thereafter, an intimate friendship developed between the two. In London, they attended the meetings of an organization known as the Communist League. The League assigned the task of drafting a manifesto for the organization to Marx and Engels. Both of them produced the famous "Communist Manifesto" in 1848 in London. It contains the ideas of communism. Marx's other works include *Critique of Political Economy*, *Das Kapital*, *The Poverty of Philosophy*, etc. For about 34 years, Marx lived in England. He spent his time in writing pamphlets and treatises on socialism. Marx was in great financial distress and his friend, Engels, came to help him most of the time. Marx died in 1883 after passing through difficult years of illness and poverty. But after his death, Marx gained a worldwide reputation as the father of revolutionary socialism or communism.

### Three Major Ideas of Marx

The theory of Marxism has been influenced by three major ideas, namely the German idealism, the English economic doctrine and the French revolutionary and socialist thought. Marx derived the idea of dialectic from Hegel, the famous idealist thinker of Germany. The idea that labour is the most important factor of production" and the labour is always paid less, has been derived from the British economists of the 18th and 19th centuries. That society can be changed through revolution and force is required to bring about the desired changes is the product of the French revolutionary and socialistic thought. The theory of Marxism is a curious mixture of above three philosophies. It is true that Marx collected stones from various places but he used them to build a house which was very much according to his own design. As Laski has rightly said, "the Communist Manifesto" is one of the outstanding documents of all times.[31]

Lenin made few changes over Marxism. The present philosophy of communism is the result of what is known as "Marxism-Leninism". Sabine has rightly observed, "The philosophy of communism is a revised version of Marxism, largely the work of Lenin and therefore, often called Marxism-Leninism." A detailed discussion on communism what is otherwise known as "Marxism-Leninism" is given below.

Marxian theory in international relations is mainly based on the following principles:

- Dialectical Materialism
- Materialistic Interpretation of History
- Theory of Surplus Value
- Class War
- Destruction of Capitalism
- Dictatorship of the Proletariat
- Withering Away of the State
- Theory of Revolution
- Dynamics of Social Change.

### *Dialectical Materialism*

Dialectical Materialism is one of the features of Communism of Marx. The word "dialectic" was used by the Greek philosophers to denote a method of discovering truth. The term dialectical materialism was probably invented in 1887 by Joseph Dietzgen, a socialist tanner who corresponded with Marx. Casual mention of the term is also found in Kautsky's *Frederick Engels: His life, His work and His Writting* written in the same year, 1887. Georgi Plekhanov, the father of Russian socialism, later used it and it thus entered Marxist theory. Marx had talked about the "materialist conception of history", which was later shortened to "historical materialism" by Engels. According to Engels, dialectic was "our best working tool and our sharpest weapon". It is a guide to action and our activities within the working class movement. It is similar to a compass or map, which allows us to get our bearings in the turmoil of events, and permits us to understand the underlying processes that shape our world. Engels exposed the "materialist dialectic"—not "dialectical materialism"—in his *Dialectics of Nature* (1883). Diamat was debated and criticized by many Marxist philosophers, which led to various political and philosophical struggles in the Marxist movement in general and in the Comintern in particular. It involved the conflict of ideas, ultimately leading to the discovery of truth. Conversations were held between persons, each upholding a different set of ideas and thus each one tried to justify his own ideas. "Dialectic" has been derived from the Greek word "dialego" which means to discuss or debate. Such discussions led to the discovery of an acceptable idea in the long run. Hence, dialectic implies a dynamic process or a process of change. After the Greeks, it was Hegel, the famous German philosopher, who made a scientific use of the term dialectic. For Hegel "dialectic" is the method by which human history is unfolded. Historical changes take place in a dialectical process. According to Hegel, this process or pattern of dialectical change has three stages, what he called as, (a) Thesis, (b) Antithesis and (c) Synthesis. Each period of history is a thesis. But in due course, it develops into an antithesis, which mutually contradicts each other. Now, as a result of this contradiction, both thesis and antithesis may give rise to higher project known as synthesis. This process keeps on repeating itself and historical changes occur through this process. According to Hegel, in this dialectical movement of human history, "ideas are conceived to be principal causes of historical process and material conditions of society are derived from the motivating ideas". Hence, dialectical change in history is due to impact of ideas. Dialectic is defined as the "theory of union of opposites" or the theory of the study of contradictions. Karl Marx agreed with the dialectical process of historical change put forward by Hegel, but he differed in substance. He said that dialectical changes are not due to "ideas" but due to "material conditions". In other words, ideas are not the motivating factor in human history, but ideas are the product of material conditions of society. Hence, the real motivating factor in historical change is 'matter' or mode of producing material things.

While Hegel's dialectic is known as "dialectical idealism", Marx preferred to call his dialectic as "dialectical materialism". Marx believed that Hegel had wrongly interpreted dialectics by making material conditions dependent upon ideas. Through his "dialectical materialism", Marx claimed that he was placing "Hegel right up". Marx said, "I find Hegel standing upon his head. It is my task to make him stand upon his feet."

The dialectical method implies the dynamic process and Marx, being a revolutionary, has been naturally attracted to this method. Marx puts in his own words. "In the social production in which men carry on they enter into definite relational that are indispensable and independent of their will, these relations of production correspond to definite stage of development of their material power of production. On the economic structures of society, rise legal and political superstructures. The mode of production in material life determines the general character of social, political and spiritual processes of life." At a certain stage of their development, the material forces of production come into conflict with the existing relations of production. Then comes the period of social revolution with the change of economic foundation and it brings about a complete transformation history. At the foundation of Marxism is the belief that everything can be explained by one thing—Matter. This qualifies Marxism as a fundamentally materialist philosophy. According to materialism, matter is the total explanation for space, nature, man, psychic consciousness, human intelligence, society, history and every other aspect of existence. Marxism then assigns the task of knowing all truth to science. If science can get to know everything about matter, then it can get to know about everything. Conclusively, matter is accepted as the beginning and ending of all reality. Matter's sovereignty in determining the course of nature is a vital part of Marxist thought and what separates dialectical materialism (the Marxist dialectical method) from dialectical idealism (the Hegelian dialectical method).

***Materialistic Interpretation of History***

The materialistic conception of history is the application of the principles of dialectical materialism to the study of the development of society. Marx's theory of Historical Materialism, which lays a lot of emphasis upon the economic factor of social evolution, is also known as the theory of Economic Interpretation of History. Historical materialism starts from the view that in order to exist human beings collectively work on nature to produce the means to live. Not all human beings, however, do the same work; there is a division of labour in which people not only do different jobs, but also some people live from the work of others by owning the means of production. How this is done depends on the type of society.

According to this concept, all the phenomena of society have their origin in material conditions of life. Thus, as Sabine remarks, his materialist interpretation meant first and foremost secularism.

According to Marx, all fundamental historical changes are determined by the mode of production or the economic forces. Change in the mode of production brings a corresponding change in social relations. "In changing the mode of production, mankind changes all its social relation. The hand will creates a society with the feudal lord; the steam will, a society with the industrial capitalist". According to Marx, the efforts of man to secure life's necessities can be grouped into four main stages:[32] the primitive, the ancient, the feudal and the capitalist. In the primitive stage, the means of production[33] being slight were communally owned; but in the rest of the three stages, the class which controls the means and implements of production, dominates and exploits the rest, which leads to tension and conflict. To quote Marx, "All the social political and intellectual relations, all religious and legal systems, all the theoretical outlooks which emerge in the course of history and derived from the material conditions of life." The supersaturate of society is erected on the foundation of productive forces. "Legal relations as well as forms of state", wrote Karl Marx, "could neither be understood by themselves, nor explained by the so-called general progress of human mind, but they are rooted in the material conditions of life.... The mode of production in material life determines the general character of the social, political and spiritual processes of life. It is not the consciousness of men that determines their existence, but on the contrary, their social existence determines their consciousness."[34]

According to Engels, the central part of the materialistic interpretation of history is that in a history epoch the prevailing mode of production and exchange, and social organization necessarily following from it, from the basis on which can be built up, and from which alone can be explained the political and intellectual history of that epoch. The economic system thus explains the political institutions and practices of a country, its social structure, its law and traditions, its philosophy as well as its religion and morality. According to Marx, the class which controls the material force of society is at the same time its ruling intellectual force. There is, however, a possibility of theory, theology, ethics, philosophy, etc. coming into contradiction with "the existing social relations". This would happen when the existing social relations have come into contradiction with "the existing forces of production". In other words, the forces of production, the state of society and conscious may come in to contradiction with another particular when condition are changing.

Marxism does not deny the significance of ideas, social ideals, human passions and aspirations. It only affirms that the origin of particular, idea is solely linked up with the requirements of development of the material of society. New ideas calling for a change in the social order arises and spread only when the development of the material life of society confront people with new task. These tasks are comprehended ideas. Having arisen, they in turn exercise an influence on the course of social development. If they correspond to the current needs of social life, sooner or later, they reach the consciousness, of the broad masses and lead to organized movements and struggles. The existence of revolutionary ideas in a particular period presupposes the existence of a revolutionary class.

The history of man is the history of an increasing power of man over nature; and the social cause of historical change is to be found in the mode of production: "Since the mode of production constitute the material basis of the life of society, the history of society is primarily the history of the development of production, the history of various modes of production that succeed one another with the growth of the productive forces." The source of this development is to be found in the necessities inherent in that development. It is the production techniques—labour skill and the instruments of labour—which are the most active elements of production and are always in a state of change and development. As for the production relations, although during the existence of a given mode or production, they undergo certain changes, these changes do not affect their essential nature. The technique of production and distributions thus constitute the primary factors in the dialectic of history.[35]

This is not to deny the significance of other material factors of life, including geographical environment, population and its growth, the principles of legislators, the whims of the politicians in power, etc. Marx and Engels, however, insisted that these factors could only delay or accelerate change, but they were secondary to the basic economic forces which controlled the process of history. It is necessary to point out that, according to Marxism, the human society has passed through only a few socio-economic formations, i.e. definite historical types of society with their own characteristics modes of production bases and superstructures. There are primitive-communal, slave, feudal capitalists and socialist. For the study of theory of value according to which the value of a commodity is determined by the value of labour spent on it. By this doctrine of surplus value, Marx tried to show the exploitative nature of capitalism. It is surplus value which is the source as well as the measure of the extent of economic exploitation.

Marx defined value as the 'crystallised labour' and pointed about that the value of a commodity equals to the value of labour necessary for its production. Of the four factors for productions—land, labour, capital and organization—only labour is variable. While the other factors do not change their value in the process of production, labour power produces a surplus over and above its equivalent. The value which the labourer gets for his services is much less than the value he produces. This difference between the value paid for the labour power and the value received by the capitalists, Marx calls it as surplus value. The value created over and above what the labour power is paid for, is appropriated by the capitalist for himself which is simple exploitation. This difference unpaid labour is precisely the share which fall to the capitalist. The rate of surplus value indicates the degree of exploitation of labour by the capitalist. "The essence of capitalist exploitation is the production of surplus value. Capitalists are not interested in producing means of production and consumer goods that are useful and needed by society but in extracting as such surplus value as possible."

In the existing structure of society, labour stands at a disadvantage. The instruments of production—machinery, tools and materials upon which labour can be performed—are owned by the capitalists. The labourer owns merely his ability to work, which is highly perishable. The labourer must, therefore, sell his labour power for whatever wages he is offered. The capitalist knows it and takes advantage of workers' disabilities. By paying him less the capitalist earns more profits. To earn more profits, he must pay less to the workers. The surplus value which is created by labour power is appropriated by the capitalist. Marx says, "For exploitation, veiled by religious and political illusion, it (bourgeoise) has substituted marked shameless direct, brutal exploitation."

The Marxian theory of surplus value has been criticized by many economists. It is pointed out that labour power alone does not create value and consequently the labourer is not entitled to the whole of value fetched by a commodity. The capitalist has to pay not only the labourer but also he has to make other payments for machinery, for the rent of the building and interest on money he invested. He has also to pay for the raw-material and to provide for depreciation charges. Thus, it is too much to say that labour alone creates value. Nor is labour power, the most important factor of production. All the factors—land, capital, labour and enterprise—are equally important and it is difficult to say how wealth can be created without anyone of them. Marxists deny the validity of such criticism and refer to the view of Marx that machines, tools, raw-material, etc. all represent "congealed labour".

However, the critics insist that Marx's theory to surplus value has the significance of a political slogan rather than of an economic truth. By using this theory he wanted to highlight the exploitative nature of capitalism and demonstrate that capitalism is doomed by the general law of capital accumulation and concentration.[36]

Marx applied his theory of "dialectical materialism" for the interpretation of historical phenomena.[37] Historical materialism is the methodological approach to the study of society, economics, and history which was first articulated by Karl Marx. Marx himself never used the term but referred to his approach as "the materialist conception of history". He also distinguished "philosophical materialism" from what he called "popular materialism". Before Marx, history had been interpreted in different ways. Some philosophers attributed historical changes to divine will. Some other scholars provided a political interpretation of history by saying that historical changes were due to kings, legislators, parliaments and so on. Hegel interpreted history in terms of "ideas", which in his opinion, motivated changes in society.

Historical materialism looks for the causes of developments and changes in human societies in the way in which humans collectively make the means to live, thus giving an emphasis, through economic analysis, to everything that co-exists with the economic base of society (e.g. social classes, political structures, ideologies). Although Marx said, he was only proposing a guideline to historical research, by the twentieth century, the concept of historical materialism became a keystone of modern communist doctrine. But Karl Marx, by applying his theory of dialectical materialism, wanted to interpret human history by taking into consideration of material factors. It is generally-known as Marx's "materialistic interpretation of history". It is the application of "dialectical materialism" to the interpretation of historical phenomena. It says that economic factors determine social existence of men. Historical events are, therefore, the products of economic factors.

No society is static, it changes through materialistic conditions. It is a matter and not an idea that shapes the society. Marx said, "It is not the consciousness if men that determines their existence, but on the contrary, it is their social existence that determines their consciousness." Marx discovered as simple truth that three basic needs of human being, namely food, clothing and shelter, should be fulfilled before he pursues any higher objectives.

In other words, it can be said that the economic sub-structure determines the political super structure. Social evolution takes place through materialism. The various stages of social evolution in history were primitive economy, slave economy, feudalism, capitalism and socialism. Primitive economy was the thesis, salve economy was its anti-thesis. This process of social evolution will go on till perfect socialism or classless society is established. This is known as Marx's materialism. Wayper rightly observes, "In all stages of human life the forms or conditions of production determine the structure of society. Thus, the hand-mill gives you society with the feudal lord; the steam-mill society with the industrial capitalist." The structure of society will in its turn breed "attitudes, actions and civilizations. Therefore, all the social, political and intellectual relations, all religious and legal systems, all the theoretical outlooks which emerge in the course of history, are derived from the material conditions of life."

The theories of Marxism are based on a scientific method of thought called dialectical materialism. Marxist and neo-Marxist international relations theories are positivist paradigms which reject the realist/liberal view of state conflict or cooperation; instead focusing on the economy and material aspects. It makes the assumption that the economy trumps other concerns;

allowing for the elevation of class as the focus of study. Marxists view the international system as an integrated capitalist system in pursuit of capital accumulation. Thus, the period of colonialism brought in sources for raw materials and captive markets for exports, while decolonialization brought new opportunities in the form of dependence. Marxist theories receive scant attention in the United States where even moderate socialist and social democratic parties lack mainstream political influence; elsewhere, especially Africa, Latin America, South and East Asia, and some parts of Europe, Marxist and other progressive theories are more incorporated into political discourse.

Marxian view treats international politics as an extension of the class war in global perspective. There are certain basic assumptions of the Marxian theory. Economic factors play a decisive role in international relations. Class instead of nation-state is the basic unit in international relations. Proletariat or working classes do not belong to any other particular nation. So they unite at global level and proletariat internationalism would lead towards world revolution. Capitalism culminates into imperialism. Lenin concluded that imperialism is the last stage of capitalism.

With the passage of time, imperialism, which is the highest stage of capitalism, would suffer from three contradictions. First, there would be contradictions and conflicts when capitalist nations clash with each other to build their colonies in different parts of the world to serve as markets for their products. Second, class conflict between capitalists and workers. Working class would demand more rights and facilities. Third, struggle between imperial powers and the people of colonies. Colonial people fight of their independence. These three contradictions would lead the world to the brink of revolution causing imperialism to collapse. Lasting peace can only be established after world revolution and the goal is international disequilibrium in order to change the world to establish world socialism. It may take a long time for world revolution to be successful at global level. In the meantime the principles of national self-determination and peaceful co-existence will continue to occupy an important place.

According to the Marxists, the contemporary world is essentially divided into two sub-systems of states—imperial-bourgeois and socialists. The relations among the socialist states are determined by the principle of socialist international and are called new type of international relations. The Communist Weltanchuaang (world view) of the international community also affirms the existence of a third force consisting of anti-imperialist socialist forces operating outside the socialist state system and within the imperialist-bourgeois state system. Applied to the field of international politics, Marxian view implies conflict between the communist and the non-communist world. Politics is seen in terms of class conflict at the national as well as international levels. International political reality can be understood only by laws of social development as laid by Marx, interpreted by Engels and applied by Lenin.

### *Class War*

The doctrine of class war is a corollary of historical materialism. If the latter contains the theory of social change, the former describes its mechanism. According to Karl Marx, the theory of class war provides a key to the understanding of history. As he writes: "The mechanism of the process of capitalistic socialization of labour at last reach a point where they become incompatible with their capitalistic husk. This leads to open revolt. The knell of capitalism sounds. The exploiters are expropriated."

Coker beautifully sums up the foregoing account of the way in which capitalism creates conditions of its own decay: "Thus the capitalist system enlarges the number of workers, brings them together into compact groups, makes them class-conscious, supplies them with means of inter-communication and co-operation on a worldwide scale, reduces their purchasing power, and by increasingly exploiting them arouses them to organized resistance. Capitalists, acting persistently in pursuit of their natural needs and in vidication of a system dependent upon the maintenance of profits are all the time creating conditions which stimulate and straighten the natural efforts of workers in preparing for a system that will fit the needs of a working means society."

The inevitable end of the class struggle will be victory of the proletariat. As a result of this victory class distinctions will disappear from society, and with their disappearance class struggle too would come to an end. The proletariat will use its political power to eliminate very remnant of capitalism. When all class distinctions would have vanished, the society would become free from class antagonism and classes. In this classless society the motto would be: "From each according to his capacity to each according to his needs."

The doctrine of class war as given by Karl Marx has been criticized on a number of grounds. Firstly, it is difficult to endorse the view that the history of all hitherto existing society is the history of class struggle. No one can deny the existence of classes in society; but it is wrong to identify these classes with economic classes. Oligarchs and democrats, Kshatriya and Brahmins are social classes rather than classes. Nor it is correct to say that the class struggle in history has always been between the exploiter and the exploited. Moreover, within each main class, there are numerous groups. It is difficult to point out to any periods of history when society was divided into two clear-cut classes. Experience shows that in all periods of history human being have freely intermingled. Karl Marx has simplified the class doctrine too much. As Popper writes, "Indeed, the divergence of interests within the ruling and the ruled classes goes so far that Marx's theory of classes must be considered as a dangerous over-simplification, even if we admit that the issue between the rich and the poor is always of fundamental importance. One of the great themes of medieval history, the fight between the popes and emperors, is an example of dissension within the ruling class. It would be probably false to interpret this quarrel as one between exploiter and exploited." Even capitalists of all over the world do not constitute a single class in the sense of being inspired by class in common with the capitalists of India; rather their interests clash. Similarly, the antagonism existing between the skilled and unskilled labour beliefs the myth of workers solidarity.

Secondly, the theory of class struggle has not developed along lines anticipated by Marx. While there has been a trend towards larger enterprises and concentration of wealth, Marx's prophecy about the increasing misery and degradation of the working class has not proved true. The worker at least of the affluent societies in the West has shared in the growing prosperity of the bourgeoisie and now enjoy more amenities than his predecessors a hundred years back. In between the working class and the capitalist class, there has arisen a fairly large middle class. Thus, instead of becoming sharply divided into two classes, the society has come to be divided into three or more sections. Most of the people belonging to the middle class reflect the ideas of the bourgeoisie and do not feel very enthusiastic about the proletarian cause. Capitalism has also hitherto been showing signs of growth and expansion. It has adjusted itself to the changing circumstances. Moreover, Marx's prophecy that the proletarian revolution will take place in an advanced capitalistic country has also not come true. There has been a revolution in Russia where it could be least expected under the Marxian analysis.

Lastly, the Marxian belief in ultimate victory of the proletariat is a mere pious wish on his part and does not rest upon any scientific basis. If and when capitalism might result no in communism, but in anarchy from which there might emerge some dictatorship unrelated in principle to communist ideals. Further the theory of the final victory of the proletariat may be a good propaganda, but it is only a theory.[38] There is no assurance that technocrats and administrators will not occupy positions of vantage and privilege in a future socialist society.

As a corollary of the materialistic interpretation of history and the surplus value, Marx enunciated his theory of class war. In each society, according to the system of production to cite an example, in feudal society, barons exploit the series. Class struggle is the active expression of class conflict looked at from any kind of socialist perspective. Karl Marx and Friedrich Engels, leading ideologists of communism, wrote "The written history of all hitherto existing society is the history of class struggle." Marx's notion of class has nothing to do with social class in the sociological sense of upper, middle and lower classes (which are often defined in terms of quantitative income or wealth). Instead, in an age of capitalism, Marx describes an economic class. Membership of a class is defined by one's relationship to the means of production, i.e. one's position in the social structure that characterizes capitalism. Marx talks mainly about two classes that include the vast majority of the population, the proletariat and the bourgeoisie.

Other classes such as the petty bourgeoisie share characteristics of both of these main classes. When the mode of production is capitalistic, two classes are created. These classes in a capitalistic system are bourgeois and proletariat or the haves and have-nots. Thus, Marx wanted to prove that class struggle has been permanent feature of human history. This is because the economic system makes on class, "exploiter" and the "exploited". Marx writes: "Freeman and slave, patrician and plebian, baron and serf, guildmaster and journey man in one word oppressor and oppressed, standing constantly in opposition to each other, carried on uninterrupted warfare now hidden and now open, a fight that each time ended either in revolutionary reconstruction of society at large, in the common ruin of the contending classes."

### *Destruction of Capitalism*

"Capitalism", says Marx, "contains the seeds of its own construction." Capitalist economy has a tendency towards concentration of capital. Marx's primary concern was the intellectual destruction of capitalism. Wealth accumulates in the hands of a few capitalists. All the producers are thrown of business by cut-throat competition. Labourers are equally exploited. The law of concentration of capital leads to increasing miseries of the poor or the have-nots. Despite his belief in a progressive history, and in the inevitable downfall of capitalism, Marx thought that in destroying capitalism's intellectual support he could hasten its real demise and usher in a socialist era. Many of his works can be seen as reactions to the growing status of the relatively new field of political economy, pioneered by figures like Adam Smith, David Ricardo and Thomas Malthus, whose increasingly laissez-faire theories promoted an extension of exactly the features of capitalism that Marx thought were most defective. Hence, his critique ranges from attacks on the complacent liberal bases of capitalism to complex analyses of the economics of the day and of leading theorists.[39]

Capitalism results in localization of industry. A large number of labourers working in a particular industry reside in a particular place. This increases the strength of labourers. Constant mutual contract helps organize labour. Again, the capitalist system of production brings out development of international trade and commerce. This provides opportunity for workers of the world to unite.

The process of alienation, however, is not specific to capitalism. Marx identified three stages of development in the history of society: "oriental despotism, ancient slave-holding society, and feudalism". In each of these we can find, to some extent, alienation taking place; under despotism, men are arbitrarily coerced by the ruling despot, and so their production will not be under their control; in a slave-holding society, slaves are wholly alienated, neither having control over their productive processes, nor ownership of their products; under feudalism the serf is given some land, but either the entirety or a portion of the proceeds are taken by coercion by the land owner. So, one could object that Marx's theory of alienation seems not to be a specific criticism of capitalism, but a general criticism of economics, and that alienation is an unfortunate result of the productive process in general. But Marx thought that not only was alienation a necessary component of the economic superstructure, but also that it was in capitalism that humanity suffered the most profound form of alienation, when the bourgeois consolidate control over our labour and commodify it, and when the product of our labour becomes the commodity of the capitalist.

The concept of commodification is unique to capitalism. Whereas in the former three stages of development, the products of labour are either enjoyed by the worker or taken directly by the property owner for their own use, in capitalism the products of all labour become commodities, traded on an open market. Once on the market, commodities only have value insofar as they are useful, and so their labour-based value is forgotten or annulled, and the new basis for value becomes their utility for the bourgeois who happen to buy the particular product. Thus, capitalism enlarges the number of workers, brings them together into compact groups, makes them class-conscious, supplies them; with means of inter-communication and co-operation in a worldwide scale, reduces their purchasing power and by increasingly exploiting them, arouses them to organized action. This is how capitalism is destroyed by the Proletariat Revolution. The destruction of capitalism is, in fact, the construction of socialism and finally the classless society.

### *Dictatorship of the Proletariat*

Although according to Marx, capitalism process to its destruction, it will not at once create communism. After the proletarian revolution has given a final blow to the decaying capitalism, the communistic society will not be born immediately thereafter. The capitalist system will be succeeded by the establishment of the dictatorship of the proletariat as a necessary prelude to the withering away of the state. The state during this interim period will be a revolutionary dictatorship of the proletariat. This transient dictatorship is necessary for completing the tasks of revolution, i.e. to hold down the efforts of the bourgeoisie to regain their lost power and privileges and also to prepare the way for the final victory of socialism. Engels writes, "Since the state is only a temporary institution which is to be made use of in the revolution in order forcibly to suppress the opponents, it is perfectly absurb to talk about a free popular state. So long as the proletariat needs the state, it needs it not in the interests of freedom, but in order to suppress its opponents: and when it becomes possible to speak of freedom, the state as such ceases to exist."

Thus, the first stage in the realization of communism will be 'quasi-state', popularly called the dictatorship of the proletariat. This new state will be a class organization and it will function as the representative of the revolutionary working class. It will expropriate the bourgeoisie, centralized all instruments of production, and increase the total production as rapidly as possible. In short, the proletarian state will follow revolutionary measures leading to the complete destruction of capitalism. It is thus a means to an end, and is transitory in character. Once the bourgeoisie has been suppressed and all the remnants of capitalism have been removed, the proletarian state will also become superfluous and thereafter wither away. In place of the bourgeois society, with its classes and class antagonisms, there shall come into being an association in which the free development of each is the condition for the free development of all. "In the communistic society, people will become gradually accustomed to the observance of the elementary rules of social life without compulsion, without subordination, without the special apparatus for compulsion which is called the state." When socialism blossoms into communism, mankind will make the ascent "from the kingdom of necessity to the kingdom of freedom".

The philosophy of Karl Marx has been criticized on many grounds. Some points of criticism suffer from one-sidedness. Marx has exaggerated the importance of the economic forces and oversimplified the complex social phenomena. Marx's conception of class struggle has also been assailed. It is pointed out that the growth of capitalism in the West has not placed the capitalist and the proletariat into hostile camps. His prophecy about the increasing misery of workers has also not come true. His concept of the withering away of the state after the overthrow of capitalism has not yet been realized in the USSR and the Soviet state shows no sign of withering away. The Marxists moreover do not make any allowance for inter-class conflicts and focus their attention almost entirely on inter-class conflicts. Marxism is thus somewhat removed from political and historical reality. It is also accused of ignoring the psychological aspects of politics. Though Marx view the state in terms of force, he has not given an adequate treatment of the problem of power. Nor does he show any consciousness of the defects in human nature like his selfishness. Lastly, critics doubt in a violent revolution can provide a secure foundation of the socialist order of society. The latter requires that the people should be permeated by the spirit of fellow-feeling and be guided by the motive of social service. According to Joad, "there seems to be good grounds for believing that the policy of gradual reform advocated by evolutionary socialists is likely to secure advances of a more permanent, albeit of a less startling character than the methods of the revolution and of the class war".[40]

Nevertheless, the ideas of Marx had gained a powerful hold over the intellectual as well as the masses. He uncovered vital truths and foresaw important developments that were hidden from his contemporaries. He unraveled the relation between economic factors and social change and made a powerful attack on the squalor and complacency. He gave a philosophy which has changed the face of the world. To the communists he was a prophet. To socialism in general he provided a theory and a hope in the coming millennium. In the words of Wayper, "For the power of his message, for the inspiration of his teaching and for his effect upon future developments Marx can be sure of his place in any collection of the world's great master of political thought."

**Withering Away of the State**

When all remnants of bourgeois society are crushed, there is no need for the State. "The State withers away". The Stateless and classless society comes to prevail. This is the final stage of communism. As Engels observed, "When proletariat seizes the power of the State, it puts an end to all differences of class and antagonism of class and consequently puts an end to the State as a State." Under perfect communism, the State as a machinery of coercion is no longer necessary. It is a free society of voluntary-associations. There are no policemen and no military people. This is the scientific socialism of Marx and this is the ultimate stage of communism.

According to Marx, the state is used as a tool in the hands of the bourgeois for exploitation. It is commanded by the rich class in order to exploit the poor. If men are good and perfect, equality prevails, there is no necessity of the state. The state is necessary in the transitional stage in order to achieve the goal of perfect socialism. It becomes an institution for promoting the cause of the proletariat. In perfect communist society, the principle is "from each according to his ability, to each according to his needs". Communism aims at classless society and perfect economic equality. It also abolishes exploitation. If communism stands for these objectives and when these objectives are realized, there is no necessity of the state at all. Thus, Marx's idea of withering away of the state, however idealistic it may be has its own sense of justification.

### *Theory of Revolution*

Communism is a revolutionary creed. It believes in violence and force to solve the complicated social problems. In the words of Marx, "Force is the midwife of the modern State." Hence, Marx advocated evolution as the only way to get rid of mankind from inhumanity and exploitation caused by capitalism. He gave a clarion call to "the Yorkers of the world to unite and revolt as they have nothing to lose it their chains".

### *Dynamics of Social Change*

Communism believes in the dynamics of social change. It is a progressive philosophy. It opposes various forces including religion which hinders the human progress. Marx was convinced that religion regards the progress. Hence, he said that "religion is the opium of the people". Marx is a great humanitarian and a philanthropist. He has advocated rapid progress for the poor and downtrodden in the society.

### *Alienation*

Marx's theory of alienation refers to the alienation of people from aspects of their human nature. Marx believes that alienation is a systematic result of capitalism. His theory relies on Feuerbach's *The Essence of Christianity* (1841). Marx's *Theory of Alienation* is the contention that in modern industrial production under capitalist conditions workers will inevitably lose control of their lives by losing control over their work. Workers thus cease to be autonomous beings in any significant sense.

The class of the proletariat feels annihilated in estrangement; it sees in it its own powerlessness and the reality of an inhuman existence. It is, to use an expression of Hegel, in its abasement the indignation at that abasement, an indignation to which it is necessarily driven by the contradiction between its human nature and its condition of life, which is the outright, resolute and comprehensive negation of that nature. Within this antithesis the private property-owner is, therefore, the conservative side, the proletarian the destructive side.

### *Uniqueness of the Theory*

This approach has a unique place in the study of politics as it is different from both traditional and modern approaches. It, however, possesses certain points of both the approaches. It deals with a wide range of social phenomena with a past, present and future perspective.

The Marxian approach has been called political analysis by proxy as economics dominate the scene and politics figure incidentally. The other disciplines like History, Sociology, Psychology and Ethics become its offshoots. Moreover, it seeks for the abolition of politics as it views politics as not a fundamental activity of human beings. It emphasises stateless condition as the final stage of social development, because it views 'state' as a consequence of class contradictions. It calls for deeper scrutiny of meaning and nature of politics by going to the roots rather than confining oneself to the base and superstructure. It assumes a deterministic character as it brings out not only social contradictions but also solutions. It becomes an ideology based on a certain set of propositions that are not open to question.

Marxist analysis starts with distinctions between the base and the superstructure. The base is responsible for the evolving of the superstructure. It says economic structure of society is the base, whereas the social structure, including the legal, political and religious dimensions, is the superstructure. Thus, it insists on analysis of the economic structure of society, rather than the political system as the latter is dependent on the economic structure. In order to understand the character of the political system, it is important to know about the historical stages of development of the economic structure and the class structure prevailing at these stages. At every stage, it says, the society is divided into two antagonistic classes: of the haves and the have-nots. Politics, as such, becomes a process through which these classes try to attain power.

Marx presented in detail five stages of historical development. Primitive communism is the first stage where the mode of production involves hunting, fishing, and food gathering. At this point, the classes have not yet merged. The second stage is the slave system where the mode of production is animal husbandry along with domestic agriculture and small industry, with masters and slaves as the classes in society. Feudal system is the third stage where agriculture on a large scale is the mode of production. The dominant classes are the landlords and the serfs. This stage is succeeded by the capitalist system where the mode of production is large industry. The class structure has capitalists and workers. Finally, there is the socialist system where, though the mode of production is the large industry, there are no classes; all the citizens belong to one class known as workers.

Marxist approach assumes that the state of contradictions can each end only in the establishment of a socialist society. Once this is established, it will lead to a phase of communism which is classless and stateless society.

Marxist approach claims to be scientific and progressive. It also assumes normative character. But the weakness in this approach lies in conforming to an ideology with utmost rigidity. It has been criticized for culminating in the 'pseudo scientism of generated Marxism'. Further, there is practically no scope of independent analysis. Neo-Marxist like Antonio Gramsci and Ralph Miliband realized this and attempted an independent analysis.

Gramsci, conceding the relative autonomy of the state and realizing the importance of the superstructure in a capitalist system which can strongly influence the base itself, evolved a framework for the analysis of the bourgeois state. He made a clear distinction between the two levels of superstructure, i.e. political society and civil society. He opined that the structures of domination are two fold: structures of coercion and structures of legitimation. The former is exercised by the political society. Accepting the unity of state power and class power, he argued that class character of the capitalist state is perpetuated by the middle class of state officials, economic power, of the capitalist class and the inherent desire of politicians and bureaucrats to continue the existing economic system on which their position depends.

The Frankfurt school consisting of Theodor Adorno, Max Horkheimer, Herbert Marcuse, and Jurgen Habermas being hostile to capitalism and critical of Soviet socialism evolved the 'critical theory' which is a new interpretation of Marxism in various directions and spheres of learning. They advanced a cultural critique of bourgeois society in terms of technological domination rather than capitalist domination.

This new-Marxism developed along with two directions—humanist and scientific. Herbert Marcuse was a strong advocate of the former approach while Louis Althusser belonged to the latter. The main themes of the humanist strain revolve around the problems of alienation and ways towards human emancipation while the scientific strain is of a scientific and explanatory character (interested in structures as well as in the relative importance of cultural, ideological and social factors).

**Basic Assumptions**

Economic factors play decisive role in international relations. They have been the root cause of many struggles and wars at international level in the past. Class instead of nation-states is the basic unit in international relations. The national interest is first of all the interests of master class which changes with rise and fall of classes. Capitalism culminates into imperialism. That divides the world into imperial powers and colonies such as haves and have-nots. Wars break out when capitalist nations clash with each other to build their colonies in different parts of the world to serve as markets for their products.

Proletariat or working classes do not belong to any other particular nation. So they unite at global level to fight out exploitation. Proletariat internationalism would lead towards world revolution. With the passage of time, imperialism, which is the highest stage of capitalism, would suffer from three contradictions. First, there would be contradictions and conflicts among capitalists for occupying more and more colonies resulting in world wars among them. Second, class conflict between capitalists and workers. Working class would demand more rights and facilities. Third, struggle between imperialists and the people of colonies. Colonial people fight for their independence.

These three contradictions would lead the world to the brink of revolution causing imperialism to collapse. The goal is not balance of power or equilibrium but international dis-equilibrium in order to achieve the goal of changing the world to establish world socialism. Lasting peace can only be established after world revolution. With world revolution, imperialism would collapse, there would be no classes and no states. In such a classless and stateless society, there will be no irritant left for struggles and wars. Such a society will be an ideal world.

Arun Bose firmly believes that "there is a Marxian analytical framework for analyzing situations of international political conflicts, which serves as a 'guide to action',—to work out Marxist strategies". According to him, this framework comprises of "four seminal theories" about international politics in modern era, which contain ideas that overlap to some extent and which may be regarded as offshoots of the primal theory of proletarian internationalism. The four Marxian theories described by Bose are as follows:

### Proletarian Internationalism

This term was coined by Lenin in his Preliminary Thesis on the national and colonial questions, submitted to the Communist International in 1920. But the basic ideas were formulated by Karl Marx and Friedrich Engel's in *Communist Manifesto* and adopted by the First International in 1847. These ideas are: (i) "the world proletariat have a common interest, independent of all nationality", (ii) "working men have no country;...since the proletariat of each country must first acquire political supremacy must first constitute itself the nation. It is itself national", (iii) "united action (by the proletariat) is one of the first conditions for the emancipation of the proletariat", (iv) "in proportion as the exploitation of one individual by another is put an end to the exploitation of one nation by another will come to an end".

According to Lenin, imperialism is the final stage of capitalism. This famous dictum became the basis of his critique of capitalist imperialism as a world system, his prediction of a successful October Revolution, his reformulation and amplification of the Marxian theory of national self-determination, and of the Marxian theory of proletarian internationalism. In imperialism, the highest stage of capitalism, Lenin defined imperialism as the "monopoly stage of capitalism" and listed its five basic features: (1) the concentration of production and capital develops to such a high stage that it creates monopolies which plays a decisive role in economic life; (2) bank capital merges with industrial capital and this results in the creation of 'finance capital'; a capital of the financial oligarchy; (3) the export of capital as distinguished from the export of commodities acquires exceptional importance; (4) the resulting formation of international monopolistic capitalist association share the world among themselves; and (5) as the final culminating point, the territorial division of the whole world among the biggest capitalist powers is completed.

The main ideas of anti-imperialism theory are:

- capital has become international and monopolistic,
- uneven economic and political development is an absolute law of capitalism,
- the proletarian socialist revolution is possible first not only in several countries of Europe, or at least the "civilized countries", as visualized in a somewhat Eurocentric vision of the proletarian revolution in *Communist Manifesto*—but also "even in one capitalist country, taken singly", which would form the nucleus, the base, the hegemony, of the world socialist revolution, "attracting to its cause the oppressed classes of other countries, raising revolts...against capitalism", and "engaging in the event of necessity" in "internationalist" defensive and offensive wars "against exploiting classes and states" in other countries. In re-examining the theory of proletarian internationalism in the context of imperialism of his times, Lenin thus made major new departures in the Marxian understanding of the nature of the national and colonial questions.

### National Self-determination

The *Communist Manifesto* stresses a specific Marxian "class" approach to the national question, according to which classes which attain political supremacy "constitute" the nation. In each country, the working class must acquire political supremacy (later defined by Lenin as the dictatorship of the proletariat), must constitute itself "the nation". Thus, the goal of "national self-determination" was to be realized through "proletarian self-determination" within each nation. This very basic tenet of the Marxian theory on the "national question", makes the Marxian understanding fundamentally different from any non-Marxian theory on the "national question". Taking hint from re-thinking by Marx (especially on the Irish demand for separation from the UK, which Marx had at first opposed), and on the basis of his own analysis of the "new", imperialist stage of capitalism—Lenin arrived at an assessment of the arousing of national antagonisms instead of their subduing as visualized in *Communist Manifesto*, in the days of imperialism and the world socialist revolution. In this extension of the Marxian theory on the national question "which was now explicitly and emphatically linked with the colonial question"—Lenin included three modifications, viz. (i) a distinction was made between the "oppressed nations", and the "oppressor nations", (ii) the "oppressed nations" were identified as the victims of imperialism, as "national revolutionary" reserves or allies of the proletariat in the world socialist revolution, (iii) the recognition of the right of the oppressed nations to self-determination was now explicitly interpreted to mean not only the right of the oppressed nations to secede freely, but also the desirability of secession to remove "distrust" and "prejudices" among the oppressed nations. However, all three modifications were still within the framework of the overall programmatic aim of "a United States of the world" (and not of Europe alone) as "the state form of national federation and national freedom which (is) associate(d) with socialism—until the complete victory of Communism bring about the total disappearance of the state...."

**Peaceful Co-existence of States**

As Marxian theory reiterated by Lenin during the First World War, "capitalism means war" and the task of the socialist states is to "raise revolts against capitalism", it is not evident how a theory of "peaceful co-existence of states" coincides with the Marxian theory of proletarian internationalism. But once this theory was enlarged by a theory of anti-imperialism, of "inter-imperialist contradictions",[41] and the "uneven development of imperialism", propositions about the chances of peaceful coexistence of socialist and capitalist states had to be sorted out. For the "law of uneven development of imperialism" meant: (i) the proletarian socialist revolution could be victorious first in several countries, or even in one country, (ii) it had to survive capitalist "encirclement" by relying on inter-imperialist contradictions over and above its internal and external supports from the world proletariat and its "reserves", and (iii) the best method to accomplish this was to try to work out relations of "peaceful co-existence" between socialist states and at least some, if not all, the capitalist states. On the other hand, the Marxian theory of national self-determination had as corollaries (i) the possibility of peaceful co-existence of peoples, and national freedom and equality within a voluntary union of socialist states, and (ii) the possibility of peaceful co-existence between the socialist states, and the liberated national, sovereign states of the "oppressed nations" after their secession from the imperialist states of the "oppressor nations", whether or not they become socialist in the process of their national liberation, or even if their political independence is a mere cover for economic, financial and military dependency upon the imperialist states.

### Four Model Strategies

The above seminal Marxian theories are integrated by Arun Bose in different ways to work out Marxist strategies in international politics, represented by the foreign policies of modern communist states. These four distinct "model" strategies, seem to represent the basic, logical thrust behind the foreign policy experiments adopted by modern Communist states. These strategies are: (i) "transnational" or "cosmopolitan", (ii) the "non-aligned", (iii) "the Soviet-centric", and (iv) the "Sino-centric". The last two strategies are definitely geared to the notions that the "genuine", "reliable" nucleus or "base" or "protector" of the world socialist revolution are the Soviet

Union or Communist China respectively. The other two "models strategies" carry no such "country" labels. The "transnational" or "cosmopolitan" model strategy clearly rejects the idea of "socialism in one country", and leaves no scope for idealizing the role of socialism in anyone country, or group of countries as the "base of the world revolution". The "non-aligned" model strategy is strictly "poly-centric", "insisting that socialism in each country is fighting for socialism only in one's own country". For want of space these strategies are not being discussed in detail nor is it necessary either.

#### Marxian Theory Under Attack

Marxian theory of international relations can be denounced as unscientific, impracticable, utopian, inconsistent and unhistorical. Its shortcomings can be described in brief as follows:

All the "four seminal theories" presented by Arun Bose remained in embroynic state. The propositions of these theories could not find any further development theoretically nor realize practically in all these years. Therein lies the failure of these theories. The main theory of proletariat internationalism proved wrong as proletariat of different states actually thought in terms of their nationality and national interest. During different wars and struggles, working men worked, for the victory of their own country setting at naught Marxian dictum 'working men have no country'. It seems that proletariat of the world have ignored Marx's call for "united action" at global level for their emancipation. Lenin's theory of imperialism is historically wrong, because historical facts contradict Lenin's famous saying: "imperialism is the highest stage of capitalism". Imperialism existed even before the advent of capitalism e.g. Roman and Greek empires in ancient period. According to the theory of imperialism, every capitalist country must grow into imperialist country. However, in reality, many capitalist countries e.g. Switzerland, Canada, Australia, etc. did not indulge in empire building. Economic factors are not the exclusive factors accounting for imperialism and wars. Empires were built and wars were fought on several other non-economic reasons such as religious, cultural, political, military, personal ambitions of rulers etc. Nation states remained the basic unit of analysis in international relations despite Marxists insistence on class as its basic unit. Imperialism collapsed after the Second World War but not the capitalism as predicted by Marxist theory. Contrarily, in many countries capitalism gained strength after that. Moreover, after decolonization, imperialism again raised its ugly head under the garb of neo-colonialism, economic imperialism and 'Red' imperialism. In other words, old and overt imperialism re-emerged covertly.[42]

Marxian theory may be criticised on the following grounds:

**Creed of violence:** Communism is criticized as a creed of violence and hatred. It openly preaches the theory of revolution and class war. According to Marx, history is nothing but a record of struggle between the rich and the poor. Force can bring change in society. Revolution is not illegal in the eyes of the advocates of this theory. Hence, communism is considered to be a highly revolutionary philosophy.

**Non-economic factors ignored:** Communism puts emphasis only on economic factor. According to Marx, economic or materialistic factor alone is responsible for the social, political and economic changes in the society. He has ignored non-economic factors like religion, language, political condition, science, etc. He has also denied the role of religion in the society. Religion is undoubtedly a powerful force in society.

**Undemocratic:** It is undemocratic. It is inimical to liberty or freedom. There is concentration of power in communist society.

The state is considered to be omnipotent and omnicompetent during the transitional stage. The individual is reduced to a position of mere cog in the machine. The state compels individual to do all works. There seems to be no freedom in communistic society. Churchill once said that this system is covered by "an iron curtain". Trotsky, a veteran communist leader, was disillusioned after seeing the working of communism.

He wrote, "In a country where sole employer is the State, opposition means death by slow starvation. The old principle—who does not work shall not eat, has replaced by new one—who does not obey shall not eat. The State is not withering away: Lastly, the communistic attitude towards the State is erroneous." The State is not an instrument of class exploitation or oppression. According to Aristotle, "the State originates in bare needs of life and continues for sake of good life". The state is a benevolent organization. Further, the state is not withering away; in the transitional stage of communism, there is the dictatorship of proletariat. Even in the perfect communistic society, it is doubtful whether the state will wither away.[43]

In spite of the above criticisms of communism, it has become the popular philosophy in the modern world. As A.J.P. Taylor writes, "The *Communist Manifesto* must be counted as a holy book, in the same class as the *Bible* or the *Koran*." C.L. Wayper has rightly observed, "For the power of his message, for the inspiration of his teaching and for his effect upon further developments, Marin can be sure of his place in any collection, of the world's great master's of political thought." Russia was first communist country in the modern world. It went to communism in 1917. China became a communistic country in 1949. The philosophy of Marxism has got certain modifications in the hand of Lenin. We shall examine the modifications made by Lenin in brief.

**Post-Marxian Theory in International Politics**

The humanist strain of Neo-Marxism draws particularly on the problems of alienation and way to human emancipation. Thus Herbert Marcuse has portrayed the conditions of alienation in bourgeoise society which have reduced the human being to "one-dimensional man". He gave a penetrating critique of capitalism as regards its impact on human freedom. According to him, capitalism exercises monopolistic control not only on production and distribution, it also creates the desire and demand for commodities through a clever manipulation of the mass media. In *Eros and Civilization* (1966) Marcuse has given a blue print of society where alienation will be removed and freedom will be restored. It will be a democratic community where work will become play, and necessary labour will be organized in harmony with liberated and the culture of the capitalist society comprised of two elements: (1) structures of coercion, and (2) structures of legitimation. Gramsci, paid special attention to the functioning of civil society which was exemplified in the institutions of family, school and church, etc. According to Gramsci, civil society legitimized the rule of bourgeoise so that nobody would challenge its supremacy.

Ralph Miliband and Nicholos Poulantzas are other neo-marxist thinkers who dwelled on the relative autonomy of the state. Miliband (*The State in Capitalist Society*, 1969) has accepted the unity of state power and class power. He argued that the class character of the capitalist state is perpetuated by (1) the middle class or upper class background of the state officials, (2) the economic power of the capitalist class, (3) the inherent desire of the politicians and bureaucrats to continue the existing economic system on which their own positions depends. Poulantzas, on the other hand, has drawn a clear distinction between the position of the capitalist class domination is not automatically translated into state power and the state cannot properly be regarded simply as the instrument of a class. Relative autonomy of the state helps in improving its economic performance on the one hand and promoting capitalist interests on the other. He rejected Miliband concept of state power.

Weber also rejected Marx's theory of economic determinism and stressed on autonomy of state power. Weber argued that the state has its own powerful resources. It enjoys executive control over legitimate use of force in society which is not accessible to private interests. It maintains a strong organization in the form of bureaucracy which can formulate implement and monitor the policies of the state. The state power could not be reduced to an instrument of class interests.

### Critics of the Frankfurt School in International Relations

Several camps of criticism of the Frankfurt School have emerged.

Some critics accuse that the intellectual perspective of the Frankfurt School is a romantic, elitist critique of mass culture with a contrived neo-Marxist guise.

Another criticism, originating from the Left, is that critical theory is a form of bourgeois idealism that has no inherent relation to political practice and is totally isolated from any ongoing revolutionary movement.

Both of these criticisms were captured in Georg Lukács's phrase "Grand Hotel Abyss" as a syndrome he imputed to the members of the Frankfurt School.

Notable critics of the Frankfurt School:

- Henryk Grossman
- Georg Lukács
- Umberto Eco
- Mike Godwin

## NOTES

1. Quincy Wright, *A Study of War* (Chicago, 1965), p. 140.
2. Alexander George and Juliette George, *Woodrow Wilson and Colonel House* (New York, 1956), p. 7.
3. Richard N. Rosecrance, *Action and Reaction in World Politics* (Boston, 1963), pp. 304-05.
4. Joseph Frankel, *Contemporary International Theory and the Behaviour of States* (London, 1973), pp. 72-73.
5. M.S. Venkataramani, "The Ford-Kissinger Safari in Angola", *Foreign Affairs Reports,* September-October 2008, p. 86.
6. Roudolph J. Rummel, "The Relationship Between National Attributes and Foreign Conflict Behaviour" in J. David Singer, ed., *Quantitative International Politics: Insights and Evidence* (New York, 1968), p. 187.
7. Mahendra Kumar, *Theoretical Aspects of International Politics* (Agra, 1972) 2nd revised edn., p. 37.
8. Theodore A. Couloumbis and James H. Wolfe, *Introduction to International Relations: Power and Justice* (New Delhi, 1986) 3rd edn., p. 25.
9. Karl W. Deutsch *et al., Political Community and the North Atlantic Area* (Princeton, N.J.: Princeton University Press, 1957).
10. J. David Singer and Melvin Small, "National Alliance Commitments and War Involvement 1818-1945" in *ibid.*, pp. 513-42.
11. McClelland, n. 17, p. 20.
12. Couloumbis and Wolfe, n. 4, p. 28.
13. Inis L. Claude, Jr., *Power and International Relations* (New York, 1962), p. 11.

14. Norman D. Palmer and Howard C. Perkins, *International Relations* (Calcutta, 1969), p. 213.
15. Vernon Van Dyke, *International Politics* (Bombay, 1966), p. 221.
16. Roger Hilsman, *To Move a Nation: The Politics of Foreign Policy in the Administration of John F. Kennedy* (New York, 1967), p. 542.
17. Richard Neustadt, *Presidential Power* (New York, 1960), p. 10.
18. Warner R. Schilling, "The Politics of National Defence: Fiscal 1950" in Schilling *et al.*, *Strategy, Politics and Defence Budgets* (New York, 1962), p. 23.
19. Richard Neustadt, *Presidential Power* (New York, 1960), p. 10.
20. Samuel P. Huntington, "Strategic Programmes and the Political Process" in Wesley, W. Posvar *et al.*, *American Defence Policy* (Baltimore, Md., 1965), p. 150.
21. Kenneth Prewitt, "Political Ambitions, Voluntarism, and Electoral Accountability", *American Political Science Review* (Washington D.C.), Vol. 64, March 1970, pp. 5-17.
22. The discussion here on Organizational Process Model is mainly drawn from Richard C. Snyder *et al.*, "Decision-making as an Approach to the Study of International Politics" in Snyder *et al.*, eds., *Foreign Policy Decision-Making: An Approach to the Study of International Politics* (Glencoe, 1962), pp. 104-37; Graham T. Allison, *Essence of Decision: Explaining the Cuban Missile Crisis* (Boston, Mask, 1971), pp. 67-100.
23. Snyder, *ibid.*, p. 99, emphasis added.
24. H. Sprout and M. Sprout, "Environmental Factors in the Study of International Relations", *Journal of Conflict Resolution* (Ann Arbor, Michigan), Vol. 1, 1957, pp. 309-28.
25. Charles F. Hermann, "International Crisis as a Situational Variable" in Rosenau, n. 8, pp. 409-21.
26. J.K. Baral, *The Pentagon and the Making of US Foreign Policy* (New Delhi, 1978), pp. 1-38.
27. Arthur Schtesinger, Jr., *A Thousand Days: John F. Kennedy in the White House* (Boston, 1965), p. 406.
28. Roger Hilsman, *To Move a Nation: The Politics of Foreign Policy in the Administration of John F. Kennedy* (New York, 1967), p. 542.
29. Lenin, *Marx-Engels-Marxism* (Moscow, 1947), pp. 278-90.
30. Lenin, "Preliminary Draft Theses on the National and Colonial Questions" in *ibid.* , pp. 231-35.
31. Arun Bose, "The Marxian Theory of International Relations" in K.P. Misra and Richard Smith Beal, ed., *Internatioinal Relations Theory—Western and Non-Western Perspectives* (New Delhi, 1980), p. 159.
32. For detail see *ibid.*, pp. 160-66.
33. Marx and Engels, *Selected Works*, 2-Volume ed., VoU (Moscow, 1950), pp. 44, 49.

34. Lenin, *Marx-Engels-Marxism* (Moscow, 1947), pp. 278-90.
35. Lenin, *Selected Works*, ed., Vol. 10 (Moscow, 1946), pp. 33-34, 55-59.
36. Richard C. Snyder, H.W. Bruck and Burton M. Sapin, *Decision Making as an Approach to the Study of International Politics* (New York, 1954).
37. Snyder, Bruck and Sapin, in Hoffmann, ed., n. 25, p. 155.
38. Michael Brecher, "International Relations and Asian Studies: The Subordinate State System of Southern Asia", *World Politics*, XV (January, 1963); Leonard Binder, "The Middle East as a Subordinate International System", *World Politics*, X (April, 1938).
39. Michael Haas, "Approaches to the Analysis of Systematic Factors", Chapter 9 of *International Conflict: A Prolegomenon to Peace Research* (Unpublished Manuscript), p. 103; quoted in Norman D. Palmer and Howard C. Perkins, *International Relations* (Calcutta, 1970), 1st Indian Reprint of 3rd Edn. p. XX.
40. Snyder, Bruck and Sapin, in Hoffmann, ed., n. 25, p. 155.
41. Lenin, "Prelimanary Draft Theses on the National and Colonial Questions" in *ibid.*, pp. 231-35.
42. These "antinomy revolutionary reserves" wcrl' identified by Lenin, p. 8.
43. Lenin, "Preliminary Draft Theses on the National and Colonial Questions" in *ibid.* , pp. 231-35.

# Power Analysis and Balance of Power

4

Power is the bottom line of politics or in other words, politics is the game of power-play. It has been the crux of the civilization from the time immemorial. It is rightly said that "survival of the fittest", in other words starting from the imperialistic epoch to the present day nation-state system, the very basis of a state was established on power or national power. It is the power-play that led to the most infamous wars of the world. So before we start to read other concepts in international politics or world systems, we must vitalize on the concept of power and power analysis. The concept of power analysis has been the topic of discussion between the actors and the non-actors in the field of international relations.[1]

## CONCEPT OF POWER IN INTERNATIONAL RELATIONS

Power in international relations is defined in several different ways. According to Morgenthau, power is the ability to control the minds and actions of others. He defined power as relationship between two political actors in which actor A has the ability to control the mind and actions of actor B. Thus, power in the words of Morgenthau "may comprise anything that establishes and maintains control of man over man (and it) covers all social relationship which serve that and, from physical violence to the most subtle psychological ties by which one mind controls another". Thus, power is viewed as a set of attributes of a given actors as well as a relationship between two actors. The simple way to understand the concept of power to see it as a relationship of independent entities. Similarly, the best way to operationalise and measure a state's capacity to exercise power is to look on its specific attributes and elements which can be easily measured.[2]

Robert Dahl says that power is "the ability to shift the probability of outcomes". According to him, "A has power over B to the extent that he can get B to do something that B would not otherwise do."

Schwarzenberger argues that power is "the mean between influence and force" and may be defined as "capacity to impose one's will on others by reliance on effective sanctions in case of non-compliance". He distinguished power from both influence and force by regarding it as containing a threat not present in influence and yet stopping short of the actual use of force.[3]

The relation between the state and power is very close. Hartman observes that power manifests itself along the lines of influence beginning with latent or unintended use of power (that is to say persuasion), through conscious but regulated power, (i.e. pressure) and reaching up to its final gradation (that is to say, use of force). He says that "power lurks in the background of all relations between sovereign states". Thus, all inter-state relations are ultimately the relations of power politics. Politics is nothing other than the pursuit and exercise of power and that political relations are mainly power relations. Power has been the crucial means for achieving national interests. This is why every nation wants to maintain and utilize power. The position of a state in the comity of nations is determined not by its civilization or culture or literary contribution, but its power. Every state possesses power through different amounts and kinds.

The above observations suggest that power refers to one's ability to influence the behaviour of another and hence, power and influence are similar phenomena, though there is no unanimity among writers about whether these are identical. Further, it is suggested that force or coercion is an element of power.

## DIFFERENT PERSPECTIVES OF POWER

The terms, Power, Influence, Control, Authority and Capability are all interrelated terms which are used interchangeably. We find a very closeknit relationship between power and influence. Some say that power and influence are the same while others observe that influence is a part of power. One scholar says that A can make B behave in the desired way by resorting to four means. These are persuasion, reward, punishment and force. A may succeed in prevailing upon B to do or not to do something by persuasion by forceful and convincing arguments. Persuasion is the most common element of diplomacy. Whether it is bilateral or multilateral diplomacy, one actor seeks to influence the attitude of another or others by the strength of his logic. There is no certainty that superior logic would prevail. Often under an argument lies hidden, other instruments like reward and punishment which may be determined the efficacy of argument. But no nation normally resorts to these instruments for pressurizing other nations. Rewards for compliance may include diplomatic support, economic aid and military assistance. Punishment may include, in addition to the withdrawal of rewards, hostile activities like unfriendly propaganda, diplomatic opposition and aid to the enemy of the state concerned.

Regular flow of American aid to Pakistan is viewed as reward to it for playing ball with the US and as punishment to India which often disagrees with the US on important issues. Punishment may also involve the threat of force or use of force. Use of force is obviously the extreme form of punishment. Thus, punishment and force, as instruments of eliciting compliance from other state(s) are not strictly separated from each other, though some distinction, based upon the intensity of hostility, between these two is made for the purpose of analysis. It has been observed that the first two means—persuasion and reward—constitute influence while the last two—punishment and force—form power. This argument implies that the main feature that distinguishes power from influence is coercion or force. It has been argued above that reward and punishment are interrelated. The withdrawal of one would mean the latter in the same vein, it may be argued that persuasion is not strictly separable from the other three instruments of inducing the target nation. The American arguments in UN and other diplomatic forums are judged by other countries not only by the merits of those arguments, but also by other considerations like what America can do or cannot do if its pleas are accepted or rejected. Thus, American wealth and military capability heavily weigh with other nations when the latter evaluate the American persuasion on any issue. All this leads us to the conclusion that directly or indirectly power is at play whenever A is able to induce B, even by persuasion, to do or not to do something. The so-called influence gained by resorting to persuasion and reward is also a part of power continuum.[4]

Thus, the power can be described in the following perspectives:

- Power as control over resources and capabilities.
- Power as a goal of states or leaders.
- Power as a measure of influence or control over outcomes, events, actors and issues; power as security.

Political theorists such as Machiavelli and Hans Morgenthau have primarily used "power" as a goal in international relations. Power is an inherent goal of mankind and of states among Classical Realist thinkers. Economic growth, military growth, cultural spread, etc. can all be considered as working towards the ultimate goal of international power. Political scientists principally use "power" in terms of an actor's ability to exercise influence over other actors within the international system. This influence can be coercive, attractive, cooperative, or competitive. Mechanisms of influence can include the threat or use of force, economic interaction or pressure, diplomacy, and cultural exchange. "Power" is also used when describing states or actors that have achieved military victories or security for their state in the international system. This general usage is most commonly found among the writings of historians or popular writers. For instance, a state that has achieved a string of combat victories in a military campaign against other states can be described as powerful.

Power is the capacity to direct the decisions and actions of others. Power derives from strength and will. Strength comes from the transformation of resources into capabilities which infuses objectives with resolve. Strategy marshals capabilities and brings them to bear with precision. Statecraft seeks through strategy to magnify the mass, relevance, impact, and irresistibility of power. It guides the ways the state deploys and applies its power abroad. "Power" is also used to describe the resources and capabilities of a state. This definition is quantitative and is most often used by geopoliticians and the military. Capabilities are thought of in tangible terms—they are measurable, weighable, quantifiable assets. Thomas Hobbes spoke of power as "present means to obtain some future apparent good".

Chinese strategists have such a concept of national power that can be measured quantitatively using an index known as comprehensive national power. Modern discourse generally speaks in terms of state power, indicating both economic and military power. Those states that have significant amounts of power within the international system are referred to as middle powers, regional powers, great powers, superpowers, or hyperpowers, although there is no commonly accepted standard for what defines a powerful state.[5] Entities other than states can also acquire and wield power in international relations. Such entities can include multilateral international organizations, military alliance organizations (e.g. NATO), multinational corporations, non-governmental organizations, or other institutions such as the Roman Catholic Church or the Hanseatic League. Under certain circumstances, states can organize a sphere of influence or a bloc within which they exercise predominant influence. Historical examples include the spheres of influence recognized under the Concert of Europe, or the recognition of spheres during the Cold War following the Yalta Conference. The Warsaw Pact, the "Free World", and the Non-Aligned Movement were the blocs that arose out of the Cold War contest. Military alliances like NATO and the Warsaw Pact are another forum through which influence is exercised. However, realist theory often attempts to stay away from the creation of powerful blocs/spheres that can create a hegemony within the region. British foreign policy, for example, has always sided against the hegemonic forces on the continent, i.e. Nazi Germany.

Some political scientists distinguish between two types of power: soft and hard. The former is attractive while the latter is coercive. Joseph Nye is the leading proponent and theorist of soft power. Instruments of soft power include debates on cultural values, dialogues on ideology, the attempt to influence through good example, and the appeal to commonly accepted human values. Means of exercising soft power include diplomacy, dissemination of information, analysis, propaganda, and cultural programming to achieve political ends.

Hard power refers to coercive tactics: the threat or use of armed forces, economic pressure or sanctions, assassination and subterfuge, or other forms of intimidation. Hard power is generally associated to the stronger of nations, as the ability to change the domestic affairs of other nations through military threats. In international relations, a number of concepts are used to describe powers of various types.[6]

Firstly, the hyperpower coined to describe the post-Cold War United States, and has also been applied retroactively to the British Empire, it is a term used to describe the sole superpower in a unipolar system. Secondly, superpower used to describe the United States and the Soviet Union, and has been applied retroactively to the British Empire, the term superpower describes the polar countries in a bipolar or unipolar system. Thirdly, the great power refers to any nation that has strong political, cultural and economic influence over nations around it and across the world. Fourthly, the middle power reflects a subjective description of second-tier influential states that could not be described as great powers. Fifthly, the regional power is also used to describe a nation that exercises influence and power within a region. Being a regional power is not mutually exclusive with any of the above categories.

The term energy superpower describes a country that has immense influence or even direct control over much of the world's energy supplies. Russia and Saudi Arabia are generally acknowledged as the world's two current energy superpowers, given their abilities to globally influence or even directly control prices to certain countries, as Russia has done with natural gas prices in relation to its neighbours. Sixthly, the soft power is a term used in international relations theory to describe the ability of a political body such as a state, to indirectly influence the behaviour or interests of other political bodies through cultural or ideological means. The success of soft power heavily depends on the actor's reputation within the international community as well as the flow of information between actors. Thus, soft power is often associated with the rise of globalization and neo-liberal international relations theory.[7]

**Soft Power**

Soft power has always been a key element of leadership. The power to attract—to get others to want what you want, to frame the issues, to set the agenda—has its roots in thousands of years of human experience. Skillful leaders have always understood that attractiveness stems from credibility and legitimacy. Power has never flowed solely from the barrel of a gun; even the most brutal dictators have relied on attraction as well as fear.

Popular culture and media is regularly identified as a source of soft power, as is the spread of a national language, or a particular set of normative structures; a nation with a large amount of soft power and the goodwill that engenders it inspire others to acculturate, avoiding the need for expensive hard power expenditures.

The term was first coined by Harvard University Professor Joseph Nye, who remains its most prominent proponent, in a 1990 book, *Bound to Lead: The Changing Nature of American Power*. He further developed the concept in his 2004 book, *Soft Power: The Means to Success in World Politics*. While its usefulness as a descriptive theory has not gone unchallenged, soft power has since entered popular political discourse as a way of distinguishing the subtle effects of culture, values and ideas on others' behaviour from more direct coercive measures such as military action (hard power) or economic incentives. The basic concept of power is the ability to influence others to get them to do what you want. There are three major ways to do that: one is to threaten them with sticks; the second is to pay them with carrots; the third is to attract them or co-opt them, so that they want what you want. If you can get others to be attracted, to want what you want, it costs you much less in carrots and sticks.

Soft power, then, represents the third way of getting the outcomes you want. Soft power is contrasted with hard power, which has historically been the predominant realist measure of national power, through quantitative metrics such as population size, concrete military assets, or a nation's Gross Domestic Product. But having such resources does not always produce the desired outcomes as the United States discovered in the Vietnam War. The resources from which soft power behaviour is derived are culture (when it is attractive to others), values (when there is no hypocrisy in their application) and foreign policies (when they are seen as legitimate in the eyes of others). Unless these conditions are present, culture and ideas do not necessarily produce the attraction that is essential for soft power behaviour. The extent of attraction can be measured by public opinion polls, by elite interviews, and case studies. Nye argues that soft power is more than influence, since influence can also rest on the hard power of threats or payments. And soft power is more than just persuasion or the ability to move people by argument, though that is an important part of it. It is also the ability to attract, and attraction often leads to acquiescence.[8]

### Benefits of Soft Power

Soft power rests on the ability to shape the preferences of others. Measuring power in terms of resources is an imperfect but useful short-hand. It is equally important to understand which resources provide the best basis for power behaviour in a particular context. Oil was not an impressive power resource before the industrial age, nor was uranium significant before the nuclear age. Power resources cannot be judged without knowing the context. In some situations, those who hold high office, command force, or possess wealth are not the most powerful. That is what revolutions are about.

### Hard Power

Hard power is a term used in international relations. Hard power is a theory that describes using military and economic means to influence the behaviour or interests of other political bodies. It is used in contrast to soft power, which refers to power that comes from diplomacy, culture and history.

Hard power lies at the command end of the spectrum of behaviours and describes a nation's ability to coerce or induce another nation to perform a course of action. This can be done through military power which consists of coercive diplomacy, war and alliance using threats and force with the aim of coercion, deterrence and protection. Alternatively, economic power can be used which relies on aid, bribes and economic sanctions in order to induce and coerce.

### Political Power

Political power is a type of power held by a person or group in a society. There are many ways to hold such power. Officially, political power is held by the holders of sovereignty. Political powers are not limited to heads of states, however, the extent to which a person or group holds such power is related to the amount of societal influence they can wield, formally or informally. In many cases, this influence is not contained within a single state and it refers to international power.

Political scientists have frequently defined power as "the ability to influence the behaviour of others" with or without resistance.

### Separation of Powers

Charles de Secondat baron de Montesquieu claimed that without following a principle of containing and balancing legislative, executive and judiciary powers, there is no freedom and no protection against abuse of power. Separation of power must be in such grade, that any of the branches can operate without excessive limitations from the others; but interdependency between them must also be in such grade, that one single branch cannot rule out the other's decisions. This is the separation of powers principle.

### Division of Power

A similar concept, termed division of power, also consists of differentiated legislative, executive, and judicial powers. However, while separation of power prohibits one branch from interfering with another, division of power permits such interference. For example, in Indonesia, the President (who wields executive power) can introduce a new bill, but the People's Consultative

Assembly (holding legislative power) chooses to either legalize or reject the bill.

More recently, there has been a move among academics to differentiate power from a new concept of luck. Under some conditions (particularly, when examining the third dimension of power), it becomes necessary to determine who obtains a favourable result through the wielding of genuine power and who is simply "lucky". An example might be an ethnic minority who receive favourable treatment while not intentionally seeking it. A person promoted through positive discrimination would be considered "lucky" rather than "powerful". The eventual aim of such discrimination would be to eventually convert some (or all) of that luck into power. Some groups remain serially lucky without ever obtaining power.

**Power Politics**

Power politics is a state of international relations in which sovereigns protect their own interests by threatening one another with military, economic, or political aggression. Power politics is essentially a way of understanding the world of international relations: nations compete for the world's resources and it is to a nation's advantage to be manifestly able to harm others. It prioritizes national self-interest over the interest of other nations or the international community.

Techniques of power politics include, but are not limited to, conspicuous nuclear development, pre-emptive strike, blackmail, the massing of military units on a border, the imposition of tariffs or economic sanctions, bait and bleed and bloodletting, hard and soft balancing, buck passing, covert operations, and asymmetric warfare. The English term 'power politics' is derived from the German word *Machtpolitik*.

**Great Power**

One of the hallmarks of contemporary great power status is permanent membership on the United Nations Security Council. A great power is a nation or state that has the ability to exert its influence on a global scale. Great powers characteristically possess economic, military, diplomatic, and cultural strength. Nations often consider the opinions of great powers before taking actions of their own. The term "great power" was first used to represent the most important powers in Europe during the post-Napoleonic era. Since then, power has been shifted numerous times, most dramatically during the First and Second World Wars. While some nations are widely considered to be great powers, there is no definitive list, leading to a continuing debate.

## NATIONAL POWER

The problem of defining the term 'power' in a quite precise manner arises from the fact that different writers have taken different views about it. The result is that its real meaning seems to range from Friedrich's description of it as 'a certain kind of human relationship' to Tawney's emphasis on the identification of power with the capacity of an individual or a group of individuals to modify the conduct of others in the manner which one desires. Not merely this, while a great political thinker like Hobbes identifies power with some 'future apparent good', a modern psychoanalyst like Harold Lasswell likens it with 'influence'.[9] We also find that while a great communist leader like Mao of China says that 'power flows from the barrel of a gun', an apostle of peace, truth and non-violence like Mahatma Gandhi substitutes the force of gun and bomb with the power of love and truth emanating from the hearts of the people.

The development of national power is a vital part of international politics. An investigation of international system requires the necessity of examination of the mechanism or elements of power or capability factors, available to the actors within the system. Such an examination can help us in assessing the capabilities of various actors and thus enable us to discern which states are likely to be more important in their influence on developments within the system.

National power is the ability or capability of a nation to secure a change or more particularly to control the behaviour of other nations in such a way as it would lead to the attainment of certain desired objectives of national interest. This ability of a nation depends on several factors which are together called the components or elements of national power. Frankel prefers to term them as capabilities or capability factors. Another popular, but loose designation is 'determinant of national power'. None of these factors or elements is individually a determinant of national power and because it is not merely the existence of these factors which makes a nation powerful. It is the ability to skillfully harness and use these factors that leads to national power. Hence, it is preferred to call these as the components or elements or factors of national power. Power is an unquestionable actuality of all human relationship. Power is the core of politics both domestic and international. Politics is primarily a struggle for power in which each nation seeks to accomplish the goals of its national interest by means of power.

### Categorization of Fundamentals of National Power

There are a number of elements of national power. Many political scientists have attempted to classify these. Whereas Morgenthau classifies them into two parts:

- permanent and
- temporary.

Oraganski prefers to classify the national power into two categories:

- the natural and
- social determinant.

The former including geography, resources and population and the latter including economic development, political structure and national morale. Palmer and Perkins, Charles O. Lerche, Abdul Said, Theodore A. Coloumbis and James H. Wolfe have classified these elements into two parts:

- tangible and
- intangible elements.

The former including those elements, which can be assessed in quantitative terms and latter including such elements as are ideational and psychological and cannot be quantified. Geography, raw materials, natural resources, population and technology are the tangible elements, whereas ideology moral, leadership, personality, organizational efficiency and quality of diplomacy are the intangible elements.

All these classificatory schemes are quite arbitrary. The elements of national power are so much mutually dependent and connected that we cannot evaluate one without reference to the other. Their interdependence is almost complete and power is indivisible and hence, every attempt without going into the relative merits of various classificatory schemes to classify its elements is bound to be limited in approach and scope.

## Elements of National Power

The elements of national power are as follows:

1. Geography
2. Natural resources
3. Population
4. Economic development and industrial capacity
5. Technology
6. Military preparedness
7. Ideology
8. Leadership
9. Organization and quality of government
10. National morale and national character
11. Diplomacy

### *Geography*

Geography is an important constituent of national power. Ideal geographical conditions can be a source of potency and negative and hindering geographical factors can be a source of weakness for the national power. Its role as an element of nation power is linked with several other elements, like:

- population,
- level of scientific, and
- industrial development, etc.

In fact, scientific inventions and technological developments have made it possible for man to adjust, to a very large extent, with and overcome geographical problems and hindrances. Today, Soviet Russia, despite her geographical limitations, has become a major naval power. Similarly, United States, a traditionally ocean-oriented power has, in the post-war period, become a superpower and today hold military base in all strategically important areas. Today, it has assumed a big military role in various parts of the globe, particularly in the so-called heartland of Eurasia. The missile and jet-age has helped America and Russia to be superpowers in world politics.

Geography is an element and not the element or an independent determinant of national power. The geo-politicians over-rate its importance. We have to accept its importance but at the same time weight and analyse it only in the context of other elements. The human element has to be taken into account. As such, the evaluation of geography as an element of national power has to make in relation with other factors and not independently.

The nature and role of geography as an element of national power can be analyzed through a study of the subsequent geographical factors:

- Size
- Location
- Maps
- Climate
- Topography

## Size

Size is another geographical element of national power. The large sizers of a country can accommodate a large population, offer better natural resources and raw materials and can be more helpful in the defence of the country. A large size can help the country to defend by retreat followed by an attack. It is definitely more, rather, very difficult for a state to defeat a big country. It was the large size of Russia that helped it to defeat the forces of Hitler. Large area also makes it possible for a country to establish vital industrial complexes far away from the frontiers and thereby, organize their effective defence. Thus, size is a component of national power.

## Location

Location of a nation can be a serving as well as a hindering factor for her national power. It determines whether a nation can be a sea-power or not. England could become a big naval power and thereby an imperial power because of its location. The location of Japan has helped it to be a major ship-building nation. Locations of Germany in the heart of Europe and of Russia in the centre of 'World Island' have been source of strength for these two nations. The location of USA helped it to adopt and follow the policy of isolation before the First World War. The strategic location of Pakistan in Asia has helped it to secure favourable policies from USA and China. India's location as a sub-continental power of Asia has been a source of strength for its role in international relations.[10] The location of Switzerland has been instrumental in securing for it the states of a neutralised state. Middle East and continental Europe have been the potential zones of power rivalry because of their geographic and strategic locations.

**Maps**

Maps are always geographical in nature and these are sometime used by nations to justify a particular course of policy or action as well as to reject the views of other nations. The Sino-Indian dispute is a dispute of maps regarding MacMohan Line. The Chinese claim of a large part of Soviet territory is again based on maps. The controversy between India and Bangladesh over the issue of ownership of New Moore Island involves a dispute involving interpretation of maps. Maps as such are used as instruments for justifying a particular demand or action of a nation. Padelford and Lincoln have appropriately observed, "Observers of international relations always need an atlas showing population, raw materials, communication routes and other data and the ability to interpret maps."

**Climate**

No one can deny the importance of climate in the context of national power. Climate determines the food production, economy and even the culture of a nation. It can be a source of big hindrance of help for the human capabilities. The cold climate of Artic zone and Antartica and the excessive heat of the tropical zone, and Sahara, have kept the development of life backward in these areas.[11] Extreme heat and cold are unfavourable conditions for national strength. The prosperity of India stands inseparably conditioned by monsoons. A failure of monsoons weakens India and likewise timely and good monsoon rains help India to be self-sufficient and even surplus in food production. It is a well-known fact that the great centres of power have so far arisen only in the moderate temperature zone, between 20 and 60 degrees north. A helpful climate can be a source of power and an unkind climate can be a source of weakness. Hot climate makes people slow and lethargic, whereas cold climate makes people study, hard working and efficient. Thus, climate is an element of power.

### Topography

The nature of topography is an important factor of power. A nation with plain and artificial boundaries can be an easy victim of expansionism on the part of powerful nation. Natural boundaries with strategic advantages are always a source of strength for a nation. Terrain can influence the power of a state and its potentials for offence, defence and growth. It is terrain which determines decisions concerning physical security of the state. The English Channel has been a source of defence and strength for England. The Atlantic and Pacific Oceans have provided strength to the security of United States. Amongst the elements of national power, geography is a stable, tangible, permanent and natural element. Its importance as a factor of national power can be judged from the fact that many geo-political scientists like Moodie, Spykman, Haushofer, Mackinder and others, regard geography as the determinant of international politics. The foreign policy of a country is determined by its geography.

### *Natural Resources*

Natural resources are stable factors of national power. No nation can hope to be a powerful nation if its territory is not adequately graced by natural resources. The industrial and military capabilities of a nation as well as its economic well-being are dependent upon the existence of natural resources. A self-sufficiency in certain key resources can be big source of power of a nation. Both America and Russia have been in a position to be superpowers in world politics mainly due to their self-sufficiency respect of several key natural resources. No nation can be powerful without becoming a developed industrialized nation and the chances of becoming an industrialized nation are fundamentally linked with the possession of natural resources, particularly industrial raw materials and minerals. Morgenthau, however, makes a simple twofold classification: raw materials and food.

### *Population*

Another basic element which effects national power is population. "As long as men are needed for production and fighting, other elements being equal, the state with a larger number of men and women to perform such tasks shall be more capable of becoming a major power." Man-power continues to be a key factor which determines the industrial and military capacities of a nation and its status as a power in international relations. In this age of science, machines have come to perform a larger number of functions which were previously being performed by men, yet machines have failed to completely replace men. Even today, men behind the machines continue to be more important than the machines. Man-power alone can exploit the natural resources and utilise these for the satisfaction of national needs. Large concentration of man-power in Asia, particularly China and India, has been an important factor of power structure in international politics.

### *Economic Development and Industrial Capacity*

Morgenthau has emphasised the importance of economic development and industrial capacity as element of national power when he observes, "the technology of modern warfare and communications has made the overall development of heavy industries an indispensable element of national power". The quality and productive capacity of the industrial plant, the know-how of the working man, the skill of the engineer, the inventive genius of the scientist, the managerial organization—are those factors upon which industrial capacity of a nation and hence its power depends.[12]

Effective economic organization and planning are essential ingredients of a powerful nation. It is a very important part of national power of a nation because it is the means for military power and the basis for welfare. Poverty is always a source of limitation of power. It is this factor which is forcing most of the developing countries of the Third World to live with neo-colonialism-economic dependence on the rich nations. Economic development and industrial capacity are important elements of national power. However, like other elements, these two elements are also closely related to other elements, particularly, raw material, technology, skilled man-power, scientific talent and research, economic resources, etc. Their role as elements of power has to be analyzed in relation with other factors and not independently. The modern warfare has made industrial capacity a significant factor of military power of nation. The agricultural production of a country can be increased only through industrialized farming. Increased industrial capacity increases the agricultural capacity and the power of a nation.

A nation with developed, healthy and growing economy alone can be a great power in world politics. Nations with developed economies can use the economic instruments—aid, loan, rewards, trade, grants, and denial of rewards of punishment; for securing their desired goals in international relations and thereby further increasing their national powers. The increased importance of economic instruments of foreign policy is a recognized fact of present day international relations. The level of economic well-being determines the power of a nation.

In this age of industrialization, developed industrial capacity alone can be a source of enduring and effective economic development. Only industrially advanced nations can become great powers. Today, United States, United Kingdom, France, Japan and Germany are powerful nations because of their huge industrial capacities. They have the ability to process raw materials and thereby are in a position to control international economy. A state must have surplus industrial production if it wants to be economically developed and this can be achieved only through industrialization.

***Technology***

The position of technology as a factor of power can be judged from the fact that today, technological aid or assistance, arms control, nuclear technology, communication technology, and space technology are elements of international relations and these influence the foreign policies of both the developed and underdeveloped countries. Technology is the submission of science for promoting human welfare. It is the capability to use scientific inventions for the encouragement of human welfare. Development in engineering and industrial production is directly related to the nature and level of technology. It has been the advanced technological ability that has largely contributed to the prosperity and power of the developed countries.

The level of technological development determines the power-status of a nation. A nation backed by highly developed and advanced technology alone can be recognised as a developed nation. America and Soviet Union are both highly technologically developed nations and this fact has been a major source of their power. It has tremendously increased their abilities to influence and control the behaviour of the poor and less developed nations. The development of nuclear technology has been a source of tremendous influence on international politics. Initially, monopoly over atomic secret was sought to be sued by America for maintaining power superiority over Russia. The Russian success in acquiring the nuclear technology in early 1950s, however, made the Soviet Union successfully compete with American power in international relations. The overkill capacity achieved by both the superpowers, resulting from the huge stockpiling of nuclear weapons of mass destruction, has been a source of limitation for other nations. The nuclear technology, missile technology and space technology have given a big boost to the power of superpowers.[13]

### *Military Preparedness*

Military preparedness is directly dependent upon such factors as technology, industrial capacity, economic development policies of the government, etc. and hence it is not an independent determinant of national power. While evaluating military preparedness as a factor of national power we have to take into account three factors:

(i) War technology or technological innovations,

(ii) Military leadership, and

(iii) Quantity and quality of soldiers.

Military power is not national power, nevertheless it is an important part of national power which contributes to its strength and effectiveness. Military preparedness is a background factor for the success of foreign policy. Military preparedness is the most noticeable and tangible factor capable of supporting the foreign policy and promoting national interest. It influences the level of success in achieving foreign policy. Major powers of our times are big military powers. By virtue of being a major military power, India, besides other factors, is considered a major power with the potential to be great power in future.

War technology is an important factor but it can be fruitful only when backed by efficient planning and systematic and effective use. It refers to the nature and type of weapon system that is available with the army of the state. Modern warfare is a sophisticated technological warfare. The quantity and technical quality of weapons and military equipment is a major factor that determines the level of military power of a nation. Advanced military technology is always a source of potency and strategic advantage. The submarine technology available to the German Army was responsible for the initial success that Germany secured in First World War. However, the convoy system and use of bit tank battle technique adopted by Britain, successfully met the German threat and made possible the British victory over Germany. In Second World War, atomic technology helped America to inflict a crushing defeat on Japan. Thus, the weapon system and war technology is an important factor in military preparedness.

In a war, weapons and equipment play a key role but their role and effectiveness is dependent upon the quantity and quality of soldiers. Military equipment and weapons system is important, but not as much as the soldiers who actually use these weapons and equipment. War technology brings into focus the role of military leadership. Military planning is a valuable factor of military action in a war. Skilled, trained, experienced, dedicated and disciplined military leadership alone can make the best use of available weapons, equipment and man-power. A war victory can be possible only under effective and efficient military leadership. The number, skill, training, discipline and dedication of the soldiers are essential factors, which can make possible an effective and successful use of military weapons and machines.

Pakistan had superior weapon system, tanks and aircraft in both the 1965 and 1971 wars with India, however, it failed to use this superiority to its advantage because of inadequately trained and less skilled men behind these machines. Indian soldiers could provide a decisive and befitting answer to Pakistani attack because of their superior qualities which made it possible to use a relatively lower level machines and equipment for securing the desired objective and best possible results.

### *Ideology*

Ideology is closely linked with national power. Ideology has been a source of unity and strength both at home and abroad. The ideology of nationalism has always been a source of internal strength for nations. The ideology of liberalism has helped America to spread its influence in Western Europe and other parts of the globe. These are elements in the power of a state. The ideology that a government upholds is spruce of unity and support of the people at home and abroad. The ideology of communism has been a big source of strength for the communist states. Ideology has helped them to influence the development and use of command over power and violence. Similarly, the adoption of democratic socialism has helped India to establish friendly and cooperative relations with the democratic West and the communist East. It has also been a source of popular support for the Government of India.

A choice of wrong ideology can be a source of weakness. Nazism destabilized Hitler's Germany and Fascism did the same to Mussolini's Italy. Further ideological differences within a nation, and among nations can be a source of weakness. These differences have smashed the relations between Russia and China. A suitable popular ideology can increase the power of a nation to explain, justify and secure the goals of national interest. In practices, a nation uses a number of particular ideologies for securing support for its foreign policy objectives. These provide cover to the real intention of the state.

### *Leadership*

Leadership of a nation is an important human building block of national power. The operation of natural resources, raw materials, technology, industrial competence, military power and ideology for strengthening the national power of a state is reliant upon the qualities of leadership that runs the government of the state. Civil and military planning is a function of the political leaders. The responsibility of the leader is to make and implement foreign policy of a state. National power is really the power of the decision-makers—the leaders. The quality of leadership determines the nature and extends of power that a nation uses for securing its national interest. Efficient, devoted and grown-up leadership can be a source of national power in the sense that a judicious use of power can surely augment the national power and its operational usefulness.

### *Organization and Quality of Government*

Government is obligatory for a judicious and proper use of possessions and exercise of power. It can effectively mobilize the element of national power and thereby increases it. Lack of effective and well-organized government can seriously edge the power of a state. It is the business of government to coordinate men and material resources and secure power fulfilling goals of national interest. Effectiveness of government organization and administration within a state is another element of national power. There are many examples which highlight the importance of this factor of national power. For decades, China remained a weak power because, among other reasons, the central government lacked effective control over major portions of the country. Similar was the case of France. Until de Gaulle took control in France in the year 1958, political power had for several decades been divided among a number of political parties. This not only brought crisis to the cabinet but also made it difficult for the French government to pursue policies on an enduring basis. Democracy or dictatorship proves a power advantage is a question on which opinions differ.[14] The arguments advanced in favour of democratic government are: that it provides its citizens with the greatest spiritual, political and scientific freedom, and public criticism and widespread participation in the decision-making process make it more probable that the decisions will be sound. The usual argument in favour of dictatorship is that it makes it easier to form a single, unified, specific policy, since disagreement within the government is suppressed.

### *National Morale and National Character*

National morale is also an element of national power. National morale refers to the extent of determination with which a nation ropes the foreign policies of its government in peace and war, it permeates all activities of a nation, its agriculture and industrial productions as well as its military establishments and diplomatic survey. The success in 1965 and 1971 wars, the successful green revolution and the entry into nuclear club through a peaceful nuclear explosion in May 1974, and in 1996 gave vital strength and reinvigorated the national morale. A high and healthy national morale can be a big source of power which can lead to successful use of power for securing the national interest. High national morale kept the Britishers in high spirits which finally helped them to win war, even after having lost many battles. The high morale of Indian army has been a factor in the victory in 1971 war with Pakistan. It is the extent to which the people support their leaders believe in the superiority of their state and in the rightness of their cause. It depends upon a combination of circumstances and the quality of leadership and can be subject to frequent and sometimes sudden fluctuations. Indian morale became quite low after severe revises in Sino-Indian War of 1962. Their evaluation as factors of national power must be done with reference to other human and material factors. The intangibility of these factors particularly national character must also be kept in mind.

National character is a shared name for referring to the traits of the people, their attitude and aptitude towards work and national needs. Sociologists advocate that Russians are known for their durability, elementary strength and persistence; Americans for their inventiveness, initiative and spirit of adventure; Britishers for their undogmatic common sense; Germans for discipline and industriousness; Japanese for their nationalism; Indians for their tolerance and faith in rich cultural traditions; and Chinese for their cosmic unchangeability. Traits of national character definitely influence the national power of a nation. The stereotypes of national character can be grossly misleading, there is some foundation for the observation that different nations tend to develop their own peculiar ways of thinking and acting, some of which are more useful than others for the power of the state. National character are elements of national power but their role can be both positive and negative.

***Diplomacy***

Diplomacy of high eminence can fetch the ends and means of foreign policy into synchronization with the available resources of national power. It can catch the hidden sources of national strength and transform them fully and securely into political realities. Diplomacy is the brain of national power, which can bring all the power sources of a nation.

Hans J. Morgenthau regards diplomacy as the most important, though unstable, element of national power. Diplomacy is the means of foreign policy and as such helps it to achieve better results through judicious hard work and influence in international relations. In the words of Morgenthau, "the quality of a nation's diplomacy combines those different factors into an integrated whole, gives them direction and weight, and awakens their slumbering potentialities by giving the breath of actual power". British diplomacy has been instrumental in projecting Britain as a major power in world politics, even after the loss of its status as a mighty imperial power.

The role of diplomacy as an element of national power has undergone a change in recent times. The emergence of new diplomacy—open and conference diplomacy, has somewhat limited its role as a factor of national power. We cannot accept Morgenthau's thesis that diplomacy is the most important of all the elements of national power, nevertheless, we cannot deny that diplomacy is a factor of national power which, when of high quality, can effectively contribute towards the effective and successful exercise of national power.

**Assessment of National Power**

The dimension of power is a tricky task because it involves the task of measuring, quantitatively and qualitatively, a large number of tangible and intangible elements of national power. The need to analyze the actual and potential power of a nation makes the task difficult. To assess the power of a nation in peace and war involves still bigger difficulties. The relativity of power relations again pose a problem to measure the power of a nation in comparison with the powers of other nations is a highly difficult exercise which becomes all the more difficult due to the highly dynamic nature of several elements. Extent and growth of national power is fundamentally essential for international relations because this can help them to scrutinize the nature of struggle for power among nations. The ability to measure and assess national power can greatly augment the understanding of international relations.

Many scholars have tried to use various techniques for measuring power of a nation. Some scholars advocate the study of history of past relations as they try to measure power. This technique is unacceptable because it ignores the highly dynamic nature of power. Many scholars regard performance in war as the criteria for judging the power of a nation. This is a limited and unreliable basis. Power in peace and power in war are two different things.

The results of war cannot provide an adequate criterion of power because power revealed in the war is not the only kind of power. A militarily weak nation may have a good influence in times of peace. The examples of Switzerland and Sweden are before us. External domain includes those territories and population outside a nation-state that belong to its 'sphere of influence'. The internal domain can be measured in terms of population, area and gross national product. The external domain can be analyzed in terms of sphere of influence, alliances, dependencies and the degree of penetration in the political processes of other countries. The external domain of USA can be measured in terms of its alliances, etc., NATO, SEATO, ANZUS, OAS, and the number of military bases abroad. Similarly, Russian external domain involves a judgement about Warsaw Treaty Organization and Soviet military bases abroad.

National power cannot be measured or weighed physically in terms of meters, litres, kilograms, tonnes, etc. The problem of measurement lies both in the subjective limitations of the analysis and in the very characteristics of the elements themselves. It would be a gross over-simplification to say that any one of the elements determines by itself the power of a nation. An evaluator may ignore the relativity of power by erecting the power of one particular nation into an absolute. Power is never absolute. A state cannot be considered to remain powerful all times to come. Power keeps changing and history is a record of this statement. Britain, Germany and now Russia are the examples of past great powers of the world. Rise and fall of nations is a common phenomenon in history. Power is, therefore, not a simple and stable phenomenon.

The nature of power is ever changing and is dynamic. Some scholars contend the power factors like military force, population, size, raw materials, geography are declining in importance as part of the power equation while other factors like technological excellence, education and economic growth are gaining in importance. Nye believes that 'coercive power' is declining, 'co-optive' power is increasing. While war earlier was a technique to increase national power, the idea of a total war is a risky proposition in the context of a nuclear age. The interdependence of all elements is so complete that power is actually indivisible. The gap between estimate and reality of power also makes measurement difficult. The possibility of the underestimation or overestimation of one's own power and overestimation of that of others result in policies of peace and status quo. While over-estimation of one's own power and underestimation of that of others pave the way for policies of war and change. Power is relative and situational. If China is considered powerful, it can be powerful only if we specify the comparison. A county's situational power is often less than the total inventory of its capabilities.

In Iranian hostages crisis, American military power had little value in getting the hostages released. Power is also linked with the specificity of power. That is to say, that no particular type of power can be such that it can be applied in any form and in any condition. Even huge stock of nuclear weapons will be meaningless deterrent if the rival thinks that those weapons will not be used.

Finally, power is multi-faceted and the error occurs by giving one-single factor a decisive role to the disregard of all other factors. Sometimes, an evaluation is made on the basis of geo-politics or nationalism or military capability. All aspects of power need to be considered and placed in their proper relative and situational contexts. To conclude, with all its complexities, a complete understanding of power is crucial to a sophisticated analysis of international relations. The successful pursuit of international relations is based on a realistic assessment of both national interest and power.

### Control of National Power

National power operates within certain restrictions. The major limitations of national power are as follows:

**1. International Organizations:** It is true that United Nations has also kept the power of the states within limits. The United Nations cannot intervene in the internal matters of any state except when they pose a threat to the peace, but it certainly acts as a check on the unfair and unlimited use of power by the states and hence is a limitation on national power.

**2. Balance of Power:** In international politics, the power of one nation or a group of nations is worn to avert a particular nation from magnificent its will upon others. When a state has predominance of power, it must be balanced or checked by the combined powers of the other states. The common patterns of balance of power are direct opposition to other state by one state with a view to preserve status quo. In the second one, two nations compete with each other to establish control over the third nation. The other common methods used to maintain the balance of power are 'divide and rule', compensations and acquisitions, armaments and intervention, alliance and counter-alliance and buffer state formation.

**3. International Laws:** To keep away from international anarchy, a code of conduct in the nature of international law is essential to edge the national power. The execution of these laws by consent or use of external force restricts the scope of use of national power by any state.

**4. Disarmament:** An effort has been made through several agreements, treaties and conventions to control the use of nuclear and conventional weapons that have the potentialities to destroy the entire world. This has inevitably resulted in the curtailment of the national power.

**5. International Morality:** To safeguard international society, certain moral precepts have been frontward such as keeping of promises, trust in other's world, fair dealing, respect for international law, protection of minorities, repudiation of war as an instrument of national policy, international morality protects human life in peace by renouncing the policy of assassination of the leaders of the opponent countries, techniques of giving poison, treachery, etc.[15] Similar moral limitations operate in items of war. They protect civilians and those combatants who are unable or unwilling to fight. It is undesirable to make civilian population major target of attack. The Geneva Conventions of 1864, 1906, 1929 and 1949 as well as Hague Conventions of 1899 and 1907 laid down certain specific conditions regarding the treatment of the sick or wounded soldiers (prisoners of war) by the other side. There is moral condemnation of war and war as an instrument of foreign policy has been repudiated. The two Hague Peace Conferences of 1899 and 1907, the Leauge of Nations of 1919, the Briand-Kellogg Pact of 1928 and the United Nations in the present times all have avoided war itself as their final goal.

**6. World Public Opinion:** Modern history testifies that the world public opinion had never acted as a deterrent against any state which insisted on following a particular policy. These instances are—the Japanese aggression against China in the thirties; the German foreign policies since 1935; the Italian attack against Ethiopia in 1936; the Russian suppression of the Hungarian Revolution in 1956, Czechoslovakian revolution in 1968, and intervention in Afghanistan in 1980, China's annexation of Tibet in 1959, Iraq's annexation of Kuwait in 1990 and Taliban's rule in Afghanistan from 1996 to 2001. However, because of the technological unification of the world because of the rapidity of communication by inventions in ocean, land and air transportation and in the press, postal service, telecommunication and satellite communication system, a world public opinion tends to develop and influence government actions.

## BALANCE OF POWER

Balance of power is an overused concept in international politics. It means many things to different people. As has been said by Claude, it is an "ambiguous concept" and it has got many meanings. Sometimes, it is used as a policy. It is also used as a symbol. It is also used at times as a propaganda ploy. If in the 19th century the theory of balance of power took strong roots, in 1970s it gained immense popularity due to the effort of Henry Kissinger, the "star" of the foreign policy establishment of the US in the first half of 1970s. Kissinger, who has all along been a keen student of the balance of power, went on theorizing on it even after he joined the Nixon administration. His attachment to Metternich and Bismarck whom he studied extensively did not diminish with the passage of time. On the other hand, his faith in balance of power and his admiration for these original protagonists of this theory were reinforced by his active association with "real politics" of the world.[16]

To understand balance of power, we may take the analogy of a balancer with a pair of scales. If the weights in the two scales are equal, there is balance. The same analogy may be extended to international politics. The two states or two coalitions of states are in balance if they are equally powerful. Morgenthau rightly says that the balance of power is "an actual state of affairs in which power is distributed among several nations with approximate equality".

Balance of power refers to "equilibrium" in international politics. In a normal human body, there is equilibrium. When an individual suffers from a serious disease, this equilibrium is disturbed. But different organs of the body would automatically react to prevent such disturbance. Further, an external input like medicine is injected into the body to maintain equilibrium at the original level or at a different level. Thus, the maintenance of equilibrium in the body in the face of external attack requires automatic internal reactions and at times, external intervention duly planned and executed. Similarly, the equilibrium in the international system is not an automatic process only. It involves human choice and decision planned and implemented. It has been described as "diplomatic contrivance". A similar process occurs in the economic system. It is described as "countervailing power".

The main aim of the balance of power is the preservation of the stability of the international system. But this can be done if one element is too strong for others. In such a case, the former can destroy the latter, without destroying the systematic stability. But the theory of balance of power would not allow it as it requires that the stability is to be maintained without any element being lost. That is why one of the conditions of balance of power is some sort of equality among its elements. Thus, its two goals are the stability of the system accompanied by preservation of its elements and these goals are to be accomplished by ensuring approximate equality of power among the constituting sub-systems. Vernon Van Dyke is right in pointing out that security and peace are the main purposes of balancing power. "Though peace is often stated as the purpose, security is usually the more fundamental concern." When a potential enemy suddenly increases its military capability, a state is more concerned about the possible impact of the enemy's increased strength upon its security than about the danger to the peace, although it would generally justify its security-oriented response in the name of the preservation of peace threatened by the enemy. A state plays the balancing game with a view to removing such possible danger to its vital interests. Dyke observes, "...the prime object of the balancing of power is to establish or maintain such a distribution of power among states as will prevent anyone of them from imposing its will upon another by the threat or use of violence". In a balance of power system, no state or combination of states should be so powerful as to endanger the security of others and resultantly the stability of the system. Castlereagh described the balance of power as "the maintenance of such a just equilibrium between the members of the family of nations as should prevent any of them becoming sufficiently strong to impose its will upon the rest". In the same vein, it has been observed by Palmer and Perkins that the concept of balance of power assumes that through shifting alliances and countervailing pressures no one power or combination of powers will be allowed to grow so strong as to threaten the security of the rests."[17] Sidney Fay who holds a similar view of balance of power describes it as "just equilibrium in power among the members of the family of nations as will prevent any one of them from becoming sufficiently strong to enforce its will upon the others".

Theoretically speaking, balance of power assumes equality of contending powers so that neither of them would be inclined to be aggressive. But realistically speaking, every power, while professing balance of power, would be aiming at preponderance of power on its side. It would seek to maintain a clear margin of power over its adversary. The motivations may be of twofold. It would be confident that its superior power would deter the opponent from invading it. Secondly, if the need arises, it may take punitive action against the opponent. In either case, its efforts would be directed at ensuring military superiority *vis-à-vis* the opponent. It has been observed by Nicholas J. Spykman: "The truth of the matter is that states are interested only in a balance which is in their favour. Not an equilibrium, but a generous margin in their objectives. There is no real security in being just as strong as there is a potential enemy; there is security only in being a little stronger. The balance desired is the one which neutralizes other states leaving the home state free to be the deciding force and the deciding voice."

**Definitions of the Balance of Power**

Fenelon in 1835 defined it as: "action by the state to keep its neighbours from becoming too strong because the aggrandisement of one nation beyond a certain limit changes the general system of all the other neighbours attention to the maintenance of a kind of equality and equilibrium between neighbouring states".

In 1886 Stubbs stated: "The Balance of Power, however it be defined, that is, whatever the powers were between which it was necessary to maintain such equilibrium, that the weaker should not be crushed by the union of the stronger, is the principle which gives unity to the political plot of modern European history."

### Uniqueness

- The balance of power game is mainly a big power game and the small powers are used as mere weights in the scales.
- The balance of power implies dealing with diplomatic contrivance and not historical causation.
- The balance of power is concerned with equilibrium as well as international disequilibrium.
- Nations have mostly desired preponderance of power.
- It is subject to constant changes, to shifting political patterns and powers relationships.
- It is not a gift of God but is the result of diplomatic activity.
- Balance of power normally favours the status quo, but to be effective, the policy must be changing and dynamic one.
- When a balance of power has been accomplished real balance of power seldom exists. Its real test is war. If war takes place it means that real balance of power was not there.

### Patterns of Balance of Power

The pattern is one of direct oppositions when there are two nations confronted with each other. One nation wants to establish its power over another while the other refuses to yield. It results directly from the desire of either nation to see its policies prevail over the policies of the other. Morgenthau in his book *Politics Among Nations* (1973) mentions two main patterns of the balance of power:

- the pattern of direct opposition and the pattern of competition where the balancing of opposing forces goes on until the weaker nation yields or war decides the issues, and

- The pattern of competition exists when one or the other nations tries to establish its domination over the third power and neither of the two powers allow each other to disturb the status quo. The competition between the United States and China for control of the countries of South-East Asia offers an example of this pattern.

## Category of Balance of Power

There are three types of balance of power, as under:

1. Local, regional or worldwide balance of power
2. Simple and multiple balance of power
3. Flexible and rigid.

### *Local, Regional or Worldwide Balance of Power*

Balance of power can be local, regional or global depending in terms of their geographical coverage (i.e. the area of its operation). The balance is local, if it is at the local level, like of the balance of power between India and Pakistan. It is regional, if an area or a continent, say Europe of Asia, is involved. The struggle amongst the European powers in the nineteenth century aimed at maintenance of regional balance of power. The balance of power is regarded as worldwide or global if it concerns more than one region. During the two world wars, the principle of world balance of power motivated the actions of various states.

### *Simple and Multiple Balance of Power*

If power is concentrated in two states or in two opposing camps, the balance of power is said to be simple. The United States and the Soviet Union individually, and the Eastern and Western blocs respectively, were the examples of the simple balance in the post-war period of bipolarism. When there is a wide dispersal of power among states and a number of states or groups of states balance each other, the balance is called multiple or complex. With the decline of bipolarism after the end of the Cold War, multipolarism has been on the rise. Germany, Japan, China, India, France, Britain are major powers on the rise today, thus, creating a favourable environment for balance of power to operate.

### *Flexible and Rigid*

In the monarchical days when princes could make sudden and radical shifts in their alliances, the balance was generally flexible. With the coming of ideologies and greater economic interdependence, patterns of balance of power have tended to become rigid.

## Techniques and Strategy to Take Up Balance of Power

The balance of power is an uncertain regulator for it creates an equilibrium that is best temporary and improvised. The balance of power is not a natural phenomenon and requires special efforts. The techniques and devices, which contribute to its operation, are as under:

**Break up:** The device has been resorted to by nations who want to keep their competitors weak by keeping them divided. Britain often used it to keep her large empire intact, or the policies of the Soviet Union from the twenties to the end of the Cold War in opposing a closer and political integration of Europe, and the policy of Western countries to keep India and Pakistan divided by propping up the Kashmir issue very often.

**Alliances and Counteralliances:** Alliances have been the most convenient institutional device to increase one's insufficient power. The alliances are built out of community of interests for its foundation, directed against a common enemy and may break up after the objective is achieved. Alliances generally lead to counteralliances, e.g. Triple Alliance of 1882 was countered by Triple Entente in 1907. When a state feels that it cannot defend itself against another big state, it enters into alliance with another weak or powerful state for achieving its goal. The alliances are of two types:

(1) offensive

(2) defensive.

Both are concerned with the balance of power. An offensive alliance seeks to upset the balance in favour of its members and a defensive alliance aims at restoring the balance. Similarly, the

Axis formed in 1936 was a counterweight against the alliance between France and East European nations. It is the post-Second World War era, the USA with its allies formed NATO, SEATO, CENTO, etc. and the USSR countered them with Warsaw Pact.

**Compensation and Partition:** When some powerful nation occupies the territory of small nations, the powerful rival nations cannot tolerate this act. They place a condition either to share its prey with them or to allow them to compensate themselves elsewhere. Under such conditions, the powerful rival nations divide small nations and swallow their share of the prey. Thus, Poland was partitioned between Russia, Prussia and Austria-Hungary in 1972 is an example of compensation and partition. After World War II, Vietnam, Korea and Germany were partitioned for similar reasons. This involves a method of redistributing power in a way that international balance of power remains unaffected. "The bargaining of diplomatic negotiations, issuing in political compromise is the principle of compensations in its most general form, and as such it is originally connected with the balance of power".

**Intrusion and Non-interventionism:** Under such circumstances, a major power tries to regain a last ally by intervening in its domestic affairs and establishing a friendly government there. Allies may shift their loyalty from one power-bloc to another. Britain intervened in Greece in the end of the World War II to see that Greece did not fall into hands of Communists. After World War II, the United States intervened in Guatemala, Cuba, Lebanon, Laos, Kuwait, etc. and the Soviet Union in North Korea, North Vietnam, Hungary, Czechoslovakia, Afghanistan, etc. Non-intervention suggests neutrality or guarantee of neutrality for certain states, or efforts to localize war or protect the rights of neutrals in time of war.

**Armament and Disarmament:** The arms race of USA and the former USSR in the post-war period is the most recent example of this kind. To maintain local balance of power, India and Pakistan also indulge in arms race. Like armaments, to attain balance of power consistent efforts at disarmament are essential. The states may agree on proportionate reduction in their arms so that balance of power between them may be stabilized. In the twentieth century, the steps in the direction was taken by the Treaty of Versailles and Washington Naval Conference in 1922. After 1987 and especially after the end of Cold War, the USA and Russia have taken certain disarmament measures.

**Traditional Buffer State:** Buffer state is a state set up between two large and unfriendly nations and it always keeps them safely apart, to minimize the chances of conflict between them and thereby contributes to the maintenance of balance of power. In the 19th and early 20th centuries, Afghanistan had been a traditional buffer state between the Imperial Russia and British India, as Tibet was a buffer state between Imperial China and British India.

**Household Method:** If the state feels that the balance has been tilted in favour of the rival, it can become powerful by cultivating power domestically like developing related industries and other aspects of science and economy whose total effect world make it stronger and help it in restoring the balance.

### Relevance of Balance of Power System

The principle of balance of power has greatly contributed to the preservation of peace in the absence of system of collective security. According to Carr, peace in Europe in the nineteenth century was largely due to balance of power. The theory and practice of the balance of power has been a subject of great debate and discussion. It has greatly contributed to the preservation of the modern state system by guaranteeing independence of smaller states. Balance of power makes it difficult for any single state or a group of states to become so powerful as to overwhelm the rest. It helps in the preservation of multiple nature of international society and its stability.

Morgenthau has criticized the balance of power on three counts—its uncertainty, its unreality and its inadequacy. This was due to certain defects in this system:

- The balance of power pre-supposes the presence of three or more states of roughly equal power, but the bipolar system which emerged in the post-World War II period gave a serious set back to the system of balance of power.

- The ideology has undermined the possibility of readjustment of any kind in the international political and multiple state system. Where the foreign policy of a state is guided by ideology, the state is usually not much interested in the balance of power, and is poorly equipped to pursue it.
- The balance of power does not bring peace. On the other hand, it has encouraged wars. Organski has expressed that the periods of balance were periods of war, not periods of peace.
- The threat of war is of limited utility in the nuclear age due to the nuclear stalemate.
- While the superpowers are becoming more and more powerful, the poor Third World states are becoming weaker.
- The emerging importance of collective security, international law and international organizations like United Nations has further relegated the balance of power to the background.
- Decline in the relevance of the alliance system, which is the cornerstone of the balance of power, has further made it obsolete.
- It is difficult to measure the power positions of states at a given time of history and claim that a balance of power exists. It is difficult to make a correct assessment of the power of China, India or Japan.
- The growing uncertainty lies in the fact that one cannot always be sure who are one's allies and who are the opponents. It does not provide suitable measures to recognize the real intention of other states.
- The post-War period created unfavourable conditions for the working of balance of power system.
- In view of the above developments, certain scholars have contended that the concept of balance of power has become obsolete and is incompatible with present conditions.

- But it would be too much to assert that it has ceased to be a factor in the power struggle and that the balance of power is nothing but a device of management of power.

So long power continues to be a factor in the conduct of international relations, the balance of power shall continue to have relevance. Its relevance would depend on how far its mechanisms is modified to suit the new conditions. There are two other objective factors of the international reality that proved the existence of balance of power even in the days of bipolarism.

The role of non-aligned nations is maintaining balance between the two superpowers. These un-recommitted nations behave like what Richard Rosecrance calls the "multiple buffer". The other is the role of the superpowers in maintaining an equilibrium between the countries directly involved in a situation of crisis.

As long as multi nation-state system exists, balance of power politics will continue in practice, however, roundly they are dammed in theory. In all probabilities, they will continue to operate, even if effective supranational groupings, on a regional or world level, are formed.

After the end of Cold War, the influence of ideology has been on the wane. With the collapse of Soviet Union and disintegration of Communist bloc, ideological struggle lost its edge. Consequently, ideology as a negating factor of balance of power has disappeared.

With the decline of bipolarism, multipolarism has been on the rise. Germany, China, Japan, India, EU, South-East Asian countries have regained their lost power, thus, creating a favourable environment for balance of power to operate. The success of the United States in liberating Kuwait from Iraq and removing the Taliban regime from Afghanistan, is now the only superpower and militarily and economically matchless. Thus, in the present world the USA can be regarded as a balancer.

Balance of power is a measure of the amount of the military power states or blocs held in relation to each other. The theory that peace and stability are most likely to be maintained when military power is distributed so that no single power or bloc can dominate the others. Balance of power theory is also founded on the realist premise that weakness invites attack and that counterveiling power must be used to deter potential aggressors. Competition is proper because it leads to the equalization of capabilities among the major competitors.[18] We can identify three models of the balance of power in the second half of the twentieth century (since 1945)—Unipolarity—the United States, Bipolarity—the United States and Russia, Biploycentrism—Cold War Satellites (the continued military superiority of the two superpowers and their allies' continued reliance on their respective patrons for security), with a fourth probably emergent in the early twenty-first century—Multipolarity. Since 1989, we are moving towards a multipolar world. Such multipolar system is likely to consist of the United States, China, Japan, Russia, Germany and the European Union. In this way, the above factors and developments prove that the balance of power is still relevant, valid and meaningful.[19]

### Characteristics of Balance of Power

The balance of the power system has the following characteristics:

1. **Equilibrium:** The balance of power aims at maintaining equilibrium in the international system. There may be minor changes now and then, here and there. But these changes should not threaten the equilibrium of the system. When this equilibrium is lost, the balance of power has failed. If there is any threat to the stability of the system by one or more members, other members would automatically react and seek to counter it. However, occasional disequilibrium is not ruled out in a balance of power system.

2. **Temporary and Unstable**: The balance of power system is unstable and temporary. From time to time, it would be vulnerable to instability. When the system is subjected to severe stress, one balance of power system may be replaced by a new one. Deutsch and Singer have pointed out: "No balance of power system has lasted longer than a few centuries, and most of the original powers contending in such systems have survived as independent powers only for much shorter periods."

3. **Active Intervention:** Balance of power is not a "gift of the God". It is the result of the active intervention of the man. Whenever a state fears that the balance is being tilted against it, it would immediately try to counter it. It cannot afford to wait till some other force intervenes on its behalf to maintain or restore the balance. It must be ready to take necessary steps, including risking a war, if it is determined to safeguard its vital interests which would be jeopardized if it remains silent.

4. **Status Quo:** Balance of power is oriented towards status quo. The privileged nations would favour maintaining the status quo, whereas those who feel deprived or underprivileged would seek to change the system-radically if necessary. In fact, several wars have broken out in the past due to these contrary motivations of the states.

5. **Subjective and Objective Approaches:** There are two approaches to balance of power, namely the subjective approach of the historian and the objective approach of the statesman. In the eyes of the historian, there is balance between two states if they are equally powerful. On the other hand, a statesman would take a subjective look at it. He is inclined to be biased by nationalism. Only when his country is more powerful than its potential enemy, he would say that there is balance of power between them. Thus, when he speaks of balance, he really means imbalance in favour of his country having more power than its adversary.

6. **Big Power Game:** Balance of power is essentially a big power game. They are not so much interested in peace as in stability of the system. In other words, they are primarily concerned about their own security. It follows that small states do not count much in balance of power system. They are used as mere weights in the scales. They are objects rather than subjects. However, of late, small states seem to be asserting themselves. Some of them refused to be objects of big power game. Their efforts would bear fruit if there is solidarity among them. The South-South linkage would decrease, if not eliminate, the practice of small powers being exploited by big powers in the interest of the latter.

There are mainly two patterns of balance of power, namely the pattern of direct opposition and the pattern of competition. The pattern of direct opposition means that there is direct conflict between two adversaries and either of them is trying to grow more powerful than the other and become able to control the actions of the latter. The latter would also seek to gain more power in order to be able to resist the design of the former to control it and if possible be able to control the former. Thus, balance ensues from their direct opposition to each other. We may cite the examples of the "balance between India and Pakistan, and the same between Iran and Iraq." In the pattern of competition, balance between two adversaries results from their common desire to control a third state. For example, A and B are opponents and A is trying to control the state C. But B fears that if A's plan succeeds, it would be stronger than it and the balance between them would tilt in A's favour. So, B would try to prevent A from controlling C or it would seek to control C itself so that it would grow stronger than A. But, for the same reason, B would not be allowed by A to control C. Thus, neither A nor B, due to their mutual conflict and check, would be able to control C. This indicates that the independence of C would remain unimpaired due to the competition between A and B to control it. Whether they directly oppose each other or seek to contain each other through their competition for a third country, the fact remains that they are adversaries and the motive of each one is to grow stronger than the other so that it would be able to control the policies and actions of the latter.

Balance of power may be divided into two types, namely simple balance and multiple balance. Simple balance involves approximate equality of power between two states or coalition of states. The main adversaries are very powerful when compared to other states who may or may not be the members of the rival camps led by them. Thus, these two are the unchallenged leaders of their respective blocs and power gap between them and their followers is very wide—almost unbridgeable. In other words, simple balance involves bi-polarization The world power structure in the aftermath of the Second World War was characterized by simple balance. The US and the Soviet Union, the only two nuclear powers for first few years after the Second World War, emerged as the superpowers. They led the Western bloc and the Communist bloc respectively. In the multiple balance of power system, the power is dispersed among several countries.[20]

The balance of the system is not controlled by the equation between two dominant powers. The inter-relationship among several power centres helps in maintaining the balance. The Concert of Europe which came into being on the heels of the Congress of Vienna was an ideal example of multiple balance. The major powers were Great Britain, Prussia, Austria, Russia and France and their inter-relations were marked by change and flexibility. Further, the lines of their alignment were not rigidly drawn. So, the response of anyone of them in a given situation was far from predictable. It is argued by a few scholars that the present international system is increasingly tending to be a multiple balance system. Instead of two, there are now five confirmed nuclear powers and there are also many "threshold" powers which are reported to have already manufactured or expected to make soon nuclear weapons. Moreover, there are economic giants like Japan and West Germany whose technologies are very advanced and who have the capacity to go to nuclear. Thus, the world is no longer strictly bipolar. The US and the Soviet Union are, no doubt, pre-eminent powers, but they are not in a position to dictate terms to their allies. On the contrary, they are often seen cajoling and persuading them. This is especially true of the Western camp. France defies the US on several occasions. China is no longer subordinate to the Soviet Union. Thus, in terms of power, the world is changing towards a pluralistic structure.

At the geographical level, the balance of power can be divided into three types. The first is local balance which refers to the approximate equality of power between two local adversaries. We may speak of local balance between Iraq and Iran, India and Pakistan, Ethiopia and Somalia. The second is regional balance. It refers to the balance between two important forces in a region. Such forces may be individual nations or a combination of nations. For example, one may speak of balance in Southeast Asia because both the sides—Vietnam, Kampuchea and Laos on the one side and ASEAN on the other—are more or less equally powerful. If all the Arab nations can combine together and present a countervailing force to Israel, then we can speak of regional balance prevailing in the Middle East. As the things stand now, Israel enjoys a lead over its Arab adversaries in respect of power. Thus, the regional balance in West Asia is at present tilted in favour of Israel. Lastly, we can refer to the central balance. This implies that there is balance at the centre of the world power structure and the two adversaries—the two superpowers in particular, and the two power blocs in general are more or less equally matched and neither side is strong enough to make the other kowtow.

Power may be balanced either by making oneself stronger to counter the apprehended increase in the power of the opponent, or by weakening the opponent. No country, in practice, aims at equality; it tends to achieve some degree of military superiority over its adversary. To achieve this objective, the following devices are normally resorted to.

7. **Armament and Disarmament**: Armament is the most common device of maintaining balance of power. The state which apprehends that the balance is tilted in favour of its opponent would first think of arming itself with more powerful weapons to restore balance. Once it starts procuring such weapons, the opponent may also think that it is losing the game to the former. With the fear that balance is against it, it would also go for arming itself to the teeth with more powerful weapons. Thus, follows a cycle of armament and rearmament, and the main motivation for this is caused by deep-seated mutual suspicion. This would explain why both the superpowers are engaged in constant efforts at arming themselves with increasingly deadly weapons. The same is true of the arms race between India and Pakistan. The moment Pakistan finalized the F-16 deal with the United States, India lost, so to say, not a single minute to try to procure Mirage-2000 from France, Mig-27 from the Soviet Union, and Jaguars from Britain. It is also alleged that both Pakistan and India are making serious efforts to develop nuclear weapons. It is also argued that disarmament may help in maintaining balance of power. The states concerned

may agree on proportionate reduction in their arms so that balance of power among them may be stabilized. That will also enable them to save a lot of money which they can divert towards development. But it is not an easy task. It involves two difficulties. First, the state which feels that it has the preponderance of power may not agree to reduce its arms to such a level where its military superiority would be lost. Secondly, it is not easy to determine one's proportionate portion of military power to be decreased. Power is constituted by many elements including military capability. How will one determine the size of cut in the industrial capability of Japan which would be proportionate to a specified amount of cut in the number of arms of China? The only great success in this regard, however, has been the Washington Naval Treaty of 1922, in which Great Britain, the United States, Japan, France and Italy agreed to a proportionate reduction and limitation of naval armaments.

8. **Domestic Measures:** If a state feels that the balance has been disturbed in favour of the opponent, it would tend to increase its power. Power has many elements. The state concerned would try not only to acquire more powerful weapons, but also to develop related industries and other aspects of science and economy whose cumulative effect would make it stronger and help it in restoring the balance. Domestic measures required for this purpose may also involve introduction of compulsory military training and allotment of more money in the defence budget. It may also include development of indigenous capability to manufacture sophisticated weapons and related defence instrumentalities including ICBMs.

9. **Compensation:** Compensation, as a method of balance of power, may take two forms. First, when a big power occupies a part of a small country, other big powers, fearing that the balance is tilted against them, demand their shares at the cost of that small nation or some other type of compensation. Thus, the big powers gain extra territories at the expense of a small state and divide the latter in such a way that the balance of power among them is not disturbed. In 18th century, this is how Poland was partitioned among Prussia, Austria and Russia. If an aggressor nation is defeated, the victors, while concluding the

Peace Treaty, demand compensation from the vanquished so that it will not be able in future to disturb the stability of the system by launching a new aggression. However, care is taken to ensure that such compensations would be distributed among the victors in such a way that the balance among them is not disturbed. This was done at the Congress of Vienna in 1815, after the defeat of Napoleon.

10. **Alliance and Counteralliance:** A country enters into an alliance with another country generally in its own interest, and an alliance is directed against a third force—a country or a combination of countries. Not necessarily are all the members of the alliance hostile to its targeted nation. For example, the alliance between A and B is directed against the state X. A and X are hostile to each other while B is not the direct enemy of X. But still then B may agree to be a member of the alliance if it gets sufficient reward from A in the form of economic, military/diplomatic help against its enemy, Y. To take a concrete example, Pakistan was a member of SEATO and CENTO whose ostensible targets were the Soviet Union and China. But Pakistan was not their enemy. Still then, it agreed to be a member of these two alliances as it was apparently assured to get sufficient economic aid, and military as well as diplomatic help from the US against India, its main enemy. Thus, different members of the alliance may have different calculations. While the dominant ally may think of using it for maintaining balance or tilting balance in its favour at the central level, a minor ally may hope to use it for maintaining local balance or bending it in its favour. Alliances may be classified into two categories, namely, defensive and offensive. One country, fearing an attack by a stronger foe, would try to forge an alliance with another country to defend itself against such an attack. It is also possible that a country, with a view to ensure its success in its planned offensive against its enemy, would be inclined to enter into an alliance with another country or a group of countries. However, this distinction between defensive and offensive alliances is not easy to establish. In fact, the members of every alliance would describe their alliance as defensive in nature. Palmer and Perkins have rightly observed: "Every alliance is defensive from the point of view of

those states which participate in it, and aggressive from the point of view of those states which are opposed to it." Whether an alliance is defensive or offensive in nature can better be known, not from its declared objectives which mostly would be identical in tone, but from subsequent happenings. If an alliance is used for initiating a war, it is offensive in nature. The Tripple Alliance concluded by Germany, Austro-Hungary and Italy on the eve of the First World War was offensive. It was confirmed by their aggressive and provocative postures which resulted in the outbreak of the First World War.

It is debatable whether alliances and counteralliances are conducive to peace or they breed war. No doubt, they provide check and balance between adversaries. But they are also largely responsible for intensification of mutual suspicion which help in aggravating enmity between nations or groups of nations. The spiral of alliance and counteralliance tends to create an environment which, far from establishing peace and stability, significantly contributes to the negation of peace. Further, it expands the area of military tension instead of shrinking it. The efforts of both the superpowers to rope in allies in different areas in the post-war period greatly enlarged the area polluted by the Cold War. Military alliances are not so much based upon ideology as upon "expediency". Nations are attracted towards each other within an alliance system not mainly by their ideological affinity. Ideology, in international politics, is mostly a rationalize—a cover to hide reality. Nations enter into an alliance if they perceive it beneficial for them. Perceived interests would determine who "will be whose ally at what time". The US embraced Pakistan as a close ally in 1950s even though one was the leading democratic nation while the other was a dictatorship. Some members of NATO concluded in 1949 do not share, till today, the democratic heritage and values. These are characterized by anti-democratic features like feudalism and military rule.

11. **Intervention:** Intervention may be resorted to as an instrument of maintaining balance of power. If a state feels that the loss of another state from its sphere of influence will tilt the balance against it, it would be inclined to intervene in that country for tightening its grip over it. On several occasions, the

US has intervened in Latin American countries in defense of pro-American regimes in those countries. After the fall of Nicaragua to the Communists, the US is now much concerned over the Left insurgency in another Central American Republic, namely El Salvador. If things further deteriorate from the American point of view, there is every possibility of direct and open US intervention in El Salvador in near future.[21] There are now frequent reports to the effect that the US is planning to invade Nicaragua to overthrow the pro-Soviet regime ruling that country. In 1979, the Soviet Union intervened in Afghanistan and placed in power, a pro-Soviet regime when it feared that Kabul was about to slip away from its control. Vietnam recently intervened in Kampuchea and put in power a pro-Vietnam-, a pro-Soviet-, regime with Heng Samrin as the head of the government with a view to maintaining balance between it and the ASEAN in South East Asia. Intervention may lead to war. The Chinese intervention in Vietnam in 1979 to "teach the latter a lesson" led to a limited war between the two. Similarly, the American intervention in Vietnam in 1960s led to a long, protracted war between the US and North Vietnam which came to an end only in 1973.

12. **Divide and Rule**: The policy of "divide and rule" as a means of maintaining balance of power is practiced both at the central level and at the local level. For last many years, the Soviet Union has been trying to sow the seeds of dissension within the NATO and wean away France and a few other Western countries from the American influence. Ironically, the US also is interested in the absence of perfect harmony and unity among its Western allies because of its fear that the latter may be united against it and try to throwaway the "American overlordship" over them. The US is even allegedly encouraging misunderstanding and suspicion among France, Britain and West Germany so that the balance between the US and its West European allies is kept tilted in favour of former. The US is also keen to keep the Soviet Union and China divided, because it is afraid that the unity of two Communist giants would bend the central balance against it. At the local level, the big powers also apply the principle of divide and rule to maintain balance of power.[22] From the

beginning, the United States has been trying to win over Pakistan and use it against India so that the latter does not emerge as the preponderant power in the Indian sub-continent. As India refused to be its ally and as India and the Soviet Union are on good terms, the US fears that the preponderance of power in South Asia in India's favour may contribute to tilting the central balance in favour of the Soviet Union.

13. **Buffer State:** A buffer state is usually a small state sandwiched between two potential adversaries who normally do not interfere in the internal affair of the buffer state. It is a check on the aggressive design of either adversary. Thus, the buffer state helps in maintaining the local balance. For a long time during the 19th and early 20th centuries, Afghanistan was the buffer between Russia and British India. So was Tibet between China and British India. To some extent, Nepal can be described as a buffer between China and India both of which seem to be trying to keep Nepal in good humour. Taking advantage of this, Kathmandu has been trying for last several years to maximize its leverage *vis-à-vis* both India and China.

### Implication of the Term 'Balance of Power'

- Balance of power is a certain kind of arrangement for the working of international relations in a multi-state world.
- Balance of power is a description or a condition in international relations.
- Balance of power indicates three things. These are mainly on:
    - an equality or equilibrium of power among states resulting in balance,
    - a distribution of power in which some states are stronger than others, and
    - any distribution of power among states.
- As a policy, balance of power means that an imbalanced power is dangerous and that in a multi-state system, the only policy which can check the erring behaviour of other states is that of confronting power with counteracting power.

- As a symbol of realism, the balance of power imply the existence of power factor in international politics and indicates the reality of power politics.

**Balance of Power: An Overview**

1. Balance of power has mostly been a big power phenomenon. It is assumed that the equilibrium among great powers would ensure world peace. In the name of peace, the Concert of Europe was used for policing the little Europe. During the first half of 19th century, any national uprising was mercilessly suppressed by them in the name of "peace". Kissinger, in a way, repeated the Concert of Europe logic when he said a few years back that world peace hinged on the equilibrium among the five major centres of powers. In the Kissingerian model of world politics, small countries matter little. They are required to play to the tune of these great powers. Thus, the balance of power theory has an inherent bias for the big powers and contempt for small powers. Further, the cause of nationalism is likely to be crushed under the chariot of balance of power.

2. Nuclear balance between the two superpowers has, of course, helped in maintaining international peace in the post-war period. But such peace has been partial as well as precarious. Both superpowers are afraid of initiating a war against each other. Thus, the balance of terror is a preventive mechanism against the outbreak of war between them. But the nuclear balance may be disturbed any day if one side gains the first strike capability. Further, till that possibility materializes, the two superpowers are in constant tension—far from being in a state of peace. They lack peaceful existence, even though there is peace on the surface. Thirdly, even if we concede that this poor quality of peace is worth having, what about the rest of the world? Nuclear balance does not remove the possibility of the outbreak of local wars among small and middle powers. On the other hand, such wars are fomented by major powers in their vested interests. They would not mind to sacrifice their small allies/supporters so long as they are not directly dragged into the war and so long as that would serve their more important interests. It is logical to argue that the frequency of local wars would increase with the intensification of nuclear stalemate.

3. It is contended that peace in the 19th century was due not so much to balance of power as to the preponderance of power. So long as an aggressive state feared that the opposite side was much more powerful, it did not initiate an attack. But the moment it seemed to feel that both sides were more or less equal in strength, it tended to indulge in aggression. For a long time in the post-Napoleon era, the preponderance of British power helped in preserving peace. It was a restraint on the aggressive design of Russia on the Turkish empire. But when Germany felt confident that it was as much powerful as others, it launched aggression which led to the outbreak of the First World War. The same pattern of behaviour was repeated by Germany after a few years which resulted in the outbreak of the Second World War. Thus, a big war has started whenever there appeared to exist some sort of balance of power. In other words, the disappearance of the preponderance of power posed immediate threat to international peace. Thus, it is erroneous to argue that balance of power is a guarantee for peace. A.F.K. Organski says that periods of balance are periods of warfare and those of preponderance of power are periods of peace. He believes that in a situation of preponderance of power on one side, the weaker party resigns itself to the preponderance. Thus, according to him, "imbalance of power", not "balance of power", is the preserver of peace.

Organski's argument needs some further analysis. Peace that could be maintained in Europe after 1815 was mainly due to two factors. First, Europe lacked a clear line of alignment. There were five great powers—Britain, France, Prussia (later Germany), Austria and Russia. Not any two of them were sure of their alignment. Everyone felt free to join one side or other. It was difficult to know who was the biggest enemy of other. Thus, there was frequent change and modification in the alliance arrangements.[23] Because of this loose alliance mentality everyone of them seemed to fear that if it tried to disturb the system, all others might combine against it. This was the main reason why none of them dared disturb the system for a long time.

These five states which were members of the Concert of Europe were more or less equal in strength. None of them including Britain, the "balancer", was overwhelmingly more powerful than others. It is true that because of its geo-strategic positional advantage and stronger navy, Britain was difficult to be defeated by any other power. But it is doubtful if Britain single-handedly had the capacity to easily defeat anyone else of the other four. Thus, this military equality among the Big Five and the lack of clear alignment were conducive to the preservation of peace between 1815 and 1914. These factors deterred potential aggressors from attacking others.

Thus, it is not enough to say that the preponderance of power is the preserver of peace. In fact, if one side is preponderantly powerful, it will be tempted to be aggressive because it will have less fear of reprisal. It may be inclined to believe that it can escape with some gains. Only when a prospective aggressor fears that others who may combine against it are overwhelmingly more powerful than it, will it not commit any aggression. Thus, aggression tends to become a function of any side strongly believing that it has the preponderance of power whereas peace is the result of no side being confident that it has preponderance of power.

Is balance of power an automatic process? Is it a semi-autocratic process? There is some truth in such assertions. But these do not constitute the whole of the reality. When a particular side becomes very strong, another side which is the possible victim of the former's increased power, would try its best to get stronger so that it does not suffer. The reaction of the second side to the former's changed military status is natural, spontaneous and therefore, automatic. The move to counter the former is a choice deliberately made by the latter. But the choice is apparently rational and this rationality largely contributes to the automatic dimension of the reaction. Because of this mix of automatic reaction and rational choice Inis Claude regards balance of power as semi-automatic. However, it may be emphasized that the policy of balance of power is largely automatic, whereas the actual balance of power is not necessarily so. A state has the tendency to take steps to counter its stronger enemy. But such steps may not yield the desired result; these may not restore the balance between the two states.

As the big powers in the 19th century were not divided into hostile camps with check and balance, it was difficult for small powers to assert themselves. On the other hand, there was apparently some unity among big powers on their common need not to allow any small power to rise higher in the power ladder. Further, as all of them were conservative powers, they had a great stake in the maintenance of the status quo. As a result, nationalism hardly could raise its head during those years. Any new wave of nationalism was immediately suppressed by the Concert of Europe. Things are much different now. Taking advantage of the deep cleavage between the two superpowers, the small and middle powers are now able to make a lot of independent maneuvers in international politics. As the superpowers need them in their global competition, they have some leverage *vis-à-vis* the former which their predecessors in the 19th century hardly enjoyed. During those years any rising nation was the likely object of the common wrath of big powers. Today, a rising nation is almost sure to get the support of one camp even if the other camp may oppose it.

It has been argued that peace would ensue if there is "preponderance of power in the hands of the satisfied". The question is, who is "satisfied" and what is the limit to such satisfaction? At what point would an aggressive/expansionist/ambitious nation be satisfied? Chamberlain, the famous appeasement Prime Minister of Britain, followed this logic when he went on appeasing Hitler with the hope that the latter would be content with some specified concession. But such concessions, instead of satisfying Hitler's expansionist appetite, resulted in whetting it. Thus, the "satisfaction" of a state is not only subjective, but highly uncertain and dangerous. The limitations of the above contention are further exposed when we take into account the behaviours of many states which are widely regarded as peace-loving countries. Britain and France which have reputations as "peace-loving" launched aggression against Egypt in 1956. Similarly, the United States, the "torch-bearer of peace and liberty", was the villian of the piece in the drama of the Bay of Figs crisis of 1961 and has indulged in several aggressive and interventionist activities. Thus, peace is seldom guaranteed if there is preponderance of power in the hands of the so-called peace-loving countries. In either case, whether there is equilibrium, or disequilibrium, peace and security are not safe.

Two of the essential elements of the game of balance of power are that the party concerned is able to accurately measure its power and the power of the potential enemy, and divine the latter's intention. Measuring one's power is not an easy task. Power has got several components and one has to weigh the importance of each individual component and the result of their interaction. It may be possible with some degree of accuracy, to assess the strength of objective elements of power. But it is extremely difficult to exactly assess the objective elements of power like leadership, will power and operational capability.[24] Morgenthau says: "The uncertainty of power calculation is inherent in the nature of national power itself. It will therefore come into play even in the most simple pattern of the balance of power; that is, when one nation opposes another. This uncertainty is, however, immeasurably magnified when the weights in one or the other or in both scales are composed not of single units but of alliances. Then it becomes necessary to compute not only one's own and the opponent's national power and correlate one with the other, but also to perform the same operation on the national power of one's allies and those of the opponent." Moreover, assuming that a state is able to know that its potential enemy has become more powerful, how will it be sure that the latter would attack it? One's fear about a possible threat to its vital interests may not come true. Such threat may not be in existence at all. Thus, one's estimate of one's power *vis-à-vis* the power of the opponent, and divination of the intentions of others may often go wrong. This logic exposes some limitations of the theory of balance of power. The uncertainty of all power calculations, in addition to making balance of power impractical, may also lead to its very negation in practice. As no state can be quite certain of the power equation between it and its opponent, it would tend to increase its approximate margin of safety so that the opponent cannot dare initiate an attack. Once it feels that such a margin has been maintained, it would be inclined to turn this safety margin into a permanent feature. For that, it would seek to maximize its safety margin by being too strong for the opponent. This plan may warrant a preventive attack by the state to permanently cripple the opponent. Balance of power may also lead to both anti-imperialistic war and imperialistic war. Such wars would arise out of the opposition between imperialistic powers and status quo powers. The former would go on increasing their strength and the latter would fad to keep peace with the increase in the military capability of the former. A time would come when the status quo powers would feel that the order to redress the balance war is the only course left. This was the position in which Britain and France found themselves *vis-à-vis* Germany in September 1939. But the restoration of balance does not ensure permanent stability. On the other hand, it carries within it seeds of disturbance. The status quo power of yesterday becomes an imperialistic power today which is opposed by the one which was itself imperialistic yesterday. Such imperialistic wars frequently occurred in Europe in 18th and 19th centuries.[25]

Balance of power is often resorted to for defensive as well as for offensive purposes. Whenever a country takes military action against another country, it generally tries to justify its action in the name of balance of power. Thus, balance of power has often been used as an euphemism for aggression. The US sent its soldiers to North Korea beyond 38th Parallel on the Plea of restoring balance there threatened by Communist powers. The Soviet Union sent its troops to Afghanistan in 1979 as a "countervailing measure" against the growing military tension in the area created by the US and Chad which endangered the local balance. Thus, the balance of power, virtually turned into an ideology, tends to "disguise, rationalize, and justify international politics".

### Contemporary Balance of Power

The post-war period is much different from the earlier periods. It is the nuclear dimension which makes it qualitatively different from any other period in history. This is the first time that there are only two great powers—rather superpowers—which are more or less equally strong, but much more powerful than others including France, Britain and China which are also clubbed as great powers. However, they fade away when compared with the superpowers. Thus, the world is essentially bipolar, with the two superpowers leading the rival power blocs and many other countries are members of one bloc or the other. This development militates against the balance of power system which, for its success, requires the presence of several big powers which should share power and prevent its concentration in the hands of a few. But the concentration of power, not its dispersion, is the reality today. In the central power structure, there are only two power-holders and this significant new reality tends to create obstacles for the successful operation of the balance of power system. In the wake of the Second World War, the colonies of Asia and Africa, one after another, were liberated from the European rule. With few exceptions, colonialism is almost extinct today. The spurt of nationalism in these continents resulted in the sudden decline of colonialism. This created a serious problem for the operation of balance of power. In the past, one easy way of acquiring power on the part of main players—obviously belonging to Europe—was to gain some territories in Asia, Africa and Latin America. The absence of that option takes away one of the main pillars of the structure of the balance of power.

There is not a single balancer today in the sense in which Britain was for a long time till the 19th century. Britain is no longer the most powerful naval power. Nor does it enjoy, in the nuclear age, the geographical immunity it used to do due to its physical separation from the main continent of Europe by the English Channel. Further, Britain is not necessarily the best player in the game of diplomacy today. In this game, it may face serious challenge even from new nations of Africa. Thus, Britain has ceased to be the "balancer". Nuclear balance which is described as the new balancer may prevent a nuclear war—even a direct conventional war—between the two superpowers for a long time to come. But there is a great deal of difference between the old balancer and the new balancer. Britain's moves were not predictable. This provided a lot of space for maneuverability by great powers and injected a great deal of dynamism into the balance of power system. The moves of the two superpowers on the chess board of international politics are, to a great extent, predictable. They tend to play zero-sum games and each of them counters the other because in the international relations conflict virtually eclipses competition better not to speak of cooperation.

Another factor which contributes to the decline of balance of power is the difficulty in calculating the power potential of states concerned with the improvement in military technology, this difficulty has greatly intensified. Further, the dynamics of coalitions—formal or informal—add to the difficulty in measuring the powers of adversaries. Miscalculation in this field would lead to no action, or over-reaction, both of which may prove dangerous to the balance of power system.

The operation of the balance of power is smooth so long as it does not face any challenge from any "revolutionary" power which aims at radically altering the system—even destroying it, if necessary. At present, there are several "revolutionary" states of different brands. The Western countries construe the Communists as bent upon destroying them. So also do the latter feel about the former. However, in reality, there are several countries which pay little respect to peaceful co-existence and would like to eliminate some countries which do not fit into their models. By and large, China is one such country. It is highly ideologically oriented and inclined to take resort to military steps against its opponents. Another "revolutionary" power of a different type is Libya which, in the name of Islam, helps in fomenting political instability and rebellion in other countries which are not sufficiently "Islamized" in its eyes. The plurality of such "revolutionary powers" which repose much faith in military solutions to please their "one-track minds" tends to militate against the balance of power system. What to speak of small and middle powers having "revolutionary" goals, it is doubtful if the big two have developed sufficient stake in the status quo. On the other hand, it may be plausible to argue that at the first opportunity each one would love to deal a deadly blow to the other. Thus, Zbigniew Brzezinski who thinks that the balance of power is an "illusion" says that the big three—the two superpowers and China—"do not share even an approximate commitment to the status quo".

The above discussion suggests that the balance of power system is faced with some big hindrances which are likely to incapacitate it. On the other hand, it is difficult to ignore the long spell of peace at the centre, primarily caused by deterrence. Because of the prospect of nuclear holocaust, neither superpowers would dare initiate a nuclear attack against the other in near future. Even a direct confrontation between them with conventional weapons which might lead to nuclear war is also very unlikely. There is a strong compulsion on them to make their ends as well as means localized. They seem to be very particular about avoiding any direct confrontation. No doubt, local balance is often endangered and disturbed due to direct/indirect involvement of the superpowers. But they take every care to ensure that such disturbance in the peripheral balance does not lead to the disturbance in the central balance. While the nuclear demon sufficiently frightens the big two not to start a mad-nuclear-war, it hardly inhibits them to pinprick local balances. Thus, the coming years will be, in general, characterized by the preservation of central balance and periodic disturbances in local balances.

**Critical Estimate of Balance of Power**

Balance of power is an idea which in a historical sense refers to a distribution of power between states so that no single state or alliance has an overwhelming or preponderant amount of power. There has been much historical debate as to what the term means in practice. We need to begin by considering power as the capacity of an individual or an organization to achieve its objectives. It may take many forms: political, economic and military. In a basic historical definition, the balance of power is linked to the nation-state. A problem is that the balance of power can often actually just mean the distribution of power at a given time. For example, as enshrined in the Treaty of Vienna in 1815 this is slightly different to there actually being a genuine balance. But what it does indicate is that the balance of power is a shifting phenomenon. This is quite clear post-Cold War with the USA left as the only world superpower whilst other powers such as the EU and the United Nations attempt to create a more stable international system.[26]

Balance of power is defined as a state of dynamic equilibrium characterizing relations among nations. The balance of power is defined as the maintenance of such a just equilibrium in power between the members of the family of nations as should prevent any of them becoming sufficiently strong to enforce its will upon the others. Thus, it assumes that through shifting alliances and countervailing pressures, no one power or combination of powers will be allowed to grow so strong as to threaten the security of the rest. It rests on the basic assumption that excessive power anywhere in the system is a threat to the existence of other units and that the most effective antidote to power is power.

There have been many ways outlined to classify the balance of power. Dougherty and Pfaltzgraff (1990) see four key tenets:

- Nation-states are the key actors in an international system composed of independent sovereign states
- Domestic and foreign policies are clearly separated areas of national policy
- International politics is a struggle for power in an anarchic international environment
- States have different capabilities to achieve goals and defend interests.

What one can see from this is the significance of the idea of a balance of power for international politics. Further, one can also see the possible problems that can occur when an attempt is made to challenge that balance,[27] for example World War I or World War II. One also needs to bear in mind the problems that can be caused by an artificial balance of power such as that prior to World War II. A balance does not mean no change at all, rather it reflects an ordered change which is consented to by the major and lesser powers at a particular time. But in reality, it often means lesser powers accepting the decisions made by greater powers, for example, the Munich Agreement which saw Adolf Hitler and Germany being given Czechoslovakia. It is often just a means of expressing power politics. To understand the balance of power, there is a need to distinguish the balance as pattern from the balance as process. A state that follows the pattern of the balance of power makes an organizational choice, entering alignments to counter the power of other rival groups.[28] But states that pursue a strictly unilateralist pattern, refusing all alignments, may yet play a crucial role in the development of a particular balance of power. Britain, whose "splendid isolation" from almost all alignments for nearly a hundred years after Waterloo ended with the Anglo-Japanese Alliance, played a great part in the continental balance of power during the whole period. Her role has been described as 'balancer' of the balance —a part she has often played since the time of Henry VIII: To the extent that she was uncommitted to either bloc, she was able to shift her weight as need arose to the weaker side to balance the stronger. She was of the balance but not in it—as is the case with every unilateralist state. Furthermore, states pursuing a pattern of collective security necessarily affect by their choice, the functioning of the balance.

When we say that between even two states roughly equal in power, there will be a certain balance and counterbalance, although rigid, we are discussing the balance of power as a process. We are referring to their rival power relationship rather than to an alliance which links them together on the same side. With three or more states the process is natural and inevitable, the possibilities become more varied, and the power structure more flexible. There is more opportunity for shifting and regrouping; there is greater room for adjustments in the strength of rival blocs. This very flexibility may save the balance for long periods of time from disintegrating into area. Even when war comes, the balancing process is not an end, but unless the end of the war leaves the pre-war basic power of the opposing blocs unchanged—a relatively rare although not unknown possibility—a new balance emerges from the ashes of the war. The changed power status as a result of the decisions of the battlefield and the victory or defeat that has come to each belligerent makes for a new post-war balance. Thus, we customarily reckon the duration of a balance from war to war.

Since the balance periodically disintegrates into war, the charge has often been made that the pursuit of the balance causes war. It would be more accurate to say that the inept handling of a balance pattern may bring war bought. But this is true of the use of other patterns as well. It is obvious at even the most causal glance that the duration of general balance of power varies widely in modern times. When we come to our studies of the balance of power in action, we shall be especially concerned to note the conditions under which the peace disintegrates and a new balance is brought in the flame of war. We shall also be concerned to establish, if possible, why the length of particular balances has varied so from the maximum of one hundred years without a general war (between 1815 and 1914) to a minimum of twenty years (between 1919 and 1939). If any given general balance is doomed to ultimate disintegration in the crucible of war, it does not follow that its end could not by deliberate measures be postponed almost indefinitely.

The process of the balance of power is natural and inevitable in any multi-state system. Simply by existing and by possessing power, each nation plays a part in it. Even so, the states that follow a pattern of balance-of-power alignments, by entering into alliances and understandings with other states, form the magnetic poles around which the power relations of unilateralist states revolve in varying degrees of attraction and repulsion. The alignments of these states form the hard core of the balance of power, and it is to this hard core that we must now turn our attention.

## NOTES

1. Inis L. Claude, Jr., *Power and International Relations* (New York, 1962), p. 11.
2. Hans J. Morgenthau, *Politics Among Nations: The Struggle for Power and Peace* (New Delhi, 1985), p. 187.
3. Cited in Lenox A. Mills and Charles, H. McLaughlin, *World Politics in Transition* (New York, 1956), pp. 107-08.
4. Palmer and Perkins, n. 3, pp. 212-15.
5. Hans Morgenthau, *Politics Among Nations: The Struggle for Power and Peace* (New York, 1973), p. 9.
6. George Schwarzenberger, *Power Politics* (London, 1954), pp. 3-22.
7. James N. Rosenau, ed., *International Politics and Foreign Policy* (New York: Free Press, 1969), 2nd edn. rev.
8. Ole Holsti, "The Belief System and National Images: A Case Study" in *ibid.*, pp. 543-50.

9. Marie Jean Antoine Caritat Condorcet, Marquisde, tr., Jane Barraclough, *Sketch for a Historical Picture of the Progress of the Human Mind* (London, 1955).
10. Stanley Hoffmann, "Theory and International Relations" in *International Politics and Foreign Policy,* 2nd ed. rev., James, N. Rosenau (New York, 1969), p. 30.
11. Karl W. Deutsch et. al., *Political Community and the North Atlantic Area* (Princeton, N.J.: Princeton University Press, 1957).
12. Ole Holsti, "The Belief System and National Images: A Case Study" in Janes Rosenau, *op. cit.*, pp. 543-50.
13. Inis L. Claude, Jr., *Power and International Relations* (New York, 1962), p. 11.
14. David S. McLellan et al., ed., *The Theory and Practice of International Relations* (Prentice-Hall of India, New Delhi, 1977), p. 100.
15. Palmer and Perkins, n. 3, pp. 212-15.
16. Karl W. Deutsch and J. David Singer, "Multipolar Power Systems and International Stability", *World Politics* (Princeton, N.J.), Vol. 16, April 1964, p. 403.
17. Zbigniew Brzezinski, "The Balance of Power Delusion" in David S. McLellan et al., ed., *The Theory and Practice of International Relations* (Prentice-Hall of India, New Delhi, 1977), p. 100.
18. Morton, A. Kaplan, ed., *New Approaches to International Relations* (New York: St. Martin's, 1968), p. 90.
19. Ray S. Cline, *World Power Assessment: A Calculus of Strategic Drift* (Colorado, 1975), p. 8.
20. Hans J. Morgenthau, *Politics Among Nations: The Struggle for Power and Peace* (New Delhi, 1985), p. 187.
21. Vernon Van Dyke, *International Politics* (Bombay, 1966), p. 221.
22. *Ibid.*
23. A.F.K. Organski, *World Politics* (New York, 1958), pp. 292, 297, 316-38.
24. Morgenthau, *Politics Among Nations, op. cit.*, p. 201.
25. Theodore A. Couloumbis and James, H. Wolfe, *Introduction to International Relations: Power and Justice* (New Delhi, 1986) 3rd edn., p. 25.
26. *Ibid.*
27. Ole Holsti, "The Belief System and National Images: A Case Study" in *ibid.*, pp. 543-50.
28. Rudolph, J. Rummel, "Libertarianism and International Violence", *Journal of Conflict Resolution,* 27, I, March 1983, pp. 27-71.

# National Interest

5

National interest is one of the most fundamental and vital concepts on international relations. National interest is a collective state of mind or consciousness of the people that make them believe that their primary duty and loyalty is to the nation-state.[1] National interest is the starting point in foreign policy making. The task of a foreign policy is to defend national interests peacefully, restrictively and rationally. All nations formulate their foreign policy on the basis of their national interests, determined by the needs and circumstances in which a state is placed. It means that every nation should protect its sovereignty and territorial integrity. Protection refers to preservation of physical, political and cultural identity against encroachment. Welfare of the nation also needs to be placed as an important interest of the nation in policy formulations. Hughes, American Secretary of State admitted in the 1920's that "Foreign Policies are not abstractions but the results of practical concepts of national interest". National leaders as a rule never pursue national policies that are in the interests of any nation other than their own. In short, national interest is the predominant factor in the formulation of a country's foreign policy. On the other hand, Prof. Reynolds argues that the foreign policy of a state can be based on national interest only if the interests of the various nations are homogeneous. It shall be a costly proposition to pursue a policy based on national interests, when the interests of the various nations are of a heterogeneous character. As each state shall try to resist the implementation of the alien values, this is inevitably likely to lead to a war. Prof. Reynolds further argues that in essence national interest "should relate to the real interests of the people, and this interest is not to be seen as being necessarily contained within the state context". Whatever the opinions and views, national interest is a part of international reality. At times, national interests are subject to drastic change due to change in a nation's value, internal power shifts, important personalities or economic groups. Quite often, national leaders use foreign policy to strengthen their internal position.[2] For example, Sukarno of Indonesia diverted the attention of the people from the acute economic and, social problems adopting the policy of confrontation towards Malaysia. Likewise, Pakistan has consistently raised the bogey of danger from India to divert the attention of people from internal problems. National interest is the key concept of foreign policy. Decision-makers in foreign policy should keep in mind their country's national interest while giving due weight to interests of other state.

## LIMITATION ON NATIONAL INTEREST

According to Morgenthau, national interest must be determined in the light of possible usurpation by sub-national, other national and supernational interests, which are indeed serious constraints on the national interest. At the sub-national level, we find group interests which identify interests like ethnic and economic as national interests. Similarly, the other national interests can usurp the national interest of a state in two ways, viz. through treason and criminology. Here, an individual may supply certain information to foreign governments for money. Again, the national interests of a country may be usurped by the supernational interest in two ways—through religious bodies and international organizations. While religious bodies ceased to be effective, international organizations certainly operate against the national interests of the states by compelling them to pursue only such policies which do not operate against the interests of member-states. As a unit of the international community, the state is bound by certain regulations—conventional, customary, ethical, legal or institutional and the framers of the foreign policy have to operate within these limitations. Prof. Morgenthau has asserted the need of compromising the national interests with the interests of other nations. In a multi-national world this requirement of political morality and in an age of total war it is also one of the conditions for survival. Thus, while formulating goals of national interest, the policymakers should make honest attempts to make these compatible with international interest of peace, security and prosperity.[3]

The concept of 'national interest' is an ever present feature of contemporary diplomatic discourse and has been widely analyzed by political scientists in international relations. The national interest is a key explanatory tool in the analysis and understanding of contemporary foreign policy. Scott Burchill argues that beyond the narrow aspect of security policy, the national interest has little residual value as an insight into the motivations of state policy in the external realm.

According to Naom Chomsky, "The topic of 'National Interest' has been central to the study of international affairs for a long time, and is of great current concern, as part of ongoing discussion and controversy concerning the role of the state in the evolving international political-economic order. To my knowledge, this is the first comprehensive study of the topic within the various frameworks of international relations theory that have become a very productive area of research in the post-World War II period. Burchill provides a lucid critical account of leading ideas of the major perspectives that have been developed, tracing their origins back to the enlightenment and beyond. He carefully analyzes the place of the concept of national interest within these perspectives, arriving at conclusions that are well-argued and thought-provoking. It is a very valuable study, with many implications for policy and interpretation."

National interest is central to any attempt at describing, explaining, predicting, prescribing and understanding international behaviour. Brooking's Institute defined national interest "as the general and continuing ends for which a nation acts". Lerche and Said define it as "the general, long-term and continuing purpose which the state, the nation and the government all see themselves as serving". Dyke defines it as "that which states seek to protect or achieve in relation to each other". According to Frankel, national interest "amounts to the sum total of all the national values".

Hegemony has many faces. In the early 1990s, Washington set itself three objectives: to maintain the global balance resulting from the end of the Cold War, to ensure its technological lead and military supremacy, and to create an economic environment favourable to its own interests. For the most part, these objectives have been achieved. Admittedly, international balances are not static and hegemony does not mean absolute freedom of action. But no country or group of countries appears able to constitute a political counterweight to the US in the foreseeable future, let alone call into question its primacy in the hierarchy of nations. As political pundit Thomas Friedman puts it: "In the globalization system, the United States is now the sole and dominant superpower and all other nations are subordinate to it to one degree or another. In other words, they ought to accept America's 'benevolent global hegemony'."

Every nation has a foreign policy to ensure that its needs are represented in the global community. However, in the past, especially during the Cold War, and throughout history, power has used in the international scene to push forward national interests and agendas, sometimes without any regard to the nations and people they may directly or indirectly affect. This has sometimes resulted in a rise in resentment against some of these nations who are then seen as bullies, getting away with many acts of hypocrisy. In the increasingly smaller global community, "national interests" do not necessarily mean that they are good for the international community. It is sometimes difficult to decide when national interests and international concerns should be addressed in a balanced way.

The United Nations, an international body to tackle various global concerns, as an example, has been constantly abused by those who have the power to act unilaterally when the international community's views and opinions do not agree with their own national interests. The foreign policy of some Western states have been harshly criticized by many who claim that the objective is to simply ensure that they remain as the power and authority in the world and to ensure that the "new world order" goes along the lines of Western ideals, with little consideration for other cultures.

Morgenthau analyses the concept as "the political tradition and the total culture context within which a nation formulates its foreign policy". Rostow explains that national interest is the concept which nations apply in trying to influence the world environment to their advantage. Thus, national interest determines the nature of the long as well as short-term efforts in foreign policy. It is, therefore, a generalized value synthesis to the overall international situation in which the state has to act, pursue and execute its foreign policy. In Morgenthau's opinion, the minimum requirement of nation-states is to protect their physical, political and cultural identity against encroachments by other nation-states.[4]

Basically, the determinants of national interest can be classified into two major categories: (1) Domestic, (2) External. The domestic variable mainly include the personality, ideals and role of decision-makers, the political lobby and groups of the country, the kind of government structure and political process, customs and perceptions of societies, ideology of state, pressure groups and interest groups within the state. The external factors that play a role in the formulation of national interest consist of the nation's geo-strategic environment, its place in the world community in context of capability, the relations with the neighbouring states, role of great powers, international organizations and the general nature of international society prevailing at the time. Coloumbis and Wolfe have given the following criteria of determining national interest—operational-philosophy criteria, ideological, moral and legal, pragmatic, professional-advancement, partisan, bureaucratic-interest, ethnic and racial, class-status and foreign-dependency criteria. Thus, national interest decisions seem to be the outcome of opposing wills, ambitions, motivations, needs, demands and factors.

Taken together, the vital and secondary interests of states are important in international relations, because they form the raw material out of which foreign policy is made. An ideal foreign policy contains a systematic formulation of national interests in which inconsistent interests have been weeded out. The interests have been judged against one another in terms of priorities, and the interests as a whole have been budgeted against the power of the state of achieve those interests. Once this process of modeling national interests into an overall foreign policy is consummated, the state is most probably ready, in its dealings with other states, to pursue a logical and consistent policy. There is no magic formula which ensures the interests and therefore the foreign policies of states will prove compatible. Assuming the continued existence of sovereign states, the hope of preventing war must lie either in a willingness of states of formulate mutually compatible foreign policies or in the ability of nations to adjust conflicting policies peacefully, once conflicts are found to exist.

## TYPES OF NATIONAL INTEREST

National interests envelop categories of desires on the part of sovereign states that vary enormously from state to state and from time to time. There is an irreducible core for any state at any time. This core consists of the 'vital' interests—those for which a state is normally willing to go to war immediately or ultimately. Such vital interests include for all states, as a minimum, the protection and preservation of their existing territory. In the very broadest sense, the term international relations embraces all intercourse among states and all movements of people, goods, and ideas across national frontiers. As a field of study, its focus is on the process by which states adjust their national interests to those of other states. In turn, national interests may be defined in terms of what states seek to protect or achieve *vis-à-vis* other states. Thomas D. Robinson (1961) has divided national interest into six categories. These are only based on following parameters.

**Permanent Interest:** Permanent interest includes a state's long-term and stable interests which rarely changes. If there is a change, it is rather stready. For example, India's desire to peacefully develop as an economically self-reliant and powerful nation over a period of time.

**Variable Interest:** In this sense, the variable interest can diverge from both primary and permanent interests. These changeable interests are mainly determined by the factors like personalities, public opinion, sectional interests, partisan politics, political and moral folkways.

**General Interests:** They comprise positive conditions which apply to a large number of states in such areas as trade, economics, diplomatic intercourse, etc.

**Specific Interest:** It is the commonsensical outgrowth of the general well-being but defined in terms of time and breathing space. For example, Britain regarded it as a definite national interest to maintain the independence of the new countries for preserving balance of power in Europe.

**Primary Interests:** Primary interests are also known as central part interests of a nation. These interests relate to security and survival and the state must constantly defend them at all costs. These interests cannot be compromised. These include the preservation of physical, political and cultural identity of state.

**Secondary Interests:** Secondary interests are fundamental to the continuation of a state but are not so decisive as the primary ones. These include protection of citizens abroad and ensuring diplomatic protection to the diplomatic staff.

**Matching Interests:** These refer to interests which are held in common by a number of states. For example, the United States, Great Britain and other Western European countries did not want the expansion of Soviet Power and its ideology in their region during the Cold War era. Third World countries have a common interest in asking for New International Economic order. The area of commonness is always subject to change.

**Complementary Interests:** They are not indistinguishable but form some kind of a basis for agreement and compromise on some specific issues, e.g. the United States and Pakistan served complementary interests of each other at the time of Soviet intervention in Afghanistan.

**Disagreeing Interests:** The chief responsibility of every state is to promote its national interest, and to acquire power for this purpose. The world has changed profound ways since the end of Cold War. No country can long afford to pursue its own welfare in ways that reduce the security and welfare of its competitors. A new, broader definition of national interest is needed which put human interests and global security ahead of national interests and national security. Such interests fall in the category of opposed interest.

## INSTRUMENTS FOR PROMOTION OF NATIONAL INTEREST

National interest forms the foundation on which foreign policy of a country is formulated. Today, after the end of the Cold War there is a exemplar shift from military to economic in terms of power. The totaling of the economic orientation to the concept of essential national interest assumes more importance in the context of the trends towards globalization and the new world order. A nation's foreign policy functions for the fulfillment of its national interests.

There are number of factors for the promotion of national interest. These are discussed below:

### 1. Psychosomatic and Political Warfare

Psychological warfare is associated with the "struggle for the minds of men". Political warfare includes such resources directly operating against a state, e.g. embargoes, deferment of treaties, disjointing of diplomatic relations. These measures are off-putting in character and non-violent and do produce any international crisis.

### 2. Imperialism and Colonialism

From 16th century to the middle of the 20th century, European nations used imperialism and colonialism as a tool to further their national interest. World War II did see a collapse of imperialist powers along with decolonization, colonialism. It seeks its entry in the garb of neo-colonialism or economic colonialism in many parts of the world.

### 3. Coercive Methods

Hostilities is the ultimate method used by a state in pursuance of its national interest. The measures operating directly upon the state to be coerced, actually engross the use of physical force or actual put on show of force. These methods can take the shape of assault, military maneuver and military profession to weaken the enemy state. However, war is mostly used as a last resort when all other means and methods prove ineffective.

**4. Diplomacy**

Diplomacy negotiations are used to reconcile the conflicting interests of states through the mutual process of give and take. It can be two-pronged as well as polygonal in nature. Diplomatic set of connections function through a network of foreign embassies, consulates, missions all over the world. The diplomat is the eyes and ears of his government abroad. He has to look after the interests of his country as interpreted by the policy-makers back home. Diplomatic negotiations prove fruitful only if the interests of the concerned states are harmonizing or similar in temperament.[5] In case of disagreeing interests, e.g. India and Pakistan diplomatic negotiations are not successful.

**5. Alliances**

Alliances are concluded by two or more states for the fortification and encouragement of common interests. The conclusion of an alliance imposes a legal obligation on states to honour its clauses. The character and tenure of the alliance will depend on the nature of interests sought to be protected. Alliance is mostly used for securing identical and complementary interests. Accordingly, the alliances are either military or economic in nature. The need for securing the security of capitalist democratic states against the expanding 'Communist Menace' led to the creation of military alliance like NATO, SEATO, CENTO, ANZUS, etc.

**6. Misinformation**

In international relations, half truth is used to "persuade either household groups or overseas states to accept policies favourable or at least not unfavourable to their own". Twentieth century misinformation (propaganda) is a major instrument for the promotion of national interest. Permanent agencies are set up for its efficient functioning. Importance of propaganda as a method has greatly increased in recent years due to the revolutions in the means of communication. In the post-Second World War period, propaganda became a major component of the Cold War between the Soviet Union and the United States. In case of India and Pakistan too, propaganda is used to further their own national interest.

### 7. Economic Methods

Quota system, embargo, blockade, international cartels dumping, exchanging control, economic sanctions, loans and grants are some of the means regularly employed by the states for such purposes. Developed states provide economic aids and loans to the developing countries to promote their national interest.

## RESTRAINT ON NATIONAL INTEREST

At the sub-nationwide level we locate group interests which make out interests like ethnic and economic as national interests. Similarly, the other national interests can usurp the national interest of a state in two ways, viz. through treason and criminology. Herein, individual may supply certain information to foreign governments for money. Again, the national interests of a country may be usurped by the supernational interests in two ways—through religious bodies and international organizations. While religious bodies ceased to be effective, international organizations certainly operate against the national interests of the states by compelling them to pursue only such policies which do not operate against the interest of other member-states.

According to Morgenthau, national interest must be determined in the light of possible usurpation by sub-national, other national and supernational interests, which are indeed serious constraints on the national interest. As certain regulations —conventional, customary, ethical, legal or institutional and the farmers of the foreign policy bind a unit of the international community, the state have to operate within these limitations. Prof. Morgenthau has also asserted the need of compromising the national interests with the interests of other nations. In a multi-national world, this is a requirement of political morality and in an age of total war, it is also one of the conditions for survival. Thus, while formulating goals of national interests, the policymakers should make honest attempts to make like-minded with international interests of peace, safekeeping and affluence.

It may be said that national interest is the key concept of foreign policy. Decision-makers in foreign policy should keep in mind their country's national interest while giving due weight to interests of other state.

## NATIONAL INTEREST AND NATIONAL SECURITY

The end of the Cold War, the mitigation of rivalries between the two superpowers and the disappearance of bloc politics heralded a seminal change in the nature of threats to national security. All over the world these days, security is no longer restricted to safeguarding a country's territorial integrity and sovereignty as it is used to be done some time ago. Today, the chances of a country invading another country and seizing its inhabited territory and subjugating its population are very low. Security threats are defined more in terms of international terrorism, ethno-nationalism, proxy wars, societal turbulences, technological dominance through various technological denial regimes, imposition of unequal treaties by dominant powers, narco-terrorism, narcotic traffics, organized crime and associated money laundering, etc.

National security needs to be defined in a holistic way to include, besides military security, economic and technological security, social stability and foreign policy. All over the world, economic component of security dominates thinking. Effective management of national security involves a forward looking long range assessments of threats that are likely to arise and action plans to forestall the threats. There are four areas that would command its attention. First, how to ensure the security of the country from threats of proxy war, terrorism and associated narco traffic. The second most important area in national security that needs to be focused on is the country's economic growth.

Conventional wisdom is to look at security and development as two mutually exclusive issues. This is a totally outdated concept. Without security, development cannot be progressed. Security by itself will be meaningless unless there is development which needs to be secured. Mutual economic dependence is the best way of reducing tensions and promote regional cohesion as is seen in the experience of the European Union. The third area of concern for national security should be good governance without which internal security is likely to suffer adversely. It is accepted that there is a politician-bureaucracy organized crime nexus which poses a serious threat to national security. Misgovernance of a country creates alienation among population, weakens the resistance of the country to external subversion and terrorism. Formulating a long-term strategy of ridding the politics of corruption and criminality and restoring good governance is absolutely essential if the country is to be rid of insurgencies, caste wars, communal tensions and accelerate economic growth. This should be a major national security priority. Fourthly, the 21st century belongs to nations which are going to fashion themselves as knowledge-based societies. Production and services are going to be increasingly knowledge-based. Therefore, the most vital aspect of a nation will be the knowledge and skill of its population. Therefore, national security should be interpreted not only in the external military security aspect, but also needs to be viewed in terms of internal security, economic security, technological strength and foreign policy.

The inadequacy of a military approach to national security has become evident in the post-Cold War world and international security regime. They include such non-traditional and non-military threats to national security as environmental degradation, resource depletion caused by overexploitation of minerals and water, unplanned urbanization, global warming, creation of environmental refugees and attendant security problems arising from their forced migration. Again concepts like human security and humane governance gain a new perspective in this milieu. Poverty and deprivation have enlarged the problem of human security in the developing world. Unfortunately, the security discourse in the developing world is dominated by military threats, and have no difficulty pre-empting scarce resources for military rather than human security. The concept of humane governance has also gained a new salience. Humane governance has three interlocking dimensions—good political governance, good economic governance and good civic governance. Good political governance requires decentralization of power to the people; accountability and transparency in public affairs; elimination of discrimination against women and minorities; maintenance of peace and social cohesion and access to prompt and affordable justice within the state. It defines good economic governance as a middle path between market-driven laissez faire and command/control economies. Thus, the inadequacy of a military approach to national security has become evident the world over. When European Union countries talk of their security, their concern is about societal stability in their peripheral areas and the impact of such turbulence on their countries. A strong, self-confident and economically and politically well-integrated country can afford to be more generous to its neighbours than a weak, vacillating and divisive country. Hence, national security needs to be defined in a holistic manner to include besides military security, economic and technological security and social stability.

National security is a country's capacity to resist external or internal threats to its physical survival or care values. A nation is secure to the extent to which it is not in danger of having to sacrifice core values—national independence and territorial integrity. National security usually means the maintenance of strong military defenses against enemy invasion and attack. National security should be viewed in terms of "environmental security" and "human security". The economic and ecological dimensions of national security have assumed relatively greater prominence. Though the danger of nuclear weapons and inter-and intra-state warfare continues, it would be foolish to neglect the dangers posed by such emergent threats as trade-bloc competition, neo-mercantilism, trade protectionism, the continuing impoverishment of the least developed countries, acid rain, deforestation, global warming, soaring population growth, the AIDS epidemic, international narcotic trafficking, the depletion of the earth's finite resources, and destruction of its protective ozone layer. These non-military threats must command attention, as human survival may depend on addressing them.

## COLLECTIVE SECURITY

The concept of collective security is regarded as an approach to peace. In the interdependent world of today, the security of one nation is no longer the exclusive concern of that nation but is the concern of the international community as a whole. The nations unite under the collective security system and take care collectively of the security of each of them as though their own security were at stake. Morgenthau puts the principle of "one for all and all for one". If A attacks B, then C, D, E, F, G, H states collectively take action on behalf of B against A. The collective security aims to defend the interests of peace-loving states by concentrating a preponderance of power against the aggressor. In essence, collective security is an arrangement among states in which all promise, in the event of any member of the system engages in certain prohibited acts against another member, to come to the latter's assistance. An attack on any state will be regarded as an attack on all states. The combined power of the collectivity will be greater enough to overwhelm the aggressor. The collective security is "a mutual insurance contract among the states". The theory of collective security accepts the two basic limitations that (i) war is a reality (ii) power is an effective means to reduce the incidence of war. Collective enforcement assumes a status quo, and must defend the territorial status quo existing at the time the system is brought into being. The system of collective security is highly laudable if certain conditions are provided for its proper working.

- The system should be an open system against any aggressor and not a specific opponent and should be capable of mustering overwhelming strength against the potential or actual aggressor so that it may not be able to pose a challenge to the order.
- The members of the international community must display a sense of confidence towards each other and should have a positive attitude towards fulfillment of its obligations. A war anywhere, by anyone and against anyone is a war against everyone and everywhere and states need to respond in such a situation. The states should be willing to subordinate their conflicting political interests to the common good defined in terms of collective security.

- Membership should be universal in a collective security arrangement and power need be distributed among states in a manner so that none may possibly become a menace to others and the combined powers of the arrangement may act as a deterrent against potential aggressor. The successful operation of collective security depends on common conception of security. President Wilson of USA is regarded as the enunciator of the concept of collective security in international politics. Whenever these conditions have been met in the light of actual working, the arrangement can be examined in the light of its functioning under the League of Nations and the United Nations.

## COLLECTIVE SECURITY AND ALLIANCES

Collective Security differs from the system of alliances. Military pacts like NATO, Warsaw, SEATO, CENTO were directed towards specific opponents or a certain state-or-states outside the systems. Whereas collective security is primarily concerned with peace among its own members, all of who are regarded as innocent until and unless anyone of them is found guilty. Alliances have been characterized by a limited membership of a limited aim. They do not offer any general guarantee against war.[6] Alliance such as NATO is a system of selective security, embodying the principle of some for some, whereas collective security is dedicated to the concept of all for all. Under usual circumstances, collective security and a balance of power are incompatible. The substance of the first is a world front against a possible aggressor. The substance of the second is the maintenance of such an equilibrium by two approximately equal and opposing fronts. Collective security is far more systematic than balance of power. Balance of power is a system only by courtesy, a most unsystematic system, whereas collective security represents the urge for systematization, the institutionalization of international relations.

The Cold War increased the differences between super-powers and, the shift was from collective security to peace-keeping but serving the purpose of peace. The UN has settled for more realistic and less risky approach of preventive diplomacy of peace-keeping rather than fighting a war. In the traditional peace-keeping, force is not anticipated. Force is involved when Security Council approves a peace enforcement operation under Charter VII of the UN. In peace enforcement, an aggressor is identified by the Security Council and it decides to take measures of coercion to stall aggression. In addition to peace-keeping and peace enforcement, what lies in between there is also peace-making.

Thus, collective security today works under a broader structure of peaceful existence and has tried to reconcile conflicting situations with pacific settlement of disputes. The system of collective security as it exists suffers from a number of serious shortcomings. Firstly, because of the advance of military technology and an all out destructive nature of nuclear war since 1945, there arise new problems. Since superior delivery systems minimize on the time front, a nation may already be destroyed before collective security actually comes into force and takes action. Secondly, the system of collective security has been rendered quite ineffective due to Cold War between the USA and the USSR and because of the absence of unanimity amongst the permanent members.

Today, after the end of Cold War, disintegration of a bipolar world and demise of the Soviet Union the current equations among existing powers gives the USA the much awaited opportunity of moulding UN as an instrument of US foreign policy. The USA's preference is that it alone should have full control over military operations taken in the name of United Nations. Thirdly, aggression is a very ambiguous term and there is yet to be a standard definition for the term. Even the League of Nations and the United Nations did not attempt to define the term due to its complexities. Fourthly, collective security is too complex to be practically implemented because under it no war can be localized, universalizing every local war. Finally, under the system there is no scope for the existence of neutral states because a state is either on the side of the aggressor or a member of the collective enforcement machinery. That is why neutral countries like Switzerland keeps out of the United Nations.[7]

In spite of the above weaknesses, the collective security system cannot be called obsolete or irrelevant. Preventive diplomacy and peace-keeping is a new development to ensure that UN collective security arrangement is not a failure like the League of Nations. Collective security is today more relevant. After the end of Cold War, apart from the United States, there are emerging other centres of powers like Germany, Japan, China, EU and it has brought the world community more closer and towards cooperation. The real significance of the theory of collective security lies in its contribution to the evolutionary development of the conditions of peace through international organization. There is a need for transformation of attitude and outlook necessary for collective security but this will take time.

## COLLECTIVE SECURITY AND THE UNITED NATIONS

Collective security is a global or regional security regime agreed to by the great powers that sets rules for keeping peace, guided by the principle that an act of aggression by any state will be met by a collective response from the rest. Instead of accepting war as a legitimate instrument of national policy, collective security advocates to inhibit war through the threat of collective action.[8] The theory proposed: (i) to retaliate against any aggression or attempt to establish hegemony—not just those acts that threatened particular countries (ii) to involve the participation of all member states—not just a sufficient number to stop the aggression and (iii) to create an international organization to identify acts of aggression and to organize a military response to them—not just to let the individual states decide for themselves whether to undertake self-help measures. In essence, collective security might be defined as "collective self-regulation" occurring when "a group of states attempt to reduce security threats by agreeing to collectively punish any member-state that violates the system's norms. The shortcomings in the system of collective security provided under the Covenant of the League of Nations and the holocaust of World War II, laid the foundations for a really effective collective security arrangement under the Charter of the United Nations. The UN Charter has elaborated both the concept and actual dimensions of collective security. Article 1 of the Charter refers to "effective collective measure for the prevention and removal of threats to the peace and for the suppression of acts of aggression or other breaches of peace". But elaborate provisions regarding collective security are made in Chapter VII (Articles 39 to 51) of the UN Charter.

Under Article 39, the Security Council can "determine the existence of any threat to the peace, breach of peace or act of aggression" and suggest measures for the restoration of international peace and security. Due to this power, the Security Council is also known as "enforcement arm" of the United Nations. It takes recourse to partial or complete interruption of economic relations, and of rail, sea, air, postal, telegraphic, radio and other means of communication as well as severance of diplomatic relations. On the failure of these measures, the Security Council can take military action by land, sea, or air as may be necessary to maintain international peace. Article 43 provides that all members make available for armed assistance and facilities to the UN Security Council for the purpose of maintaining international peace and security. Article 45 provides for availability of national air force contingents for combined international enforcement action. Article 49 states that members of the UN shall join in affording mutual assistance in carrying out measures decided upon by the Security Council. Article 51 specifically recognizes the inherent right of individual or collective self-defense if an attack occurs against a member of the United Nations, until the Security Council has taken the measures necessary to maintain international peace. Measures taken by members in exercise of this right of self-defense shall be immediately reported to the Security Council.[9]

The UN Charter has been responsible for evolving a comprehensive system of collective security. It makes the Security Council a very powerful organ of the United Nations. However, it ensures that any decision other than procedural matters must have an affirmative vote of nine members including concurrent votes of permanent members. Thus, UN Security scheme envisages use of collective force as a deterrence to end aggression anywhere. The first experiment under the United Nations of collective security was made in 1950 with the outbreak of the Korean War when North Korea attacked South Korea on June 15, 1950. The Security Council passed a resolution by 9 to 0 votes (with Soviet Union abstaining) asserting that North Korea had committed a clear breach of peace and called upon North Korea to stop hostilities and withdraw its forces to 38th Parallel. As North Korea failed to comply with the resolution, the Security Council decided to go ahead with police action. It set up a unified command under UN flag and requested the member-states to render necessary military assistance. However, the things became complicated after the intervention of the Chinese communist forces in Korea in support of North Korea and on account of Soviet veto. To overcome this difficulty, the UN established a 'Uniting for Peace Resolution' by the General Assembly. According to this resolution, the General Assembly assumes the power of maintaining international peace and security when the Security Council is unable to take any action on account of veto by one of the permanent members. Thus, in the Korean crisis, collective military sanctions were employed for the first time in an international police action. Other instances like the Russian-Iranian disputes of 1946, Dutch-Indonesian dispute (1945-49), were solved with the mediations of the United Nations. The Korean experience entailed some very important questions in the context of future relevance of collective security arrangement. The General Assembly's 'Uniting for Peace Resolution' fills the void in the inability of Security Council to take effective measures due to the veto power of any permanent member. The main features of this plan are:

- The General Assembly can meet in an emergency session within twenty-four hours and make necessary recommendations. Such an emergency session can be called at the request of the seven members of the Security Council or the majority of the members of the UNO. In such cases, the General Assembly can make recommendations to the member-states for collective measures, including the use of armed forces.
- The establishment of a Peace Observation Commission consisting of 14 members to observe and report to the

General Assembly about tension in any part of the world which posed a threat to world peace.

- The creation of the Collective Measures Committee to study and report on the ways and means to strengthen international peace and security in accordance with the Charter of the United Nations.
- A recommendation that each member-state should maintain within their armed forces certain elements so trained that they could be immediately available to the United Nations for service.

The Uniting for Peace Resolutions "marked the attempt of circumscribe the veto provision and to rebuild the UN into an effective collective defense system. Henceforth, the Assembly could determine by two-thirds majority of its members the situations which posed a threat to the peace and could make necessary recommendations for meeting the situation. In 1956 following invasion of Sinai peninsula by the Israelis and subsequent armed action by Britain and France in Suez a serious threat was posed to world peace. The "Uniting for Peace" system was successful in thwarting aggression in which two permanent members of the Security Council, Great Britain and France were involved. The Cold War increased the differences between superpowers and the shift was from collective security to peace-keeping and the UN has settled for more realistic and less risky approach of preventive diplomacy. This led to the realization of the organizational concept of the UN of using military personnel of member-states for the peace-keeping rather than fighting a war. This concept was further strengthened in Lebanon (1958), Congo (1960), Cyprus (1963), West Iran (1962), Yemen (1963), Kashmir (1965), Middle East (1967). In the late 80s due to the thaw in the relations between the USA and the former Soviet Union, the UN once again a mechanism indispensable to the resolution of international conflicts. The Geneva Accord (1988) on Afghanistan is a pointer in this direction. Other cases in the point have been the major UN efforts recently undertaken in Gulf crisis, Cambodia, El Salvador, former Yugoslavia and now in Afghanistan. Today there are conflicts within state borders and the UN has to intervene as in the case of Cambodia and Somalia. In the traditional peace-keeping, force is not anticipated. Force is involved when Security Council approves a peace enforcement operation under Chapter VII of the UN Charter. In peace enforcement, an aggressor is identified by the Security Council and it decides to take measures of coercion to stall aggression.

## NOTES

1. David A. Baldwin, "Power Analysis and World Politics: New Trends Versus Old Tendencies" in Klaus Knorr, ed., *Power, Strategy and Security* (Princeton, N.J., 1983), p. 8.
2. Ray S. Cline, *World Power Assessment: A Calculus of Strategic Drift* (Colorado, 1975), p. 8.
3. Mahendra Kumar, *Theoretical Aspects of International Politics* (Agra, 1972), 2nd revised edn., p. 37.
4. Rudolph J. Rummel, "Libertarianism and International Violence", *Journal of Conflict Resolution,* 27, I, March 1983, pp. 27-71.
5. Ole Holsti, "The Belief System and National Images: A Case Study" in *ibid.*, pp. 543-50.
6. A.F.K. Organski, *World Politics* (New York, 1958), pp. 292, 297, 316-38.
7. N.J. Spykman, *America's Strategy in World Politics* (New York, 1942), pp. 21-22.
8. Sidney B. Fay, "Balance of Power", *Encyclopaedia of the Social Sciences* (New York, 1937), II, p. 395.
9. Zbigniew Brzezinski, "The Balance of Power Delusion" in David S. McLellan et al., ed., *The Theory and Practice of International Relations* (Prentice-Hall of India, New Delhi, 1977), p. 100.

# Development Discourse in International Relations

6

The speed and extent of development depends on the availability of material, technological and financial resources, but in its essence, development is a human process that is determined by the response of people to their external environment. Development is the process by which human beings become aware of opportunities and challenges, formulate responses, make decisions, and initiate organized actions.[1] The growth of development theory is essentially a post-Second World War phenomenon. The post-Second World War development theory can be divided into the following four phases. The first phase was that of classical or neo-classical views. In this phase, development essentially meant economic development and primacy was accorded to economic growth. Development depends on a very broad range of knowledge—technical knowledge of productive processes, commercial knowledge of markets and business practices, personal knowledge of human health and nutrition, knowledge of laws and legal processes, knowledge of political and administrative processes and public policies, knowledge of organization and management, knowledge of emerging fields of science and, perhaps most important of all, a conceptual knowledge of the nature of the development process itself, so that we may have the wisdom to unleash and harness the energy, resourcefulness and creativity of the people. The most spectacular accomplishment of the second phase was the development of the modernization paradigm. It was felt that economic development and technological changes are hindered by institutional factors. Thus, modifications in the institutional framework of society and alterations in the attitudes and values were to be contemplated to facilitate the process of economic development. The third phase may be described as reactive and responsive: it was born out of a strong reaction to the inadequate paradigms of economic growth and modernization and responded positively to more successful praxis of development. The academics in Latin America, the Caribbean and a little later in Africa started a dependency theory. The capitalist system has achieved only partial penetration with the resulting disequilibrium of the dependent economy in the developing countries. What is happening in Third World countries is modernization rather than development based on the adaptation of new patterns of consumption by a minority. There is disenchantment with growth-centred development. New concepts of human-centred development and human resources mobilization and human capital formation emerged. The fourth phase is a reflective phase. A new international economic order is necessary both for the North and for the South.

### The Cultures of Development

This process follows the sequence from knowledge to inspiration to action. Human beings acquire knowledge, they become aware of opportunities and challenges. When that knowledge matures, they acquire a motivation or inspiration to translate that knowledge into action. No matter how great the opportunity or how dire the necessity, without that knowledge no adaptive response occurs.[2] Knowledge is fundamental to each step in the development process. It is essential for creating awareness of opportunities and challenges, a proper evaluation of alternatives, formulating responses, effective planning and organization of initiatives, and practical implementation of those initiatives.

The words knowledge, information and data are often used interchangeably, but a true understanding of the role of knowledge in development requires that we make a distinction between its ascending and descending levels or grades. In the ascending phase that leads from experience to knowledge, raw data is distilled into information and ideas. Raw, unprocessed physical facts or data is the lowest grade.[3] At the next higher level, these facts get categorized and organized as information. At a higher level, organized facts are processed and distilled into ideas, concepts, and theoretical propositions that provide a perspective which reveals their significance and inter-relationships. In the descending phase that leads from knowledge to action, ideas and theoretical concepts are applied to generate plans, organizational patterns, technological processes and physical skills that express in action.

Knowledge contributes to development in several different ways: as a productive resource; as an essential input for education, scientific research and industrial technology; as a catalyst for social change and economic development; and as a basis for civilization and cultural values that promote social integrity and harmony, which is the essential foundation for development.

In earlier stages of development, land and minerals constituted the principal resources for development. Technology was rudimentary. Human beings were valued mainly for their physical labour. Today, information and knowledge have become increasingly important inputs to the development process. All economic activities are becoming more knowledge-intensive. By one recent estimate, 50-60 per cent of all industrial output is based on information. Modern manufacturing industries depend as much for their success on the management of information relating to quality, cost and scheduling as they do on the management of production processes. The service sector, which is the greatest source of new jobs and economic growth in the world economy, is essentially knowledge-based. In USA, the percentage of the workforce engaged in manufacturing is now the same as it was in 1850. The phenomenal growth of employment opportunities in USA has been driven by the rapid expansion of services. The four most important service sectors—financial services, insurance, health and education—are especially knowledge-intensive.

This shift from material to knowledge-based resources opens up vast opportunities for developing countries to accelerate the pace of development. The characteristics of knowledge differ greatly from those of material and financial resources. Knowledge expands as it is shared rather than being consumed. Knowledge is not lost when it is freely given away. Knowledge is readily transportable at rapid speed and very low cost.

Development depends on four knowledge processes:

- Knowledge generation and acquisition through scientific discovery, R&D and transfer of technology.
- Knowledge adaptation through innovation to particular fields, needs and operating environments.
- Knowledge dissemination through formal and informal channels from knowledge developers and adapters to those responsible for applying the knowledge in society.
- Knowledge application through skilled action in fields, factories, classrooms, hospitals and every other field of activity to achieve practical results.

## SCOPE OF DEVELOPMENT

Development is multi-dimensional conception and it is not easy to define it or give it a precise meaning. It means different things to different writers. They look at 'development' in different contexts—political, social, economics, ideological or paradigm of modernization and accordingly, define and give a meaning to it. Thus, it could be said that, in the political context, 'development' would imply, among other things, participation, secularization and rationalism. In the social context, it would mean the culmination of social distinctions, evil, inequality and discrimination.[4] It would also imply to provide opportunity for social mobility and equality of status in society. In its economic dimension 'development' would mean a guarantee of social security, in absence of exploitative society, sustained economic growth and the attainment of plenty and prosperity.

The Brandt Commission acknowledged the difficulties of 'defining' or giving a precise meaning to development when it opined: "Development never will be, and never can be, defined to universal satisfaction."

In spite of the above said difficulties of the definition and meaning of development, we do have a common view, notion and understanding of development. By development, we mean the transformation of a 'traditional society' into a 'modern society'. The notion of development also implies a multi-dimensional process involving changes in attitudes, institutions, structures as well as acceleration of economic growth, reduction of inequality, eradication of poverty and so on.

Some of the writers of development theory have also tried to define it in precise terms. Some of their definitions are under outlined:

**Colm and Greiger:** Development means change, change coupled with growth.

**Esman:** Development is the rational process of organizing and carrying out prudently conceived and staffed programmes or projects as one would organize or carry out military or engineering operations.

**Gunnar Myrdal:** Development is 'a movement upward of a whole system of inter-dependent conditions as a complex process in which economic growth is only one of the several categories of causally relevant conditions.

**Weidmer:** Development is a process directed towards socio-economic development and nation-building.

**Hashu-Been Lee:** Development is a process of acquiring a sustained growth of a system's capability to cope with new, continuous change towards the achievement of developmentive politics economic and social objectives.

**Chaturvedi:** Development is a process which stand for 'transformation of society'.

**Riggs:** Development involves the ability to choose whether or not to increase outputs, whether or not to raise levels of per capita income, or to direct energies to other goals, to the more equitable distribution of what is available, to aesthetic or spiritual values, or the qualitatively different kinds of outputs.

## MARXIST CONCEPT OF DEVELOPMENT

The Marxian concept of development can be assessed from different perspectives. The perspectives are mainly on the basic structure of the Marxian society and polity. According to Marx, the concept of development means transitory phase in the onward march of society and its development—a transitory phase from capitalism of Marxism. Let us, therefore, examine the Marxist views on development.

The Marxists prefer to use the development in place of development. And, their concept of development is based on the dialectical theory of social development. It is inherent in the Marxist view of man, society and history, though it is now fully stated and developed. At the end of his introduction to the Grund issue, Marx refers to the relation between the development of material production and/or artistic production and says that 'the concept of development is not be understood in its familiar abstraction'. In the Preface of 1859, he arranged the chief modes of production in a series as 'developmentive epochs in the economic formation of society'. In the same text he describes the conditions in which 'new, higher relation of production' can appear. The basic components of this largely implicit conception of development are twofold. First, cultural development defined as human emancipation in the broadest sense. 'The complete elaboration of human potentialities' depends upon 'the full development of human mastery over the forces of nature'. Secondly, development is not regarded by Marx, as in the case of evolutionist theories of Comte and Spencer, "as a gradual, continuous and integrated process, but as characterized by discontinuity. Disharmony, and more or less abrupt leaps from one type of society of another, accomplished primarily through class conflicts."

It is true that Marx never attempted to discuss the conception of development in an exploit manner. Yet it is inherent in his model of a sequence of formations derived from modes of productions and containing internal contradictions which lead to development of social transformation through class struggle, crisis and social revolution. Social and cultural development occurs through a sequence of tribal, slave, feudal, capitalist and socialist societies. Marx has a dialectical view of development, which occurs through the clash of opposing elements in the proceeding and succeeding social formations. Unlike Spencer, Marx has made some allowance for the possibility of regress, i.e. change in the wrong direction which is described as refedualization. More recently, some Marxists speak of 'the development of underdevelopment'. Wallerstein and Frank have often discussed the fact that the rise of the bourgeoisie and the towns in Western Europe in the sixteenth century not only coincided with, but actually led to, the decline of the bourgeoisie and the towns in Eastern Europe. On one side of the Elbe, the rise of capitalism; on the other, what Engels called the 'second serfdom'. The development of one area exporting manufactured good, depended on the 'underdevelopment' of the other, which now concreted on exporting raw materials. A similar underdevelopment or regress centred in the colonies and semicolonies of industrialized countries.[5]

The Marxist concept of development has been criticized on many counts. It is pointed out that it does not permit men any freedom of choice; it undermined the importance and contribution of 'great men' to development; and it does not clearly identify the society of which the change and development is predicted.

However, this criticism is a little unfair to Marx, because he did predict change, development and development of concrete social formations and his concept of the mode of production is also historically determinate and specific. Moreover, Marx never thought of society as an organism. Plamenatz admits: "But let us not allow the defects of Marxian theory to blind us to its merits. Marxism is one of the richest and most suggestive of social theories. There is an ideal, common to Hegel and Marx, which has had a deep influence of many liberal and radical thinkers."[6]

## SOCIALIST CONCEPT OF DEVELOPMENT

The socialist concept of development lays emphasis and aims at the establishment of a socialist economy. In this economy, the scientific and technological developments of the one side and the application of industrial science of the other would qualitatively change the complexion of the traditional capitalist society. The socialist functions the state would perform for social development would be as under:

- The pursuit of a planned economy in order to avoid wasteful production and the evils of cut throat competitions of the capitalist society.
- The introduction of a socialist mode of production with a view to increase social welfare and fulfilling the material needs of society.
- The bringing about of land reforms and establishing co-operative and collective farms to increase production and enrich the material life of the people.
- The application of scientific and technological innovations in agriculture and industry to maximize production.
- The abolition of private property and its replacement by social ownership of the means of production.
- It would include the socialization of industries, mineral resources, forests, land and other marine and land resources, the railway system as a whole and state machine building and other industrial units.
- Providing an equitable system of distribution of consumer goods.
- Promoting welfare services of the working classes and thus regulate their working hours, wages, the right to rest and leisure and the right to material assistance of old age and in case of illness or disability.

The socialist concept of development also takes notes of the social and cultural functions of the state. In this field, the state guarantees to the citizens, the right to education and the freedom to engage in scientific research, liberty for artistic creation and other cultural activities. It promotes and encourages the creative endeavour of citizens engaged in science, education, art, journalism and other cultural work. Thus, the socialist state provides:

- established social equality and provides equal opportunity to all, and

- promotes socialist culture and morality by imbibing among the people the spirit of selfless service.

## GANDHIAN CONCEPT OF DEVELOPMENT

The Mahatma was also cognizant of the thoughtful conflict between those who owned productive wealth, on the one hand, those who laboured within various systems of production, having nothing besides their labour power as the basis of subsistence, on the other. It is important to stress all this since Gandhiji's attitude towards industry and technology is a much misunderstood subject.

The economic activity which the Mahatma sought to promote in urban society was the sort of economic activity which, in the idiom of our times, is looked upon as industry resting upon 'appropriate technology'. Gandhiji sought to stimulate economic activity which would increase production at the same time as it offered gainful employment to millions of the common folk. Hence, the attempt to popularize a more efficient charkha, that was still labour-intensive. This logic was applied to other instances of artisanal activity: since the increase of production in a country like India needed to be achieved through techniques which also provided employment to the rural and the urban classes.

Development has entered the world with two accomplishes: Modern science and colonialism. From science, development has inherited the belief that you can go on increasing the power of human beings over the non-human cosmos, for the world has enough resources to meet not only the needs but also the greed of all humans. From colonialism, development has inherited the faith that those on the higher rungs of history have the right to shape the ways of the life of those of the lower.

The growth of development theory is essentially a post-Second World War phenomenon. The theory of development in the period proceeding the Second World War was the product of the ethos in which it grew and developed. It was the outcome of social malfunctioning, social malaise had to be attended to and the social wrong had to be rectified. In the theories of the time social action was also called for, either implicitly or explicitly. But they and later theories did not anticipate the problems, latent in different facts and of development change. For example, imperialism was rarely projected as the cause of retardation of colonial societies and their economies. Some sought to justify it; others regarded it as a painful necessity. While advantages of imperialism where enumerated, its long-term harmful consequences were not. It was believed that factors and forces of history were moving human society in a pre-determined direction; human intervention could accelerate the pace but not latter the direction.

The post-Second World War development theory can be divided into the following four phases:

- The first phase was that of classical or neo-classical views. In this phase, development essentially meant economic development and economists focused their attention exclusively on economic growth.
- In the second phase, the relationship between economic development and social change was more keenly realized and, in consequence, emphasized. It was felt that economic development and technological change are hindered by institutional factors.
- The third phase may be described as reactive and responsive: it was born out of a strong reaction to the inadequate paradigms of development and modernization and responded positively to more successful praxis of development.
- The fourth phase is a reflective phase. One has to understand the world order and also the national order. Both have to be altered if human survival is to be ensured.

Following the Second World War, the economists and academics in Latin America, the Caribbean and a little later in Africa began to think of development in a completely new perspective which came to be known as 'dependency theory'. The Third World countries began articulating their misgivings about the feasibility, viability and desirability of the prevailing development approaches for attaining the social objectives that were incorporated in the national constitutions and plan documents. Undifferentiated growth was not raising the level of employment nor was it improving living standards for all the society.

The prominent writer of "Dependency Theory" are Hayade la Torre, I.C. Mariatgeu and the Brazilian writer Celso Furtado. This theory explained that industrialization, even if it is aimed at import substantiation, results in undifferentiated growth little trickle-down. Latin American experience suggests that transnationalization, in their cause at least, has led to dependent development which is concentrative and exclusive. It is argued that the 'centre' has now to be delinked from the 'periphery' and the 'peripheral' nations have to strive for collective self-reliance. This would enhance their bargaining power and the less they depended on the centres, the better they would be able to reduce dependence and handle effectively problems of skewed need-distribution, marginalization and poverty.

Further, the very situation in the Third World countries, especially in Latin America—the domination of their entire economic and financial structure by the industry based metropolitan centres led to the new line of thinking which started describing Latin American economies as 'dependent' rather than merely 'peripheral'. The writing of Celso Furtado indicated a developmentive change—towards a sharper attitude—which was gradually coming over Latin American thinking on development. Starting with treating the problem of economic development as 'but one aspect of the general problem of social change in our society which could not be understood unless we give it a historical context', he soon found himself developing a theory of 'underdevelopment', which relied on the manner in which the capitalist system had achieved only partial penetration with the resulting disequilibrium of the dependent economy in the developing countries. Furtado became more and more convinced of the need for structural changes in the developing countries and called for changes in both the systems of production and the system of distribution of income. His emphasis on structural change ultimately led to the 'dependence model', which found its culmination in the wirings of Andre Gunder Frank. What was happening in Latin America was, according to Furtado, modernization rather than development based on the adaptation of new patterns of consumption by a minority.

### The Keynesian Model

The Keynesian model of development is based on the classical work of J.M. Keynes, *General Theory of Employment, Interest and Money*, published in 1936. Keynes strongly supported the cause of governments assuming more powers particularly in matters of economic management, provided a viable alternative to those who were not inclined to take to socialist measures.

The Keynesian model had been designed to deal with employment problem in industrial countries—concepts of national income, savings, ranges of savings, averaged and marginal area, incremental rates of savings, capital investment, fiscal investment, average and marginal rates and so on. This model, says Hans Singer, was developed in an industrial country, for the industrial countries and should project a balanced present-future orientation. The difficulty with the concept was that it was rich in promises for a distant future, but its rewards were measly and unconvincing. It offered a post-dated cheque which could be enchased some time in the distant future, a point in time to which people could not relate with much enthusiasm.[7]

## DEVELOPMENT DISCOURSE: A REVIEW

Development is a multi-dimensional concept and has its political, social, economic, ideological implications. By development we mean the transformation of a 'traditional society' into a 'modern society'. The notion of development also implies a multi-dimensional process involving changes in attitudes, institutions, structures as well as acceleration of economic growth, reduction of inequality, eradication of poverty and so on. Development can be seen as a process and there are two schools of thought with regard to the strategy of development. One school advocates a "gradual approach to development and the other school advocates a big push" to economic development.

Prof. Rostow has classified the process of economic growth into five stages. These are:

- Stage of Traditional Society,
- Stage of Precondition of Take-off,
- Stage of Take-off,
- Stage of Maturity,
- Stage of Mass Consumption.

Alexander Gerschenkron attempted to explain development process in terms of "big spurts". Gerschenkron preferred to use industrial production as an indicator of his "spurts". The less developed a country, the greater the growth spurt and the higher the stimulus necessary for economic and social development. The greater the backwardness of a country, the "greater the pressure for industrialization. Dualism refers to two sectors of an economy such as agriculture and industry; two regions of a country such as the rich or leading region and the poor or lagging region; or two socio-cultural systems. This sectoral dualism, regional dualism and socio-cultural dualism is a temporary phenomenon attributed to market imperfection. Economic development through trickling down and spread effects, will eventually eliminate such differences and inequalities.[8]

The controversial discussion between economists in the post-war years centres around the problem of optimum allocation of investment. The policy of "gradualism" leads to a pedestrian process development and possibly to stagnation. What is needed is a "bigpush", a wave of investment in a large number of industries to break the vicious circle of poverty and to stimulate the market. Some economists argue that development is best stimulated by a strategy of balanced growth, that is, a programme of comprehensive simultaneous investments throughout all sectors of economy. Another group of economists support the argument of unbalanced growth and development can at best be achieved through a deliberate unbalancing process in the economy in accordance with a pre-designed strategy. Planning with unbalanced growth, is an extraordinary technique which has to be adopted by an underdeveloped economy which inspite of having a low savings income ratio, aims at rapid economic development within a short specified period. A fundamental feature of this technique is that unbalanced growth takes place between heavy industries and consumption goods industries. In India, the technique of planning with unbalanced growth has been adopted in the Five-Year plans. The whole process of development is then a chain of action and reaction between balanced and unbalanced sectoral growth.

The liberal concept of development is based on the principles of economic liberalism and in the field of trade and industry, private enterprise, free competition, the policy of 'Laissez faire', 'free economy' and therefore the specific functions which the state may perform. Malthus was responsible for introducing the question of population into economic growth. The socialist concept of development aims at the abolition of private property and its replacement by social ownership of the means of production. They believe in a planned economy, welfare services of the working classes and nationalization of industries, railways, lands and mineral resources, etc. According to the Marxist, this phase (socialist development) is only a transitory phase in the onward march of society and its development—a transitory phase from Capitalism to Marxism. Marx has a dialectical view of development and in his model internal contradictions which led to development of social transformation through class struggle, crisis and social revolution.

Most Western countries—leaving aside the USA under Reagan and the UK under Margaret Thatcher, who have come under the influence of 'neo-liberation' (neo-liberal state) —continue to place greater emphasis on the state capitalist strategy than on liberalism. They accept the state's responsibility for capital formation and investment in strategic areas where spontaneous demands does not exist.

The leaders of the Third World countries developed the faith that industrialization is the key to modernization and viewed that the state had a primary role to play in the process of modernization and industrialization in their own countries. The most richest Western countries (G-7) countries now enter a hyper-industrial society. Their development has the following dimensions—a service economy, professional and technical class, intellectual technology and it has seen a society guided by knowledge, capable of continual adjustment and freed from fundamental social conflicts. The growth of development theory "is essentially a post-Second World War phenomena. In its initial stage, development essentially meant economic development or economic growth. Later on, it came to be associated with the development of modernization paradigm. But it was tilted towards the western capitalist model and rarely sought to examine the totality of the infinitely complex development process. In its third phase, the economics and academics in Latin America, the Caribbean, and in Africa explained development in a completely new perspective which came to be known as "dependency theory". Dependency may ensue either from the transfer of resources from the periphery, or the south, to the centre, i.e. the North, or from the 'blocking' or 'distorting' effects on the economies of the periphery. A disenchantment grew with growth-centred development. New concepts of human-centred development emerged and human resources mobilization and human capital formation. In its fourth phase, it is contemplated that a new international economic order is necessary both for the North and the South. The cultures of development, thus have to be changed, a new style and a new idiom are needed and it essentially acquired a utopian character.

Development never will be, and never can be, defined to universal satisfaction: By development, we mean the transformation of a 'traditional society' into a 'modern society'. Development is a multi-dimensional concept and implies changes in attitudes, institutions and structures as well as acceleration of economic growth, reduction of inequality, eradication of poverty and so on. Development is a process directed towards socio-economic development and nation-building. It is a process of a sustained growth of a systems capability for transformation of society. Development can be seen as a process and there are two schools of thought as to the right type of strategy that can be followed. One school of thought advocates a "gradual approach" and the other advocates a "big push" to economic development.

The theory of structural-functional which gained currency during the fifties and early sixties led to modernization paradigm. The modernization paradigm developed independently of the reigning paradigms of growth and development. Its genesis can be traced to Protestant ethic and Calvinism. D.C. McCleland in his work *The Achieving Society* based on his analysis of Protestant ethic, laid emphasis on the need for achievement, a strongly felt desire on the part of the individual to do well in life, values of hard work, worship of one's ancestors had led to entrepreneurial behaviour in western societies. The modernization paradigm laid emphasis on the use of science and technology, factors propelling or hindering industrialization, the process of urbanization and its functional and dysfunctional aspects, communication and the growth of mass media received attention. In sum, the ethos of modernization was to be permeated by the growth of creative rationality and with the emergence of this trait structural transformation was possible. The modernization paradigm was Eurocentric and could not be of much use of the Third World countries. It was based on a superficial historical analysis and did not take sufficient account of colonialism as a major determinant of the retardation of economies and societies of the Third World. The prominent writers of the *Dependent Theory* are Hayade la Torre, I.C. Mariatgeu, Celso Furtado and Andre Gunder Frank. The mode of articulation of the underdeveloped economies with the world economic system results in a transfer of resources from the periphery, or the South to the centre, i.e. the North. It is argued that the 'centre' has now to be delinked from the 'periphery' and the 'peripheral' nations have to strive for collective self-reliance. This theory explained that industrialization, even if it is based on import-substitution, results in undifferentiated growth with little trickle down.

The main problem was to find out means and ways of getting economic growth started in underdeveloped economies. The policy of "gradualism" leads to a pedestrian process of development and possibly to stagnation. What is needed a "big push", a wave of investments in a large number of different industries to break the vicious circle of poverty. Rostenstein-Rodan and Raghnar Nurkse were its leading exponents. Balanced growth economists stressed a programme of comprehensive simultaneous investment throughout the whole economy. An autonomous and simultaneous advance in all sectors of the economy is the best way of escaping slowness, getting out of the rut and overcoming the frustration of stagnation. Another school of economists support the argument of unbalanced growth who argue that agricultural sector must be first in the priority scale of development. This surplus labour can be used in investment projects, or it can be channeled into nascent industries, which are labour intensive in their early stages. Lewis believed that no country could have an industrial revolution without increasing its savings in relation to national income. Underdeveloped countries were underdeveloped, because they had no capital to invest and they had no capital, because they hardly had any savings. Emphasis on the need for large scale state action was laid, and unless a critical minimum effort was made which could be done by the state alone, the rate of economic growth would not be able to exceed the rate of increase of population. Gunar Myrdal feel the trend towards geographical concentration of industries in urban centres. Incorporates the danger of retardation of development in other regions. Inter-regional inequalities are expected to be gradually reverse, that is, when the Spread Effects (the growth diffusion from the rich to the poor areas) begin. It will probably take twenty to thirty years for this process to occur, according to Hirschman.

Danie Bell has advanced the thesis of development from industrial society to post-industrial society. It has the following dimensions: a service economy, professional and technical class, creation of a new intellectual technology and it is seen as a society guided by knowledge, capable of continual adjustment, and freed from fundamental social conflicts. 'Political development' model presumes more equilibrium and often emphasized stability at the expense of change and social justice. The second is the 'dependency' model whose main emphasis is on economic forces and distinguished Third World economies as being on the periphery of the world economic system whose centre was in Europe and North America. It is the 'centre' the advanced industrialized countries, who set the terms on which the system operates. As a result, the terms of trade are unfavourable to Third World countries and flow of capital is asymmetrical, tending to flow from the periphery towards the centre. Development in metropolis and underdevelopment in its satellites are two sides of the same coin. So, development in the satellites is only possible when they break away from their metropolitan exploiters. This is a rare possibility and can take place only in moments of major crisis like war or severe economic depression. In the 1990s, the two important developments in the Third World were the growing democratization of an increasing number of formerly authoritarian polities and the collapse of the Second World. Thus, has arisen a new conceptualization of Third World polities based on state-society relationship. These typologies are four-stable praetorian regimes, multiple authority polities, quasi or pseudo democracies and finally an increasing number of viable democracies. Many new developing country democracies are being asked or pressurized to implement economic liberalization. This is based on the theory that freeing of markets or liberalization leads to rapid and sustained growth. But this theory is weak. If democracy is to succeed, it is imperative that economic policies are adjusted to fit democratic mandates.

Development is a state's ability "to produce economic wealth, which in turn transform society from a subsistence based economy to one where most of society's wealth is derived from the production of manufactured goods and services". Development is closely linked with the term growth. A 'developmental pattern' has been considered to have three dimensions: the kind of industries accorded prominence; the orientation of these industries to the world economy (whether they are oriented inward or outward); and the economic agents chosen for development. Urban population, high literacy rate, well-fed people, and economics driven increasingly by the service sector mark today's developed economies. Development is a process through which a country increases its capacity to meet its citizens' basic human needs and raise their standard of living. There are many problems including persistence of poverty, unfulfilled elementary needs, occurrence of famines and widespread hunger, violation of elementary political freedoms as well as basic liberties, neglect of women, worsening threats to our environment, neglect of public facilities. Overcoming these problems is a central part of the exercise of development. Focusing on human freedoms contrasts with narrower views of development such as identifying development with the growth of gross national product, or with industrialization, or with technological advance, or with social modernization. The ability of the market mechanism to contribute to high economic growth and to overall economic progress has been widely acknowledged in the contemporary development literature. A broad approach permits simultaneous operation of many different institutions in the process of development, including markets and market-related organizations, governments and local authorities, political parties and other civic institutions, educational arrangements and opportunities of open dialogue (including the role of media and other means of communication). Under the new economic orthodoxy, the IMF and the World Bank had concluded that economies in crisis need to attack the more deep-seated structures of the relationship between market and state through 'structural adjustment'. They now required that developing countries go beyond economic stabilization and break down the structures of regulation within and of trade barriers without, that is, shrink the state in favour of the market, both internally and externally. They are part of a larger design to decisively shift the economy from a highly insulated and controlled regime to one that was integrated with the world economy, and relied primarily on the markets. The reform packages generally include—fiscal management, austerity drive, harmonizing taxation, wage settlements, cutting subsidies, fiscal deficit, liberalization, deregulation, privatization, globalization, lowering tariffs, foreign investment, capital account convertibility, reforming labour market, dereserving small-scale sector, restructuring and privatization of public sector. Liberalization is a process, not an end-stage to be achieved in the here and now and incrementalism, gradualism, caution seem the appropriate method for policy in a democracy. Consequently, governments under democracy are led to follow a more moderate course in reform. The state will continue to be pivotal to reform.[9] A strong state remains a pre-requisite for a strong market. Besides, markets, whether internal or external, cannot be left to their own devices, for they can have destructive consequences for society.

In judging development it is not adequate to look only at the growth of GNP or some other indicators of overall economic expansion. We have to look at the impact of democracy and political freedom on the lives and capabilities of the citizens. Political rights, including freedom of expression and discussion, are not only pivotal in including social responses to economic needs, they are also central to the conceptualization of economic needs themselves. Developing and strengthening a democratic system is an essential component of the process of development.

In recent studies of economic growth, there is a much greater emphasis on "human capacity", "human capability" and the acknowledgement of the role of human qualities in promoting and sustaining economic growth. The "social development" (i.e. more education, better health care, finer medical attention, social security, women's rights, land reform, population policy, local democracy) must directly count as: "developmental" since they help us to live longer, freer and more fruitful lives, in addition to the role they have in promoting productivity of economic growth or individual incomes. Even when the need for "economic reform" in favour of allowing more rooms for market is paramount, in developing countries the need for public policy for the creation of basic social opportunities for social equity and social justice is crucially important. The success of development programmers cannot be judged merely in terms of their effects on incomes and outputs, and must, at a basic level, focus on the lives that people can lead. A developing country's failure to have an adequate public policy in education and health matters can be thus of profound significance in assessing the limited success of that country regarding developmental efforts.

A policy reform that concentrates just on liberalization and deregulation cannot deal with this part of the failure of past planning.

While libertarians have been inclined to stress negative liberty, advocates of public support have tended to concentrate on positive versions of it. A similar distinction can be made about the government's "duties" *vis-à-vis* the citizens. The negative roles consist in preventing what are taken to be bad development (for example, outlawing monopolistic arrangements) whereas positive roles concern supporting constructively the efforts of the government to help the citizens (for example, by arranging public education, by redistributing land and by protecting the legal rights of the disadvantaged people).

The rapid expansion of these capabilities depends critically on public action of a kind that has been severely neglected in developing countries. The real issue in 'uncaging' the tiger is the need to go beyond liberalization. In principle, the social role of the government seems to be widely acceptable by all. A 'people-centred' approach, which puts human agency (rather than organizations such as markets and governments) at the centre of the stage is the need of the hour.[10] The central issue is to expand the social opportunities open to the people. Public debates have to be taken away from the narrow concentration on issues of liberalization.

The focus of the government policy is to remove counterproductive regulations, while taking adequate note of the tremendous social and economic deprivations that blight living conditions and limit the actual prospects of participatory economic expansion.

## NOTES

1. A.P. Barnabas (1985), "Development Policies and Human Deprivation", *Indian Journal of Public Administration*, Vol. XXXI, No. 4, October-December, pp. 1269-77.
2. C.P. Bhambri (1994), *India's Politics Since Independence*, Sipra Publication, New Delhi, p. 3.
3. R. Billorey (1989), "Where Development and for Whom", *Land and Water Review*, Vol. I, No. 3, September, p. 9.

4. Michael M. Cernea (1996), "Public Policy Responses to Development Induced Population Displacements", *Economic and Political Weekly*, 31 (n. 24, June 15), pp. 1515-23.
5. S. Das Gupta (1990), "Review of Development and Under Development", *Frontier*, Vol. 22, No. 50, July 28.
6. Dipankar Dey (1991), "Destruction not Development", *Frontier*, Vol. 22, No. 32, March 23, pp. 12-14.
7. Rajni Kothari (1988), *Rethinking Development: In Search of Humane Alternatives,* Ajanta Publisher, New Delhi, p. 53.
8. Charles O. Lerche, Jr. and Abdul A. Said (1970), *Concepts of International Politics* (New Delhi, 1972), p. 75
9. Zbigniew Brzezinski (1977), "The Balance of Power Delusion" in David S. McLellan et al., (ed), *The Theory and Practice of International Relations* (Prentice-Hall of India, New Delhi) p. 100.
10. Joseph Frankel (1973), *Contemporary International Theory and the Behaviour of States* (Oxford), p. 95.

# Cold War and Multipolarity 7

## COLD WAR

Barnard Baruch first used the term Cold War. Walter Lippmann popularized the term in 1947. The Cold War has been a most important factor in shaping the conduct in international affairs in post-Second World War period. It envisaged an era of neither peace nor war between countries. Desmond Donnelly (*Struggle for the World: The Cold War: 1917-65*), Frederick Schuman (*Cold War: Restropect and Prospect*), etc. have focused the objectives of Cold War from different valid grounds. The Cold War in Soviet Union was officially regarded as a unilateral attack by 'capitalism' and 'imperialism'. In a broader sense, it began with the second Russian Revolution of 1917. The term Cold War has been defined by Florence Elliot and Michael Summerskill in *A Dictionary Politics* as "state of tension between countries in which each side adopts policies designed to strengthen itself and weaken the other, line falling short of actual hot war". Most of the scholars have treated Cold War as a post World War II phenomenon, although some scholars trace it back to the Bolshevik Revolution of 1917. For example, Prof. Schuman says, "The Cold War did not begin in 1945, in the aftermath of World War II and of the Yalta and of the Potsdam Conference. In a broader sense it began with the second Russian Revolution of 1917.... Within ten months after Russia's October Revolution, Soviet Union and the West were at war. And the war was not a Cold War but a hot war, marked by the many casualties and vast destruction." He says that the legacy of mutual fear and suspicion and hatred which nourished the Cold War of the 1940's and 50's originated in the hot war between East and West in 1918-21.

Cold War emerged due to Bolshevik revolution of Russia. The Western power had initially refused to recognize the Bolshevik government in Russia. Through this process, Cold War fashioned.

In order to know about the historical review of Cold War, we have to discuss the basis of Cold War, phases of Cold War, implication of Cold War, Détente and Neo-Cold War, etc.

Since World War II, the international relations have been chiefly determined by the Cold War an era of neither peace nor war, between Soviet Union and two leading Western Powers UK and USA. Although during the war the Western powers and the Soviet Union fought together against the Axis aggression, their relations, though cordial, were marked by undercurrent of mutual distrust and jealousy. The delay in opening the second front, the secrecy over the Atom bomb, and refusal to invite the provisional government to San Francisco made Soviet Union suspicious of the Anglo-American motives.

Similarly, the West felt that Russia and considerable territory by declaring war against Japan at the last moment. This mutual distrust assumed the shape of a rivalry after the World War II ended. At the end of the war, both America and Soviet Union confronted each other congeries of prostrate, exhausted and chaotic societies that provides an invitation to rivalry.[1] Britain and China been able to maintain control of their traditional spheres of influences, the Soviet American confrontation would not have assumed such threatening postures.[2]

The interest of the two clashed after World War II on the issues of Germany and Japan which slowly developed into what came to be called 'Cold War'. Winston Churchill in his Fulton Speech of March 1916 gave the first signal of this development. He said, "If the Western democracies stand together in strict adherence to the principles of the United Nations Charter, their influence for furthering those principles will be immense and no one is likely to molest them. If, however, they become divided or falter in their duty and if these all important years are allowed to slip away, then indeed catastrophe may overwhelm us all." He predicted the inevitability of post-war struggle against the

Russian barbarism. The rivalry assumed serious dimension after Second World War over the question of Germany and Japan.

### Foundation of Cold War

There are three dimensions of Cold War. These are:

- Cold War was rooted in the mutual misunderstanding.
- Cold War was rooted in ideological in compatibilities.
- Cold War as a product of mutual antagonism.

The roots of Cold War was in the mutual misunderstanding. Both the parties saw in their own action. This naturally gave rise to distrust towards each other. The countries held that the mistrust and the consequent fears were the basis of this conflict. The mutual fear and suspicion produced hostile interaction between two parties and both the parties were not willing to take any initiative to reduce tension. Secondly, Cold War was rooted in ideological incompatibilities. There was too much difference in the ideologies of USA and Russia to workout a long term programme of cooperation. The expansionist and crusading communist ideology was intent upon converting the entire world.

## PHASES OF COLD WAR

The following are the phases of Cold War outlined below:

1. First Phase (1946-49)
2. Second Phase (1949-53)
3. Third Phase (1953-57)
4. Fourth Phase (1957-62)
5. Fifth Phase (1962-69)
6. Sixth Phase (1969-78)
7. Seventh Phase (1979 onwards)

### First Phase

The first phase lasted from 1946 to 1949. During this period it was held that if strong pressure could be organized, the Red regime in Soviet Union would collapse like a house of cards. This feeling arose because America was having monopoly of Atom bomb and Russia was in very weak condition. Therefore, it was held that USA due to her superiority in military could determine the history of world and influence the internal affairs of Soviet Union. The policy of containing Soviet Union could not be implemented because the Allies of America were not yet fully armed for such a war and the memories of Second World War were still fresh in their mind, which prevented them from resorting to war. During this phase, America restored to direct military intervention through Truman Doctrine of March 1947 and economic integration of the West European Power by Marshall Plan of June, 1947. USA during this period followed the policy of intervention and defender of status quo. This phase was also marked by anti-communist feeling, which USA tried to implant throughout the world. This phase of Cold War ended with the conclusion of North Atlantic Treaty on April 4, 1949. This treaty was a sort of new Anti-Comintern Pact and was openly directed against the Soviet Union.[3] These activities of USA naturally provoked Soviet Union to take necessary measures for self-defence.[4]

The US resorted to direct military acting during this phase through Truman Doctrine of 1947. During this period, America followed two policies. These were:

(a) It pursued the policy of intervention and defender of status quo.

(b) Anti-communist feelings, which the USA endeavoured to implant throughout the world.

During this period, German problem also contributed tension between the two blocs. Yet another factor which contributed to the tension between two superpowers during this phase was refusal of USA to accord recognition to the communist government of China.

### Second Phase

The second phase lasted from 1949 to 1953. During this period USA continued her policy of military and economic assistance against Soviet Union. During this period, USA concluded security treaty with Australia and New Zealand (ANZUS) and Peace Treaty with Japan (1951). This period also witnessed the Korean War which was a major confrontation between USA and USSR. The United States intensified her anti-communist propaganda and spent millions of dollars for the purpose. She also invested huge amount to carry out subversive activities in the socialist countries. This provoked natural reaction from Soviet Union. It exploded the atom bomb and challenged the American monopoly. The Second Phase (1949-53) was characterized by America's policy of military and economic aid against Soviet Union. This was proved a major confrontation between USA and Soviet Union. That time a joint commission was held. But this could not be achieved. Lastly, Korean issues were referred to the UN. America launched intensified propaganda against communism. This period was marked by subversive activities.

**Third Phase**

The third phase of Cold War lasted from 1953 to 1957. During this phase, USA continued her policy of military and economic offensive. She organized the South-east Asia Treaty Organization (SEATO) and the Middle East Defence Organization (MEDO). These two treaties became new defence links with NATO. America also made a serious effort to perpetuate American domination in the Middle East by extending the Truman Doctrine to this area. USA also established a number of military based around Soviet territory and concluded defence treaties with 43 states. It was also during this period that USA involved herself in Vietnam, which turned out to be a grim climax of the Cold War.

During this phase, Soviet Union also increased her influence. She sponsored WARSAW Treaty with East European power as a counter measures to NATO. She concluded defence treaties with 12 states and foiled the American attempt to promote counter-revolution in Hungary. This period also witnessed the permanency of the Potsdam partition of Germany. The subsequent establishment of two German States allied to the two blocs was also the outcome of Cold War during this period. The phase also was simultaneous explosion of hydrogen bombs by USA and Soviet Union. During this period, a dialogue between the two countries was opened with forecast that the next phase of international relations would be marked by a spirit of negotiation and not mutual threats of extermination.

### Fourth Phase

The fourth phase lasted from 1957 to 1962. It had two extreme trends. On the one hand that the principles of peaceful coexistence were asserted and on the other hand, it saw the most dangerous Cuban missile crisis. During the initial years, the spirit of coexistence prevailed. The two countries exchanged cultural and political delegates. The heads of governments of two countries paid visits to each other. The agreement for Paris Summit clearly demonstrated that the Cold War attitude had ended. But this spirit was sabotaged by the U-2 incident. The damage done by the U-2 incident was partly repaired by the General Assembly Summit of 1960 and the Vietnam meeting of Khrushchev and President Kennedy in 1961. But the Cuban crisis literally brought the two countries on the verge of war. However, the situation was finally saved by an agreement between Khrushchev and Kennedy by which Soviet Union agreed to withdraw the missile base in exchange for the American guarantee never to invade Cuba.

### Fifth Phase

The fifth phase was from 1962-69. This period was marked by a deep appreciation of the futility of nuclear weapons. There was a world-wide concern demanding ban on nuclear weapons. The Partial test ban treaty was concluded in 1963. The Geneva Hot Line Agreement of 1963 brought USA and USSR more closer. The signing of partial Nuclear Test Ban Treaty in 1967 was regarded as a landmark in easing the Cold War. The Non-Proliferation treaty of 1968 could also be concluded due to the understanding of the two powers. However, even during this period the problem of Germany and Vietnam stood in the way of full co-operation between the two countries.

### Sixth Phase—Détente (1969-78)

With coming to power of President Nixon and his national security adviser, Henry A. Kissinger, the Soviet-American relations were officially termed as détente in 1969. The age of détente was characterized by a continuation of efforts by rival superpowers to reduce tension, diminish distrust, increase accommodation and ultimately move from competition to cooperation. Major important events contributing to the improvement of relations were: signing of Strategic Arms Limitation Treaty (SALT) in 1972, holding of 35 Nation European Security Conference in Helsinki in 1975 and organizing Review Conference on European Security Conference in Belgrade in 1978. In 1973, Brezhnev, the Chief of the Communist Party of USSR also visited Washington where summit talks were held. It resulted in signing of four important agreements in the field of research in agriculture, transportation and expansion of cultural and scientific exchanges between America and Russia. Following Watergate Scandal, President Nixon resigned and the new President Ford did not envisage new changes in the foreign policy and concluded an agreement with Brezhnev for limiting strategic offensive weapons for the next ten years. The two superpowers also signed an agreement on Joint Participation in Apollo-Soyuz Mission in July 1975. In 1971, Henry Kissinger, the US Secretary of State paid a secret visit to China and the Cold War between China and USA virtually came to an end with the exchange of ambassadors in January 1979. The détente between USA and USSR did not automatically lead to mitigation of all strains of Cold War. The USA favoured armed build up in Iran to counteract the growing influence of Russia in Middle East. The USA moved to convert Diego Gracia into military base and the Soviet Union submitted proposals for Asian Collective Security to replace the American sphere of influence in South-East Asia as well to contain China. During the Bangladesh crisis of 1971 and Egypt-Israel war of 1973, also the two superpowers extended support to opposite side.[5]

**Seventh Phase—SALT-II (1979 onwards)**

Certain events of 1978 and 1979—resulted in a decline in the process of détente and the two states are moving into a post-détente era perhaps best termed as Cold War or New Cold War. In June 1979, President Carter and President Brezhnev signed SALT-II limiting the expansion of the nuclear weapons till December 1985. But the US senate refused to ratify the treaty owing to Soviet military intervention in Afghanistan in late 1979. The Soviet "adventurism" in Africa (Ethiopia), the presence of Soviet military forces in Cuba were seen by US administration with suspicion. In addition, the Carter administration spearheaded a global campaign in favour of human rights that annoyed the Soviet leaders and gave them cause to question American intentions. In short, the Russian intervention in Afghan crisis added a new dimension to the process of détente and reactivated the forces of Cold War.

## THE NEW COLD WAR

The origin of the new Cold War is generally traced back to December 1979 when Soviet Union intervened in Afghanistan. There was a widespread apprehension in the mind of America that Soviet intervention might spread in the vulnerable countries neighbouring Afghanistan like Pakistan, Iran and might tried to bring the West Asian countries under its sphere of influence. This development gave a rude shock to the process of détente. In turn, the USA made an axis with China and Pakistan in this region to contain the influence of the Soviet Union. The Soviet Union's actions and interventions succeeded in the second half of 1970s in Vietnam (1975), Angola (1976), Ethiopia (1977) and Afghanistan (1979). The fall of the Shah of Iran in early 1979 was a terrible blow to the USA. For long Shah of Iran was the main pillar of USA foreign policy in this area. In Saudi Arabia there was a mini revolt.[6] There was military encounter between South Yemen aided by Moscow, and North Yemen helped by Saudi Arabia and USA. It has been argued that with the change in administration in USA and assumption of office by Hawkish Brezezinski as the National Security Adviser, the attitude of USA towards Soviet Union underwent a change. Brezezinski criticized Nixon as well as Kissinger for overselling détente. He emphasized the need of paying more attention to Sino-American relationship and great American interest in the Eastern Europe.

## BASIS OF DÉTENTE

A process of détente between the two major powers started in 1959 when Khrushchev advocated the policy of peaceful co-existence. In pursuance of this policy he visited Washington and met President Eisenhowver. He also addressed the General Assembly of the United Nations and proposed that within four years all the states should completely disarm themselves. Another important step in the direction of easing the Cold War was the three power partial nuclear Test Ban Treaty formally signed on 5 August 1963. This treaty provided for a limited ban on all nuclear tests in the atmosphere including territorial waters on high seas. On the recommendations of the General Assembly the United States, Soviet Union and Great Britain adopted the Nuclear Non-Proliferation Treaty. Under this treaty the nuclear powers agreed not to transfer their nuclear weapons or control over them to any non-nuclear power or to provide assistance in producing those weapons.

In 1972 President Nixon of USA visited Moscow and signed two agreements. These agreements included the Treaty on the Limitation of Anti-Ballistic Missile System and the Interim[7] Agreement or Certain Measures with respect to the Limitation of Strategic offensive Arms. The former treaty limited the United States and the Soviet Union to two sites for ballistic missiles defences, one to protect their national capital areas and the other to protect the field of ICBMs. The second agreement covered both the land-based ICBMs and submarine launched ballistic missiles. Both the treaties went a long way in reducing the tension between the two superpowers.

## THE END OF DÉTENTE

US President Jimmy Carter tried to move beyond the setbacks for peace and place another cap on the arms race with a SALT-II agreement in 1979, but his efforts were undercut by three surprising developments: the Islamic Revolution in Iran, the Nicaraguan Revolution, and Soviet intervention in Afghanistan.

The Iranian Revolution was an embarrassment for the United States and Carter's inability to get American hostages freed cost him the 1980 election. While the United States was mired in recession and the Vietnam quagmire, pro-Soviet governments were making great strides abroad, especially in the Third World. Communist Vietnam had defeated the United

States, becoming a united state under a Communist government. Other Communist insurgencies were spreading rapidly across Africa, South-east Asia, and Latin America.

And the Soviet Union seemed committed to the Brezhnev Doctrine, sending troops to Afghanistan at the request of its Communist government. The Afghan invasion in 1979 marked the first time that the Soviet Union sent troops outside the Warsaw Pact since the inception of the Eastern counterpart of the North Atlantic Treaty Organization (NATO). This prompted a swift reaction from the west, the boycotting of the 1980 Summer Olympics in Moscow, and the heavy funding for the Afghani resistance fighters.

Worried by Soviet deployment of nuclear SS-20 missiles (commenced in 1977), the NATO allies had in 1979 agreed to continued Strategic Arms Limitation Talks to constrain the number of nuclear missiles for battlefield targets, threatening to deploy some 500 cruise missiles and *Pershing II* missiles in West Germany and the Netherlands in case the negotiations were unsuccessful. The negotiations, taken up in Geneva, November 30, 1981, were bound to fail. In the countries in question, the planned deployment of *Pershing II* met intense opposition from the public opinion in a divisive debate. *Pershing II* missiles were deployed in Europe from January 1984. They were, however, soon withdrawn beginning in October 1988. The shooting down by Soviet fighters of civilian airliner Korean Air Flight 7 also increased tensions.

The "new conservatives" or "neo-conservatives" rebelled against the Democratic Party's leftward drift on defense issues in the 1970s, especially after the nomination of George McGovern in 1972, saying Liberal Democrats were the cause for US international setbacks. Many clustered around Senator Henry "Scoop" Jackson, a Democrat, but then they aligned themselves with Ronald Reagan and the Republicans, who promised to confront charges of Soviet expansionism.

## THE END OF THE COLD WAR

The Cold War, which dominated international relations for over four decades after World War II and was characterized by subtle military and political strategies of the superpower, a ruinous race for destructive armaments and establishment of military base on distant lands and across the seas, came to an end rather abruptly. This was accompanied by the lifting of the Iron Curtain, breach in the fortress of apartheid and demolition of the Berlin Wall. The process of end of Cold War started in the second half of the 1980s when there was softening in the attitude of the top leaders and they adopted conciliatory postures towards each other.

The first concrete manifestation of this change was the Malta Summit between President Bush of United States and Mikhail Gorbachev of Soviet Union. In this summit, held abroad ships off Malta on 2 December 1989, the two leaders made a serious bid to reduce tension and check the growing threats of conflicts in various areas like Middle East. It has rightly been asserted that the Malta Summit marked the beginning of new phase in the post-World War II international politics. It also laid the foundation of political co-operation between United States and Soviet Union in shaping the post-war order in Europe.

The Washington Summit (May 30-June 2, 1990) further contributed to the reduction of Cold War. At this summit President Bush and President Gorbachev concluded a number of agreements on nuclear, chemical and conventional arms. The two sides agreed to destroy thousand of tons of chemical weapons and reduce their stockpiles. They agreed to cease further production of these weapons in 1992 and finish it by 2002 A.D. They also agreed to cease further production of these weapons with immediate effect. Another important outcome of this summit was that the two leaders agreed on set of principles regarding the Strategic Arms Reduction Treaty (START) which was signed on 31 July 1991. Under this treaty the two superpowers agreed to effect reduction to equal levels in defined strategic offensive arms over a period of seven years from the date of treaty came into force.

The two powers also agreed to set up a joint commission on certification and inspection. This was followed by announcement of 'unilateral disarmament' by President Bush. Even indicated his intention to take nuclear tactical weapons out of European soil and reduce possibility of any accidental war. President Bush removed from alert status all missiles covered by START and ordered removal of all nuclear artillery shells from overseas based. He urged Soviet Union to match the nuclear arms cut. The Soviet leadership responded favourably and on 5 October 1991 President Gorbachev announced extensive cuts in tactical nuclear weapons, which not only matched American reduction of tactical weapons, but also announced cut of more missiles than it was required under START. Further Soviet Union also announced one-year moratorium on nuclear testing.

This process of unilateral cut of arms was repeated by President Bush in January 1992, and President Yeltsin of Russia responded equally and announced a 10-point disarmament with the objective of liquidating all nuclear, biological and chemical weapons of mass destruction. He also announced the decision to stop production of Tu-160, Tu-95 heavy members and long range air-based and sea-based cruise missiles. All this contributed the easing of Cold War.

In the meanwhile, the leaders of North Atlantic Treaty Organization (NATO) and the Warsaw Pact held a Conference on Security and Cooperation in Europe (CSCE) in Paris in November 1990 with a view to eliminate the threat of surprise attack and establish party of conventional weapons in Europe. The treaty provided for scrapping or conversion of about 40,000 tanks and equal number of armoured vehicles as well as more than 50,000 artillery pieces on both sides. It was also decided to reduce the number of fighting planes and helicopter gunships. In the wake of the above development the leaders of Warsaw Pact countries decided to dissolve the Eastern European Defence Alliance in July 1991. This put an end to East-West confrontation.

## FACTORS CONTRIBUTING TO END OF COLD WAR

A number of factors contributed to the end of the Cold War. Some of the important factors were as under:

- The changed strategic perception of the two superpowers —the United States and Soviet Union greatly contributed to the end of Cold War. As the two superpowers attained parity in nuclear weapons, they realized the nuclear weapons would be suicidal for both. None of them would be able to win the war, while both would be ruined beyond redemption.

- The enormous expenses being incurred on the maintenance of military based across the seas, was greatly straining the economy of United States and it was though desirable to curb this futile expenditure, particularly in view of the fact that the maintenance of military bases provided only nominal gains.
- The two superpowers came to realize that the regional conflicts and proxy wars (as in Vietnam, Angola and Afghanistan) has served no useful purpose. On the other hand, these wars had caused serious financial burdens on the two superpowers. This economic strain, in turn had led to deterioration of the economy of the two countries. This resulted in record trade and budget deficits in United States. Likewise, the military commitments in lands situated far away had upset the Soviet economy. All this obliged the leaders of two superpowers to climb down from the earlier rigid postures and reduce military expenditure.

## CONNOTATIONS OF COLD WAR

- The Cold War has far accomplishment implications in the international affairs.
- A large number of nations of Asia, Africa and Latin America after attainment of independence decided to keep away from the military alliances sponsored and supported by two superpowers.
- Cold War rendered the UN ineffective because both the superpowers tried to oppose the actions proposed by the opponent.
- Cold War led to the formation of various alliances during the peace times. Both the blocs formed alliances and counter alliances to counterbalance the growing power of the opponent for example—NATO, SEATO, CENTO, Warshaw Pact, etc. The existence of these alliances added to world tension.

- In the first place, it gave rise to a fear psychosis which resulted manufacture of sophisticated armaments.
- Cold War greatly undermined the chances of attaining the goal of one World.

## IMPACT OF COLD WAR

Cold War has resulted in mad race for armaments. States of both the blocs spent huge amounts to equip themselves with the latest weapons. This led to diversion of money which could have more profitably been utilized for improving the lot of the people. It also led to both the camps being armed to the teeth. Any local quarrel or misunderstanding could lead to a nuclear war.

Cold War and the consequent competition among great powers resulted in more freedom of action for the small and middle powers. Each group tried to win them over. The influence which the Afro-Asian countries are able to exert in the UN is well-known.

Cold War has given rise to permanent types of alliances which are concluded much in advance of war. NATO, SEATO, CENTO and the Warsaw Pact were all formed in the wake of Cold War. This alignment system covers most countries of the world.

Cold War has led to alignment system even during the peace times and constant efforts are made to strengthen them. However, in recent times there is a general tendency on the part of the newly independent states of Asia and Africa to avoid alignment with either of the two groups.

Cold War has stood in the way of achieving the objective of one world. The mutual rivalry has reduced the UNO to the status of a simple forum of world opinion.

Cold War has prevented some of the states from becoming members of the world body. The denial of representation to People's China in the security council for such a long time was mainly due to this Cold War.

Cold War adversely affected the economic development of the country diverting human labour and resources to the manufacture of destructive weapons.

## ORIGIN OF NEW COLD WAR

The origin of the new Cold War was traced back to December 1979 when Soviet Union intervened in Afghanistan. Cold War between Soviet Union and United States of America, which characterized their relations in the fifties, and somewhat subsided in the sixties and the seventies again hotted up towards the close of the 1970s. However, some scholars have tried to trace it from 1978. On the other hand, the Soviet view tends to blame the United States for the new Cold War. It has been argued that with the change in administration in USA and assumption of office by Hawkish Brezezinski and National Security Assistant, the US attitude towards Soviet Union underwent a change. Brezezinski did not share Kissinger's view that the only alternative to détente was war and criticized Nixon as well as Kissinger for overselling détente. He asserted that required responsible behaviour on the part of the Soviet Union. But its conduct in Angola, the Middle East and the United Nations certainly indicated that it was not so. He emphasized the need for paying more attention to Sino-American relationship and greater American interest in the Eastern Europe. He favoured a carefully calibrated policy of simultaneous competitions and co-operation which could promote reciprocal détente. This naturally evoked strong Soviet reaction and the fragile détente was shattered. Thus, they blame Carter for initiating the new Cold War by linking the Soviet behaviour with SALT process.

## DEVELOPMENT OF NEW COLD WAR

America followed a policy of détente towards Soviet Union because it desperately needed SALT to offset the loss of face in Vietnam. Further, this could help in maintaining the status quo, which was in favour of USA by acknowledging the Soviet parity in nuclear strategic capability so did not offset the global balance of power. In the mid-seventies, the Americans saw a number of laws in the position of Soviet Union, viz. the Sino-Soviet conflict, moving of Egypt under Sadat away from Soviet Union; the presence of King of Saudi Arabia and Shah of Iran as important factors contributing to the influence of USA in the area; elimination of Allande of Chile; Technological superiority of US nuclear arsenals. All this went well with national interest of USA and encouraged them to maintain status quo in the international system.

However, the development in the second half of the seventies went against the American interests. In Africa, the Americans suffered a setback when the Cubans were invited to Angola following the CIA and South African intervention with a view to protect them from the South Africa racist regime. In 1976-77, the Shah of Iran and Saudi Arabia tried to wean away Sardar Daud of Afghanistan from Soviet Union, which led to Saur revolution and subsequent Soviet intervention in Afghanistan. In Aden as a result of a coup Rubayya Ali was eliminated, and the Soviet influence increased. Similarly, the switch over the Soviet support from Somalia to Ethiopia in the Horn of Africa, helped the Soviet Union to increase its influence in Ethiopia. In view of all these developments, the attitude of USA towards Soviet Union underwent a change.

President Carter adopted more assertive policy to restore USA's international position. On the one hand, he tried to project himself as the champion of human rights campaign and wrote a personal letter to Anderi Sakharov, the leading Soviet dissident, and received Vladmir Bukovsky, another Soviet dissident. No doubt the Carter administration also criticized the leaders of South Africa, Latin American dictators and South Korea for denial of human rights, but by and large this criticism was directed against Soviet Union. Secondly, in mid-1977 Carter took decision to produce and deploy air launched cruise missile which contributed to the escalations of arms race, in 1978 USA's attitude towards Soviet Union began to get tougher. Brezezinski paid a visit to China and made a bid to involve her in various joint actions. This was seen by the Russian as an alliance aimed against them.

The normalization of USA's diplomatic relations with China was seen by Moscow as a intended move directed against it. No doubt in 1979 Carter and Brezhnev signed SALT-II treaty at Vietnam but Carter began to have doubts about it before he reached Washington. At this juncture USA discovered the presence of Soviet brigade in Cuba and demanded its withdrawal before SALT-II was ratified. As Soviet Union did not comply with this demand, the SALT-II was withdrawn by USA. It also boycotted Olympic Games in Moscow in 1980 and imposed a grain embargo on Soviet Union.

In the meanwhile, the Shah of Iran was overthrown in 1979. This imparted new urgency to the American plan for Rapid Deployment Force, which was already under consideration. American also made a bid to secure base facilities in Kenya, Somalia and Oman to protect the American interest in the Indian Ocean and Persian Gulf Region. This naturally raised suspicions in the minds of Russia that America was trying to establish its hegemony over Persian Gulf.

Towards the close of 1979, NATO took a decision to deploy American made cruise missiles and the advanced medium range Pershing II missile in West Europe from 1983. The NATO powers claimed that they took this decision to counter the threat posed by the Soviet deployment of a powerful new medium range missile SS-20, targeted in Western Europe. In its part Russia argued that it was obliged to deploy SS-20 Missile to counter the employment of British submarine based in Britain, etc. It is indeed difficult to say as to who is to blame for this East-West race, but it cannot be denied that as result of these decision the tensions between the two power blocs greatly increased.

In the midst of these developments, the decision by Soviet Union to invade Afghanistan in December 1979 further aggravated the situation. Soviet probably intervened in Afghanistan hoping that the intervention would be short and soon it would be able to withdraw. However, the things proved quite difficult. The Carter Administration with the help of the Chinese and through CIA arranged secret supply of Arms to Afghan rebels to pressurise Russia to negotiate. But as the Russians were not willing to withdraw from Afghanistan until the Americans assured that they would not interfere in Afghanistan Reagan Administration also extended greater help to the rebels.

On the other hand, in El Salvador (in Central America) where America intervened, the Soviets, Cubans, East Germans,

Nicaraguans, Vietnamese, Czechs, Bulgarians, Ethiopians and several others were accused of involvement in the clandestine supply of arms to insurgents and imparting them training in territories tactics, with a view to ultimately impose a Marxist Leninists dictatorship. US administration under Reagan tried to project the El Salvador issue as in international confrontation between West and Soviet Union, and tied to rope in Europe and Japan on its side in this struggle, though it did not completely succeed in this mission.

Apart from the above events around which tension grew between the two superpowers certain other events took place which aggravated the Cold War between the two. These included non-participation of USA and Soviet Union in the Olympic Games held at Moscow and Los Angels respectively in 1980 and 1984; shooting down of the South Korean Boeing 747 airliner by the Soviet fighters. In the field of disarmament also the two countries failed to reach any agreement. In 1983, the Soviet delegation withdraw from the bilateral arms talks with USA after the Cruise and Pershing II missiles were deployed in the three West European States—Federal Republic of Germany, Italy, and United Kingdom in December 1983.

### DIFFERENCES BETWEEN NEW AND OLD COLD WARS

The new Cold War differed from the Cold War of the 1950's in many respects:

- In the first place, unlike the Cold War of 1950's, in the new Cold War alliance partners were not actively involved. For example, China, Japan and even Western European countries were quite lukewarm in their support and the war persisted mainly between the two superpowers.
- Secondly, in the earlier Cold War nuclear armament build up was not an issue and the main stress was on quantitative build-up of conventional arms. This way largely due to the fact the United States of America was much ahead of Soviet Union in nuclear armament and technology.
- Thirdly, the new Cold War was more threatening than the Cold War of 1950s. The sheer quantity of nuclear

devices, the complexity of their new technology and the fallible sophistication of the early warning methods of detection; also increase the possibility of eventual use, by accident or design.

- Fourthly, the first Cold War was the result of struggle for world leadership whereas the second Cold War was based on the question of parity of its erosion in the relation between two superpowers.
- Finally, unlike the first Cold War, which greatly centred around ideology, the second Cold War centred around the arms race because the weapons technologies had advanced so much that they can easily be converted into deployable weapons.

## IMPACT OF NEW COLD WAR ON WORLD POLITICS

- The new Cold War left a deep impact on the international politics. Unlike the first Cold War in which the European colonial powers were actively involved and dealt with former colonies, in the new Cold War USA tended to deal with the former colonies directly. Generally, the United States sides with the reactionary regimes in the developing words with a view to maintain status quo. This has encouraged the Marxist leaders in these counters to lean more heavily on the Soviet Union. In this respect, the attitude of USA in the developing countries has contributed to the spread or Marxism in the developing world.
- The new Cold War gave a fresh impetus to the non-aligned movement and more and more countries joined it.
- Some of the countries of the Third World extended facilities to the two superpowers regarding stationing military personnel to maintain and service the sophisticated weapons and equipments, but these states showed greater inclination to maintain their autonomy. As a result more and more countries joined the non-aligned movement with a view to have greater maneuverability in their foreign policy between the two superpowers.

- The new Cold War was characterized by high-technology arms race and increasing intervention and pressure on the developing world, increased the chances of the two superpowers engaging in proxy wars in the developing world rather than having a direct confrontation.
- The new Cold War also greatly contributed to the economic difficulties of the superpower and adversely affected the international economy. The high defence spending resulted in high interest rates which in turn has brought in numerous economic, technological and political power by increasing its military power.

We can say that the new Cold War left deep impact on all the countries—developed as well as developing. In case of developing countries it adversely affected the social and political development. This in turn produced political instability and enhanced chances of superpower intervention in their affairs.

## NATURE OF THE POST-COLD WAR GLOBAL ORDER

- With the end of Cold War the security environment are likely to undergo changes. The conflicts henceforth are not likely to be of global dimension due to decoupling from the earlier superpower linkage. The conflicts are likely to have higher local and ethnic content which may involve higher levels of violence and may be more difficult to resolve. Thus, Afghanistan and Cambodian problems still continue to elude a solution.
- The enormous savings in military expenditure, would help in diverting these funds to development activities in the lesser developed regions of the world and would greatly contribute to the world peace.
- The reconciliation between USA and USSR would facilitate amicable settlement of long-standing disputes in Vietnam, Cambodia and Korea.
- End of Cold War is also bound to have far-reaching impact on the foreign policy of India, and she would be obliged to make several adjustment in her foreign policy to meet the changed conditions.

- It is bound to affect Russia's policy towards the Third World. On account of the bad economic conditions and disintegration of Soviet Union, there is greater possibility of Moscow developing close relations with the prosperous Western countries and she may not be able to make some economic-cum-military gestures towards countries of the Third World.
- The end of Cold War is bound to have far-reaching impact on the future course of international relations.
- It would necessitate a new look on the role of Non-Aligned Movement. As A.P. Venkateswaram, former Foreign Secretary of India observed: "The new alignments sin the international system call for a reappraisals of the movement that once served a valuable purpose of reinforcing the independence of the third world countries and enable them to take decision of merit."
- The end of Cold War is also bound to bring about far-reaching changes in US-Pakistan relations. In the changed context the United States no longer need China as second front or Pakistan, and indirectly contribute to better relations between India and USA.
- End of Cold War is bound to provide a new trust to Indo-Pakistan relations. As the two countries shall not be able to play USA and Russia against each other to promote their interests on account of the understanding reached between Russia and USA, they shall have to conduct their relations on realistic plane.
- It would lead to the emergence of a kind of world which shall be free from military alliances and adversaries. This would in turn curb the armament race because neither of the alliance would be facing any military or political threat. In the changed context, there would be no justification for building stocks of various type of weapons.

## THE CHALLENGE OF MULTIPOLARITY

The character of new multipolar structure may be different from the stability that has characterized the unipolar and bipolar phases of international politics. In part this is because the emergence of a number of comparatively politics equal great powers will introduce more complexity and uncertainty about allegiances and alignment. This may also be the case because international security issues will exhibit themselves in all their variety once again issues of material, resources, technology, ethnic animosities, political philosophy, and different conceptions of world order as well as armies and nuclear weapons. The multipolar global agenda will encompass continuing concerns about the great-powers' economic relations—the focus of liberal international relations theory.[8]

Many theorists point out the dangers inherent in multipolar distribution of power. The historical record, which suggests that if we look to the past of anticipate the future, inspires their warnings, we have many reasons to fear the re-emergence of this kind of system. Today's hopes for great-power co-operation in the new millennium have many precedents. The end of every previous great-power war was followed by an initial hopeful burst of collaborative institution building to forge a stable new order among the victorious powers. But each of these great-power design, constructed at the conclusion of a multipolar periods' war, ultimately proved temporary when the post-war sense of urgency faded. Precedents include the peace of Westphalia (1648), the Treaty of Utrecht (1713), the concept or Europe (1815), the League of Nations (1919) and the United Nations (1945). In each case, as the great-powers relative strength changed, collaboration gave way to competition. Sooner or later, every previous multipolar system collapsed, as one or more of the major power expressed dissatisfaction with the existing hierarchy, rejected the rules by which they had agreed to manage their relations, and attempted to overturn the status quo by force. Rivalry has routinely resulted in a hegemonic struggle for supremacy ending in a new catastrophic general war each more destructive than the last.

The diffusion of wealth predicts the likely intensification of great-power political competitions. Throughout history, changes in comparative economic advantage have preceded political competition. When multipolarity has existed, economic rivals have struggled to protect their wealth and have competed politically for economic position, with military conflict usually following.

A "new Cold War" could emerge between any pair of great powers such as the United States and China, if their competition escalates. However, this kind of armed rivalry need not develop co-operation could increase instead. Quite different and inconsistent political types of great-power relations could emerge in the economic and military spheres. The probability of economic rivalry and conflict is generally high, whereas the likelihood of security co-operation for many of these same relationships is also high. For example, the United States, Japan, and China exhibit conflict in their commercial relations but have shown a capacity to manage their security relations collaboratively.

Few observers see advantages resulting from the emerging situation. As former US Secretary of State, Henry A. Kissinger proposes in 1993 a serious challenge because "the United States have very little experience with a world that consists of many power and which it can neither dominate nor from which it can simply withdraw in isolation".

Yet we have no way to knowing whether the future will resemble the gloomy past history of multipolar systems. Patterns and practices can change, and it is possible for policymakers to learn from previous mistakes and avoid repeating them.

## RESPONDING TO MULTIPOLARITY'S CHALLENGES

What, then, can the great powers do to prevent the resumption of their rivalry? What security policies should they pursue in order to avoid the dangers of shared power and rapid translation in their position and strength in the great-power hierarchy.

The answers are highly uncertain, the methods of guaranteeing international security in Washington, Moscow, Berlin, Beijing, and Tokyo today revolve around four basic options. Each is actively under consideration, and each will become more or less practical, prudent, or problematic for each great-power depending of the circumstances that materialize in tomorrow's multipolar world.

A unilateral conception of a great-power's role represents one possible option. Acting alone is especially attractive for a self-confident great-power assured of its independent strength. With sufficient power, a potential hegemony can be self-reliant. Unilateralism can involve isolationism, an attempt to exert hegemonic leadership, or an effort to play the role of a 'balancer' who skillfully backs one side or another in a greater power dispute, but only when necessary to maintain a military equilibrium between the disputants. Unilateralism can also invite the world leader to play the role of international bully, acting in the absence of limits put to it by other as if it has a blank check to run the world. Or unilateralism can lead to a power's decision to help itself first, as Japan announced it would in November 1997 by pulling back in leadership, because it did not wish to pay the costs of acting as a locomotive for others.

Cultivation of a specialized relationship with another great-power similar to that between Great Britain and the United States in this century, illustrates a second approach that some pairs of great power might pursuer. The 1997 'Joint Declaration on the Multipolar World and a New World Order' signed in April 1997 between China and Russia suggests the kind of strategic bilateral partnership that can easily develop in a climate of fear in the future as well as the most probable reasons why such alliances may be forged between powers that have suffered from relations in the recent past. Convinced that a dominant United States aimed to contain their influence, and asserting that "no country should claim hegemony for itself or pursue policy from positions of strength the monopolize international affairs".

Moscow and Beijing announced their agreement to build warmer relations by joining in a common cause to counterbalance the United States and Japan in July 1997 to strengthen their specialized defense relationship by working on a common military project. This in turn led China at the October 1997 summit meeting with President Clinton in Shanghai to seek 'common ground despite differences', attempting to realize Chinese-American relations 'to a new level by sharing responsibility for preserving world peace'. Other types of specialized relations between pairs of great-power could follow, at various levels of mutual support and commitment.[9] There are several variants of this strategic option, including informal understanding, co-operations (sometimes termed ententes), and formal alliances concretized by treaties.

A third strategy under considerations is construction of a concert, of a co-operative agreement among the great-powers to manage the international system jointly and to prevent international disputes from escalating to war.[10] The concert of Europe, at its apex between 1815 and 1882, is the epitome of previous great-power efforts to pursue this path to peace.

Finally, some policymakers recommend that today's great-powers unit with the lesser powers in construction a true system of collective security. The principles rationalizing the formation of the League of Nations in 1919 exemplify this multilateral approach to peace under conditions of multipolarity, as did the December 1997 pledge by Russia and NATO to co-operate in building a twenty-first century security partnership.

Whichever combination of approaches predominates in the strategies forged to prevent great-power rivalries from escalating to war in multipolar future, the ultimate outcome will not depend on the great-powers alone. The policy response of other, less powerful actors is likely to be increasingly important in shaping world politics, and their role must also be examined.[11]

## NOTES

1. A.B. Sawant, "Recent Changes in Egypt's Foreign Policy", *India Quarterly* (New Delhi), Vol. 35, No. 1, January-March 1979, pp. 20-41.
2. M.S. Agwani, "West Asia: Humiliation Far from Home", *World Focus* (New Delhi), Vol. 6, No. 1, January 1985, pp. 29-32.
3. Richard D. Challener, ed., *From Isolation to Containment 1921-1952* (London, 1970), pp. 147-51.
4. Baral, n. 6, p. 33.
5. Jaya Krishna Baral, "US Involvement in Vietnam: From Cold War to 1960", *China Report* (New Delhi), Vol. 12, No. 3, May-June 1976, pp. 28-34.

6. Noam Chomsky, *Towards a New Cold War: Essays on the Current Crisis and How We Got There* (New York 1982), pp. 6-7.
7. Senator Gravel, ed., The Pentagon Papers: The Defence Department History of United States Decision Making on Vietnam (Boston, 1971), pp. 375-81: US House of Representatives, Congress 92, Session 1, Committee on Armed Services, United States-Vietnam Relations (prepared by the Department of Defence, Washington, 1971), Vols. 7-8, Book 1, Part 2, p. A-7.
8. A.B. Sawant, "Recent Changes in Egypt's Foreign Policy", *India Quarterly* (New Delhi), Vol. 35, No. 1, January-March 1979, pp. 20-41.
9. Theodore A. Couloumbis and James H. Wolfe, *Introduction to International Relations: Power and Justice* (New Delhi, 1986) 3rd edn., p. 6.
10. James N. Rosenau, ed., *International Politics and Foreign Policy* (New York: Free Press, 1969), 2nd edn. rev Theodore A. Couloumbis and James H. Wolfe, *Introduction to International Relations: Power and Justice* (New Delhi, 1986) 3rd edn., p. 25.
11. Mahendra Kumar, *Theoretical Aspects of International Politics* (Agra, 1972), 2nd revised edn., p. 87.

# Determinants of Foreign Policy

# 8

## STUFFING OF A FOREIGN POLICY

The foreign policy of a nation involves:

- the assessment of the gains and losses of the nation in respect of its goals of national interest
- the attempts to maintain continuity or change in relations as the case may be
- the analysis of the external and internal milieu under the influence of which the foreign policy of a nation is formulated, stated and operationalised
- the set of general principles adopted and followed by a nation (policymakers in reality) in international relations
- delimitation of the goals of national interest which are to be attained
- the means that are to be used for achieving the goals of national interest
- the guidelines or broad policy principles and decisions for conducting relations with other nations.

## RELATION BETWEEN FOREIGN POLICY AND NATIONAL INTEREST

**Deep Relation between Foreign Policy and National Interest:** The relation between foreign policy and national interest is indeed very deep. National interest is the key factor of foreign policy. Foreign policy acts for securing the goals of national interest. But at the same time, it is foreign policy which selects, formulates or concretises and defines the goals of national interest and then attempts to secure these goals. If national interest is a determining element of foreign policy, foreign policy is the director of national interest. National interest is characterized by ambiguity and vagueness and it is foreign policy that sorts out and defines the real nature of national interest of a nation and formulates concrete goals which are to be attained in foreign relations. Thus, both foreign policy and national interest are intimately related. National interest is the objective of foreign policy and foreign policy is the formulator of national interest.

**National Interest is the Basis of Foreign Policy**: The exact role of national interest in the formulation of a foreign policy is an object of great debate among scholars. One set of scholars advocates that foreign policy is and should always be based upon national interest.[1]

A former US Secretary of States Mr. Hughes once observed, "Foreign policies are not abstractions but the results of practical concepts of national interest." Morgenthau also holds that foreign policy always "seeks to defend national interest". Its purpose is: "To defend the national interest restrictively and rationally defined against the national interests of other nations which may or may not be thus defined." While formulating foreign policy, the decision-makers of a nation are always guided by the demands of national interest. "National leaders, as a rule, never pursue national policies that are in the interest of any nation other than their own." Analysing the process of foreign policy decision-making, D. Duchacek remarks, "in planning, formulating, adopting and executing foreign policy, national leaders and their aides are confronted with a veritable spider's web of conflicting claims and values. Yet, priorities, that is, the practical and not the ideal content of national interest, must finally be established in terms of preferred goals and in relation to power of one's own nation and that of other nations. Both national goals and national means must simultaneously be related to dangers or opportunities on the international scene; not only other nation's power but also their intentions must be properly evaluated".[2] Thus, national interest is the basis for the formulation of foreign policy.

**Foreign Policy as the Director of National Interest:** The other set of scholars, however, does not accept such a logic and is of the view that it is not always possible to base the foreign policy only on the national interest of a state. National interests of the state are general and vague. These lack clarity. For example, security is regarded as the primary interest of a state and yet no member of the government can precisely define the nature of security that is actually required by the state. National interests cannot be precisely identified and concretised. These have to be related to the values of the people as well as to the interests of other nations. Hence, national interest alone cannot be accepted as the basis of foreign policy. In actual practice, we find that very often the leaders of the state try to give priority to their selfish interests in domestic policies over the national interests of the state. They sometimes construct national interests in such a way as to make their way of ruling the state easier. Pakistani rulers have very often, rather always, used Pakistani interests in Kashmir as a means for securing their positions in domestic politics.

## DIPLOMACY AND FOREIGN POLICY

Diplomacy and foreign policy are two vitally important instruments of a nation's behaviour in international relations. International politics is the process of interactions among the foreign policies of various nations and diplomatic activity, particularly diplomatic negotiations, form the core of these interactions. Foreign policy and diplomacy have been rightly described by Dr. Mohinder Kumar as the two wheels of international relations. Diplomacy and foreign policy are so intimately related that in common usage, these are very often used as synonyms. The statement that British diplomacy in Middle East lacks vigour equates diplomacy with foreign policy. Diplomacy always works to secure the goals of national interest as defined by foreign policy and the latter gets operationalised mainly through diplomacy. The one exists for the other. However, to say that there is no difference between diplomacy and foreign policy is not an acceptable proposition in international politics. Diplomacy and foreign policy are greatly related but are different concepts. Foreign policy of a nation travels to other nations on the wheels of diplomacy. Whereas foreign policy is the plan and the programme formulated for securing the goals of national interest of the nation it presents, Diplomacy is the means and the tactics employed for implementing the foreign policy. It is the substance of foreign relations. Diplomacy is the process by which foreign policy is implemented abroad. In the words of J.R. Childs, "Foreign Policy is the substance of foreign relations, whereas diplomacy is the proper process by which policy is carried out." Policy is made by many different persons and agencies. Diplomacy provides the machinery and the personnel by which foreign policy is executed. One is the substance, the other is the method. "Diplomats do not determine the principles of their government's foreign policy but with their reports they render important help in policy formulation. During the course of the determination of foreign policy, the reports of the diplomats are always taken as raw-material."

**Views of Harold Nicholson**

While analysing the distinction between foreign policy and diplomacy, Harold Nicholson observes, "Both are concerned with adjustment of national interest. Both aim at the planned achievement of national interest. Foreign Policy is based upon a general conception of national requirements. Diplomacy, on the other hand, is not an end but a means; not a purpose but a method. It seeks, by the use of reason, conciliation and the exchange of interests, to prevent major conflicts arising between sovereign states. It is the agency through which foreign policy seeks to attain its purpose by agreement rather than by war. Thus, when agreement becomes impossible, diplomacy, which is the instrument of peace, becomes inoperative; and foreign policy, the final sanction of which is war, alone, becomes operative." While disagreeing with Nicholson's thesis that diplomacy ends when war breaks out, we do accept his overall view of the relation between foreign policy and diplomacy.

**Views of Sir Victor Wellsely**

Sir Victor Wellsely has beautifully analyzed the relations between foreign policy and diplomacy by observing: "Diplomacy is not foreign policy, but is the instrument for implementing it.

Both are supplementary to each other because without one, the other cannot work. Diplomacy has no separate existence apart from foreign policy." It is bound to behave like an aimlessly drifting rudderless ship without being guided and conditioned by foreign policy. Similarly, foreign policy, howsoever well formulated and rational, can become neither operational nor successful without being carried out by diplomacy. "Both together determine executive policy. Foreign policy is strategy, diplomacy is the tactics. Foreign policy is the soul of foreign relations, diplomacy is the activity through which foreign policy is enforced." "In order to have successful relations with other nations, a nation must combine rational foreign policy with subtle diplomacy."

## IDEOLOGICAL AND ANALYTICAL APPROACHES TO FOREIGN POLICY

The analytical approach to the study of foreign policy concentrates upon the study of the elements and objectives of foreign policy and considers them to be the results of a variety of factors, attitudes and circumstances. This approach holds that means, methods, techniques that the foreign policymakers adopt may change, the interests and objectives before them are relatively constant. The foreign policy of a nation is based upon the view and determination of the priority order of various aspects of national interests and international obligations. It is as such based upon national interests which are vital and must be defended at all costs and at all times. The theorising in the field of foreign policy is somewhat recent, yet under the influence of the new emphasis upon the study of politics and international politics, there have come to be developed a number of approaches/theories for the study of foreign policy. Dr. Baljit Singh groups these theories/approaches into two categories:

(i) General Theories;

(ii) Middle Range or Partial Theories.

In the first category, he includes: (a) Analytical; (b) Structural-functional; and (c) Decision-making theories.

The middle range theories, he writes, are more of the nature of analytical tools and include: (i) study of public opinion and related field of mass communication, (ii) official actors such as specific governmental agencies, and (iii) unofficial individuals or groups, often called pressure groups acting in the process. Such a classification is indeed very broad. On the basis of the popularity of various approaches, K.W. Thompson and Roy C. Macridis, however, suggest a discussion of two approaches to foreign policy which have been very popular and are two contending approaches of modern times. These are: (i) The Analytical Approach, and (ii) The Ideological Approach. We also propose to discuss these two approaches to the study of foreign policy.

The non-vital or variable interests are to be adjusted and safeguarded under particular circumstances. The analytical approach, as such emphasises the study of all the elements and factors, domestic as well as foreign, which are the inputs of a foreign policy.

"Analytical Approach holds", as Dr. Baljit Singh writes, "Foreign Policy is a system of activities evolved by nations for influencing and changing the behaviour of other states and for adjusting their own activities to international environment." Foreign policy is not the product of the ideas and ideologies of the policymakers. On the contrary, "it is a complex social process in which: (i) policymakers, (ii) principles of foreign policy, (iii) policy aims, interests and objectives, (iv) power inputs and outputs and (v) the contents of foreign policy, play an interacting and related roles". At the heart of this approach is the view that policy rests upon multiple factors. To understand foreign policy, the students must, therefore, study and analyze all these factors.

As such, this approach seeks to study foreign policy by analyzing inputs, interests, objectives and outputs of foreign policy. It also seeks to analyze the process by which policy-makers process the inputs into output.

### Ideological Approach

The ideological approach holds that foreign policy of a nation is the product of the beliefs and ideological commitments of the leaders and policymakers. Each foreign policy is either for or against various ideologies like, Liberalism, Totalitarianism, Communism, Socialism, etc. As against the analytical approach, the ideological approach seeks to study foreign policy in terms of the prevailing political, social and religious beliefs which are considered to be the determinants of the policies of states *vis-à-vis* other states of the world. In this approach, as Thompson and Macridis write, "Foreign policies are classified as democratic or totalitarian, libertarian or socialist and peace-loving or aggressive." It is with the help of ideological principles and preferences that policymakers give shape and meaning to national interest and the foreign policy that is formulated to secure the national interest. Foreign policy in this approach is considered as the function of the preference or convictions of political leaders who have the responsibility to carry out the programme of the system. This approach, however, offers a limited and over-simplified view of the foreign policy. No one can ignore the importance of ideology as an input of foreign policy, yet no one can accept that foreign policy is wholly determined by ideological beliefs. In the post-war period, the foreign policy of no nation has been faithfully following the professed ideological commitments. The US foreign policy, with professedly strong commitment to liberalism, actively maintained warm, friendly and highly co-operative alliance relationships with dictatorships like Pakistan and many other such countries. The (erstwhile) Soviet Union though a strong champion of communism during its lifetime 1917-91, maintained more friendly and co-operative relations, with non-communist India than with communist China. The end of ideology and the decline of ideology, theorists do not accept the importance of ideological approach to the study of politics. Hence, the ideological approach is definitely a limited approach. No doubt, ideological factors of the foreign policy have to be studied and analyzed by a student of foreign policy, yet ideology cannot be accepted as the approach to the study of foreign policy. The analytical approach, with its emphasis upon the study of all factors and forces of foreign policy, offers a better and more systematic way of studying foreign policy.

## INDIA'S SECURITY NEEDS AND FOREIGN POLICY OBJECTIVES

It is customary to begin a study of Indian foreign policy by discussing its main principles. Undoubtedly, the foreign policy of India came to have its independent character only after the dawn of independence in 1947, yet it must be admitted that India became a quasi-international entity even under the British rule and developed a sort of foreign policy of her own. Several years before her independence, India started participating in international affairs, and the nature of her relations with other nations was a source of influence on her foreign policy in the post-independence period. Hence, it is worthwhile to examine the nature of the Indian participation in international affairs in the pre-independence period.

**Impact of British Ideas on Indian Foreign Policy Decisions:** In the opinion of Charles Heimsath, "No other fact of Independent India's political tradition has the impress of British ideas and institutions stronger than its foreign policy." The very fact that India did not try to reverse or fundamentally change the pre-1947 structure of her external relations tends to prove the worth of this observation. It can also be stated that in its administrative structure for conducting diplomacy, in some of its definitions of the national interest and formulation of policies on some important subjects and in its style of diplomacy, the Government of India as led by Pt. Nehru followed some of the precedents of the British Indian Government. The decision in favour of continued membership of Commonwealth of Nations (Originally British Commonwealth) also reflected the impact of British ideas on Indian foreign policy.

The reason why India could keep up certain pre-independence precedents was that the Britishers had tacitly accepted India as a quasi-independent entity in international politics before 1947, in fact, since 1917.

After the First World War, Indian participation in international politics as a separate but sovereign entity was accepted by the British, of course, largely for strengthening the imperial voice in international relations and partly for giving some place to Indian nationalism. Some limited objectives of

Indian nationalism were pursued by the pre-independence Government of India and those objectives were naturally retained by the Government of Independent India. India's experience in the sphere of international relations of the inter-war period did help independent India to analyze and understand the post-war changes in international relations.

**India's Relations with Imperial Rulers:** The foreign relations of India before 1947 were linked to and governed by the interests of British Empire. The imperial government committed the entire empire to war in 1914 without any formal consultations with the dominions or India. But during the war, because of its own needs and dependence upon the resources of India and other dominions, it started the practice of holding consultations with dominions and India on matters of defence and foreign affairs. India was denied the dominion status but it was linked with other dominions, because of the big Indian contribution to the imperial war efforts. The August 1917 Montague Declaration, accepting the establishment of a responsible government in India as the final objective of the British policy in India, was made to ensure Indian help during the war.

In 1917, Lloyd George's Government agreed to India's participation in the war conferences. The Indian participation in war conferences of 1917 and 1918, did strengthen India's position in relations with the imperial government and, consequently, its participation in international politics increased.

An Indian delegation participated in the Paris Peace Conference and India got original membership of the League of Nations. Thus, India was in a position to achieve a recognized international entity, status and to participate in international relations during the inter-war period. The experience that India gained during this period was utilized by the foreign policy makers of free India.

**Indian Foreign Policy and the Issue of the People of Indian Origin Living in Other Parts of the World:** The issue of status, rights and welfare of the people of Indian origin, living in many other countries of Asia and Africa, which were previously parts of British empire, has been an important issue in the Indian foreign policy since 1947. In the pre-independence period too, the Government of India was actively concerned with this issue. The discrimination against Indians on the grounds of colour and race was being practised by a number of dominions of British empire. The British India Government tried hard to secure assurance from the Imperial Government for checking this discrimination. The Imperial Government, however, failed to provide this assurance. The anti-racialism, anti-apartheid content of Indian foreign policy, as such, had its origin in the pre-independence period.

**India's Economic and Trade Relations before 1947:** A study of pre-independence economic and trade relations of India and Britain and other countries also bears out the existence of quasi-independent character of India in International affairs. In the twenties and thirties of the 20th century, India was in a position to establish economic and trade links with many countries. However, the tilt in favour of the imperial master Britain was distinct. In 1919, British Government agreed to grant fiscal autonomy to India. In 1923, a tariff board was established. In 1924, Steel Industry of India was granted protection. In 1931, India signed the Indo-British Trade Agreement at Ottawa. This agreement provided for preferences in tariff rates for the Indian and British goods entering markets in other countries. In the post-independence period, Indo-British trade relations and India's economic and trade relations with the Commonwealth countries were influenced by the pre-independence economic and trade relations of India with Britain and other countries.

**India and International Organizations (1919 to 1947):** Further, the Indian participation in International Organizations had its beginning in the inter-war period. India signed the Treaty of Versailles and other peace treaties, and became an original member of the League of Nations. India also became a member of the International Labour Organization and the Permanent Court of International Justice. In 1928, Indians started leading delegations to the sessions of the Assembly of the League. India could, however, assert some measure of autonomy only in social, economic and technical matters.

Besides participation in the affairs of the League, India took active part in the organization and deliberations of various International conferences/conventions. Particularly, India played an active role in the drafting of Opium Convention. It could subscribe to the Convention on Traffic in Women and Children and the Slavery Convention. India fully supported and adhered to the means of peaceful settlement of disputes. India was in a position to participate actively in the working of International Labour Organization. India used ILO as a forum for voicing her grievances against economically more powerful states. The Indian leaders and the Congress also never hesitated to criticize the failures of the League. Later on, India participated in the San Francisco Conference 1945 and signed the Charter of the United Nations as an original member. After attaining Independence, India inherited the membership of this world body, while Pakistan had to get its membership afresh.

This participation in International Organizations also stood in good stead to Indian foreign policymakers when they settled down to formulate the foreign policy of free India.

**Indian Foreign Policy and Her Security Needs:** The defence and security policy of India also started taking shape during the pre-independence period. The Government of India and Indian leadership very often differed on the subject of defence policy, yet when the national leaders assumed power in 1947, they preferred to build upon the past rather than try to upset it. The system of having military barriers along the frontiers, the north-west land frontiers and the creation of Indian navy with the responsibility of coastal defence were undertaken. The Indian foreign policy got oriented towards security of India as a vital part of India's national interest. The British practice of looking to Himalayas as the impenetrable barrier was also accepted. This, however, proved to be a costly mistake in the years to come.[3]

In another way, India's role in international relations during the 1919-46 period helped the process of foreign policy making in the era of Independence. The training and experience that many Indians received during this period gave valuable help and support to the leaders of free India in their attempts to formulate her foreign policy. Heimsath has rightly observed, "The training and personality of the Indians in government service before independence set the style and contributed in some measure to the ideals which characterized Indian Foreign Policy after 1947. The British legacy, the continuity of tradition, had the advantage of providing a ready model from which the ideas of the Congress, particularly of its leader, Nehru, of course added, adjusted, re-shaped and amended this legacy and made it to suit and uphold the Indian national interests. Yet we must admit that the British legacy and the relations which India could establish during 1919-47 period, did contribute to the origin and initial course of Indian foreign policy."

The study of the Indian foreign policy depends on study of its bases, i.e. those fundamental principles or ideas which together provided the groundwork to its principles. In other words, the need is to understand the roots that have been the sources of the foreign policy. These are important factors but not as visible as the determinants/components of the foreign policy. For the purpose of our study, we can categorize the bases of Indian foreign policy into three parts: (i) Historical Basis, (ii) Philosophical Basis, (iii) Ideological Basis.

The history of the Indian foreign policy is short but highly active. It was after the establishment of the Indian National Congress as the political party of Indian people that the politicization of the people and formulation of policy orientations had its origin. The Indian nationalist leaders showed great interest in world affairs. As early as 1885, i.e. in its very first session, the Congress deprecated the annexation of upper Burma by the British. In 1892, it objected to the military activity around the natural defence lines of India. The use of India by Britain as a base for political maneuvring or military moves against India's neighbours like Tibet, Afghanistan and Persia was opposed by the Congress. In 1904, it opposed the British involvement in Tibet. "Thus, these were the earliest expressions," as Dr. N.V. Raj Kumar has said, "of India's dislike of getting involved in unnecessary foreign entanglements and favouring a neutral stand on matters that did not concern her."

However, it was after the First World War that Indians, led by Congress, started taking more active and articulated interest in foreign affairs. In 1920, the Congress sent a message of sympathy to the Irish People who were struggling for their independence. It was in 1921 that AICC, in its Delhi meeting, adopted a complete resolution on foreign policy and affirmed India's desire to establish good neighbourly and friendly relations with neighbouring and other states. It criticized the Government of British India for adopting a policy governed by the Imperial Interests of Britain over and above the interests of India. This was the first significant declaration made by the Indian leadership.

**Establishment of Foreign Department of the Indian National Congress:** In Madras Session (in 1927), the Congress passed a resolution against the use of Indian troops in China, Mesopotamia and Persia. The Calcutta Congress of 1928 directed the AICC to open a Foreign Department for developing contacts as well as for organizing the anti-imperialist movement of the dependent people. The Congress also sent greetings to the people of Egypt, Syria, Palestine and Iraq who were struggling against Western Imperialism.

Pt. Jawahar Lal Nehru came to head this department and became the director of the foreign policy of the Congress. It was this experience that made him retain and act with precision and efficiency the role of the architect of Independent India's foreign policy.

In 1930, the Congress came out with a thorough condemnation of the aggressive acts of Nazis and Fascists. It warned against the outbreak of an imperialist war and declared that India would not be a party to this war. In 1939, at the Tripura session, the Congress asserted the right of India to have and direct its own foreign policy. It again strongly condemned the forces of Imperialism and Fascism in international politics.

When the Second World War broke out and Britain made India a party to war on its side, the Congress strongly attacked the British policy. Later on, it demanded the recognition of right of India to be a full state on the basis of the letter and spirit of the Atlantic Charter. During 1945-47, the Congress, through a number of declarations, spoke out strongly "for the freedom of all countries and for the elimination of all traces of imperialist control by whatever name it may be called". It welcomed the formulation of the United Nations but expressed its dissatisfaction with the big power domination of its organization. In 1946, the Congress voiced concern and apprehensions regarding the consequences of the Atomic Bomb and of the continued power struggle among the imperialist powers. It further demanded an end to the foreign domination of Asian and African countries. These historic declarations of the Congress were instrumental in providing roots to the anti-cold war, anti-imperialism, anti-racialism, anti-power politics and pro-neutralism, good-neighbourliness and solidarity with Afro-Asian states, principles of Indian foreign policy. The resolutions adopted by the Congress clearly reflected the desires and commitments of the Indian people. The foreign policy of independent India drew its ideas, principles and strength from the declarations and resolutions of the Congress Party.

The study of philosophical basis of Indian foreign policy includes an account of such moral ideals and values of the Indian society which have influenced its nature and content. Indeed, the vast difference in the ideals and values of India from the western values has been responsible, to a significant extent, for the difference that exists between the Indian foreign policy and western foreign policies. Against power politics, war and domination as the western values, India stands for peace, non-violence and peaceful adjustment. India's policy of non-alignment derives strength from these values.

The high importance that the Indians give to the ultimate good of life is different from the 'immediate good life approach' of the western societies. Consequently, love for and faith in world peace and friendship with all are regarded as possible and practical values by India, whereas these are regarded as utopian values by the West. The five principles enunciated by Buddha are written large in the five principles of Panchsheel. Indian foreign policy of peace and the policy of taking independent decisions on the basis of the merits of the individual cases definitely have its basis in the Indian values of peace, non-violence and truth. We, in India, regard non-alignment, anti-imperialism, anti-racialism and anti-war principles as practical, egalitarian and realistic principles because of our faith in human goodness, equality of all men, universal brotherhood of man, unity in diversity, secularism and spirit of sacrifice, accommodation and tolerance. The land of Buddha, Ashoka, Guru Nanak, Akbar, Gandhi has faith in all these values. However, in the West-dominated foreign relations system, India has to accommodate her values along with the western values. Here, also, Kautilya's realism and his Arthashastra comes to our help.

Thus, Indian foreign policy has some of its roots in the Indian philosophy and culture. Like the foreign policy of each nation, the Indian foreign policy, too, has its source of strength in some well established and popular ideologies. In the main, it derives strength both from several general ideologies like Gandhism, Liberalism, Democratic Socialism and Internationalism as well as from several particular ideologies and ideological principles like Peace, Peaceful co-existence, Secularism, Nationalism, Anti-Imperialism and Anti-Racialism.

**Gandhism**: In their struggle for independence, Indians were guided by Mahatma Gandhi. His ideals of *Ahimsa* (Non-Violence), *Satya* (Truth), *Satyagrah* (Fight for Truth), Universal brotherhood, Unity of man and complete faith in peaceful means guided the people of India in this struggle. After independence, these very ideals of Gandhiji influenced the ideas of the policy-makers of India.

Faith in the principles of World Peace, total opposition to Apartheid and a final commitment to peaceful co-existence and peaceful means are some of the major principles of Indian foreign policy. These clearly reflect the influence of Gandhism. The direct approach to peace through such positive devices as mutual respect, mutual socio-economic and cultural co-operation among nations is a valued objective of the Indian foreign policy. The preference for several Marxian ideals minus violence in economic and political institutions and the desire for a peaceful world order which our policymakers are trying to secure also bear an influence of Gandhiji. The followers of Gandhism, as Indian policymakers had been, could not think otherwise.

**Nationalism:** Nationalism, as love and respect for the nation, has been a key characteristic of Indian political thought. It stands for positive attitude of love and sacrifice for the country. It bears no negative or extreme postures. It neither stands for imposition of national interests upon others, nor for Hindu-nationalism, and nor even for racial superiority complex and expansionism. The principle of non-alignment as one of the fundamental, rather the most fundamental principle of the Indian foreign policy, has its roots in such a view of nationalism. Non-alignment stands for the upkeep of freedom of action for securing India's national interest without involving India into power-politics and cold war. This view of nationalism has been a source of the Indian foreign policy.

The political ideals of Indian leaders like Gokhale, Surendra Nath Bannerji and many others were governed by the ideal of Liberal Internationalism—the ideology which stood for love and respect for humanity, faith in universal brotherhood, secularism, self-govornment and opposition to imperialism, colonialism, and to the use of force and domination.

The Indian foreign policy stands for the objective of free and intimate co-operation among the nations. It opposes, tooth and nail, imperialism, colonialism, neo-colonialism, racial discrimination, other unnatural inequalities and war in international relations. The faith in the sovereign equality of states, the right of national self-determination, the right to an independent foreign policy, and a firm commitment to the spirit of the Charter of United Nations is an important and valued feature of the Indian foreign policy. All these principles are based upon the ideology of Liberal Internationalism. The Constitution of India in its Part IV Directive Principles, under Article 51, clearly mirrors India's commitment to Liberal Internationalism. It reads: "To promote International peace and security, to maintain just and honourable relations among nations, to foster respect for international law and treaty obligation in the dealings of organized people with one another, and to encourage settlement of international disputes by arbitration."

Thus, the ideology of Liberal Internationalism has also been a basis of Indian foreign policy. The Indian national leaders were highly influenced by the 1917 Socialist Revolution of Russia and also by the ideology of Marxism upon which this revolution was based. However, along with this, they were influenced by the ideas of Fabian Socialists. Their own love and respect for democracy and the values of Indian culture were influenced by these two ideologies, the result came to be in the form of commitment to Democratic Socialism. The Indian leadership now describes it as the middle path.

This integration of love, both for democratic means and the socialist goals has been a fundamentally important ideological orientation of the Indian people and their leaders. Their policies, including the foreign policy, bear a clear imprint of a faith in Democratic Socialism. In the realm of foreign policy, this has led to the struggle for securing the rights of the Third World, particularly for securing a new international economic order based upon an equitable distribution of resources and wealth among all nations and fairer economic relations between the developed and the developing countries. The Indian commitment to work for friendly and co-operative relations with both the communist and non-communist countries also rests upon commitment to both democracy and socialist objectives. Since early 1990s, India has been following the economic principles of liberalization and globalization and yet the goals continues to be socialistic and means continue to be democratic.

Thus, the ideology of democratic socialism has been a basis of Indian foreign policy. Besides these key ideologies, it also stands influenced by the ideologies of peace, United Nations, self-determination, anti-imperialism, anti-racialism and Secularism. India has always supported the cause of the nations engaged in securing their independences by asserting their right to self-determination. To conclude our discussion on the basis of Indian foreign policy, we can say that it derives strength from the historic declaration of the Indian National Congress, philosophical ideas of its philosophers and a number of other popular ideologies being followed and advocated throughout the length and breadth of India.

## NOTES

1. P. Katzenstein, "Introduction: Domestic and International Forces and Strategies of Foreign Economic Policy" in P. Katzenstein (ed.), *Between Power and Plenty*. Madison: University of Wisconsin Press (1978), p. 56.
2. C. Hermann and G. Peacock (1987), "The Evolution and Future of Theoretical Research in the Comparative Study of Foreign Policy" in C. Hermann, et al. (eds), *New Directions in the Study of Foreign Policy*, Boston: Allen and Unwin.
3. C. Hermann, C. Kegley and J.N. Rosenau (eds), *New Directions in the Study of Foreign Policy*, Boston. Allen and Unwin (1987), p. 76.

# Watershed Development of India's Foreign Policy

9

India's foreign relations reflect a traditional policy of non-alignment the exigencies of domestic economic reform and development, and the changing post-Cold War international environment. India's relations with the world have evolved considerably since the British colonial period (1757-1947), when a foreign power monopolized external relations and defense relations. On independence in 1947, few Indians had experience in making or conducting foreign policy. However, the country's oldest political party, the Indian National Congress (the Congress had established a small foreign department in 1925 to make overseas contacts and to publicize its freedom struggle). From the late 1920s, Jawaharlal Nehru, who had the most long-standing interest in world affairs among independence leaders, formulated the Congress stance on international issues. India's foreign policy, ever since her independence, has been one of building bridges of friendship and co-operation with all countries regardless of the economic and political systems. It has always tried to secure India's national interests as well as to promote international peace and security, to maintain just and honourable relations among nations, and to foster respect for International Law and Treaty obligations. For securing these objectives, the conduct of India's foreign relations has been governed by several clear-cut principles and objectives like: (i) preservation of India's sovereign independence; (ii) pursuance of an independent foreign policy avoiding alignment; (iii) acceptance of the principle of freedom for dependent people and opposition to imperialism, colonialism and racialism; (iv) staunch opposition to the forces of imperialism and hegemony in international relations; (v) co-operation with all peace-loving nations and the United Nations for promoting international peace and prosperity; (vi) reduction of tensions in the international system; (vii) re-fashioning of a more equitable structure of international economic order and co-operation on the basis of justice and fair play; (viii) promotion of the unity and solidarity of the Third World for securing an equitable share in world politics; and (ix) securing a due place in the emerging international order commensurate with her size, population, economic power, participation in UN peace-keeping and the most developed among the developing states. For achieving these objectives, India has been following, since 1947, the path of non-alignment, peaceful co-existence and active involvement in international relations, particularly for protecting and securing the interests of the developing countries of the world. Since its origin, the Indian foreign policy has been characterized by a high degree of continuity but along with it, on several occasions, it has been characterised by far-reaching changes; of course, with continued emphasis upon the basic features which have been, all along, characterising the working of India's foreign policy.

## NATIONAL INTEREST AND INDIAN FOREIGN POLICY

Like the foreign policies of other countries, the Indian foreign policy has also sought to promote national interest. Jawaharlal Nehru, the chief architect of India's foreign policy, said in the Constituent Assembly of India on 4 December 1947 "Whatever policy we may lay down, the art of conducting the foreign affairs of a country lies in finding out what is most advantageous to the country. We may talk about peace and freedom and earnestly mean what we say. But in the ultimate analysis, a government functions for the good of the country it governs and no government dare do anything which in the short or long run is manifestly to the disadvantage of the country."

Nehru, however, did not consider the national interest of India incompatible with the interests of other nations. He said, "Some people may think of the interests of their country regardless of other consequences, or take a short-distance view.

Others may think that in the long-term policy, the interest of another country is as important to them as that of their own country. The interest of peace is more important, because if war comes, every one suffers, so that in the long-distance view, self-interest may itself demand a policy of co-operation with other nations, goodwill for other nations, as indeed it does demand.... Therefore, we propose to look after India's interests in the context of world co-operation and world peace, in so far as world peace can be preserved."

It is evident from the above observations of Nehru that he conceived India's national interests in the context of world co-operation and took a long-term view of India's interests. However, he was not in favour of giving up India's viewpoint because other nations thought differently.

## INDIAN FOREIGN POLICY AFTER 1962 (A BRIEF REVIEW)

The year 1962 marks a watershed in the development of India's foreign policy. This change was discernible during the prime ministership of Nehru when he openly declared that India was no more non-aligned so far as China was concerned. Lal Bahadur Shastri was succeeded Nehru as PM tried to cultivate friendly and intimate relations with neighbours like, Nepal, Burma and Sri Lanka as well as the two superpowers. He succeeded in procuring military and economic assistance from both the powers and greatly strengthened India's position. What is significant that even USA despite strong protests from Pakistan continued to provide liberal military aid to India. This aid was suspended only on the outbreak of war between India and Pakistan in 1965. Prof. Plamer and Perkins have asserted that the Chinese attack come as a traumatic shock to India. It is true that methods of foreign policy after 1962 underwent a change, but the basic principles of India's foreign policy continued to be the same. Another outstanding feature of Indian foreign policy during the Shastri era was that the emphasis shifted to "collective decision-making".

### Foreign Policy under Indira Gandhi

After the sudden death of Shastri, Mrs. Indira Gandhi became the Prime Minister. The principle of "collective decision-making" continued. During her period also, the process of developing close relations with superpowers continued. She was able to secure large financial and military assistance from USA. She also cultivated intimate relations with Soviet Union.

### Foreign Policy under Janata Party (1977-79)

With the formation of Janata Government in 1977, it was expected that a drastic change in India's foreign policy would take place. It was hoped that there would be a certain amount of cooling off of relations with Soviet Union and more intimate relations with USA. The Janata Government tried to develop very intimate relations with both the superpowers, and bring about greater balance and sobriety. A new chapter was opened in Indo-US relations with the visit of President Carter. Another outstanding feature of the Janata Party's foreign policy was an attempt to develop more closer relations with the neighbouring countries. The Janata Government also took a number of concrete steps to improve its relations with neighbouring countries like Bangladesh, Pakistan, Nepal, etc. It reached an agreement with Pakistan on the question of Salal Dam in Kashmir. The Janata Government tried to improve its relations with China for two reasons. First was heavy defence burden and second was desirable to cultivate friendly relations with Beijing. On the other hand, China was also eager to improve relations with India, because they were so much engrossed in their domestic problems that they wanted peace on borders with India.

In addition to this, the Janata Party continued the policy of improving relations with the countries of South-East Asia and West-Asia and extended full support to the anti-racial policies and liberation movements in Africa. In short, Janata Party followed a foreign policy which was highly pragmatic and aimed at promotion of national interests.

### Foreign Policy under Rajiv Gandhi

Rajiv Gandhi continued the foreign policy of Nehru and Indira Gandhi and reaffirmed his faith in the United Nations and the non-aligned movement, opposition to colonialism. He gave importance to our economic, technological and cultural co-operation with them. Rajiv Gandhi also tried to remove international economic disparities, developed closer relations with immediate neighbours, pursue policy of non-interference and promised to pursue the concept of common regional development of South Asia. He stood for arms race, to promote dialogue between the North and South to built a just world of economic order.

### Foreign Policy under National Front Government

The National Front Government in 1989 reiterated its determination to continue policy of non-alignment. It held talks with the leaders of Nepal, Sri Lanka, and Pakistan to remove some of the irritants present in the relations of India with these countries. It expressed its determination to develop more intimate relations with the US, without jeopardizing good relations with Soviet Union.

### Foreign Policy under Narasimha Rao

The formation of Prime Minister Narasimha Rao's government in June 1991 brought back the traditional Congress touch to the Indian foreign policy. Support for Non-alignment, Panchsheel, Disarmament, Nuclear Disarmament, NIEO, Improvement in Sino-Indian relations, good neighbourliness towards Nepal, Sri Lanka, Bangladesh, Bhutan, Maldives, resolution of outstanding issues with Pakistan, peaceful nuclear policy, support for the UNO, and development of relations with the Third World countries came to be emphatic features of the Indian foreign policy. Realizing fully the nature and importance of the changed international system of the post-Cold War, post-USSR, post-Gulf war and post bipolar world as well as the imperative needs resulting from the need to make the Indian economy a liberal market economy capable of attracting foreign investments and developed technologies into India, the policy-makers immediately got engaged in giving a new impetus and health to India's foreign relations.

Rao government tried to give a new orientation to the foreign relations in the light of harsh economic realities. Greater emphasis was laid on economic diplomacy. Indian peace-keeping forces took leading role in the socio-economic development of Somalia. India moved closer to resolving boundary question with China and the two agreed to reduce their military strength on the border. With US also India improved its relations despite differences on issues like NPT, Nuclear weapons free zone in South Asia, missile programme, Special 301, etc. However, American pressure on India to sign NPT and to abandon the missile programme gave set back to the process of improvement of relations with US.

The increased importance of relations with the USA, the need to keep limited the boundary conflict with China, the deep involvement in withstanding and fighting the Pakistan-sponsored terrorism in Punjab, and Jammu and Kashmir, the compulsions resulting from the state of the Indian economy, the external milieu, the need to conduct more smoothly, efficiently and actively India's economic trade, industrial and technology, relations with developed countries, particularly with Japan, Germany, European Union countries, the necessity to overcome the 'Gaps' resulting from the collapse of the Soviet Union and the inability of its successor state Russia to keep up all its commitments with India, the need to cultivate relations with the Commonwealth of Independent States and particularly with the newly emerged Central Asian Republics, the big need to secure a new balance in relations with developed and developing countries, all combined to press the new government to activate the Indian diplomacy, particularly the economic diplomacy, for securing India's interests in the last decade of the 20th century as well as for laying deep, the foundation of India's role in the international system of the 21st century.

Prime Minister Narasimha Rao lost no time in stating clearly and emphatically the main features of Indian foreign policy and he accepted that the main thrust of the policy was to be the same as had been followed in the past. But within this framework, changes have to be made for making the policy abreast with changed and still-changing international system. Non-alignment was to be followed in the light of the new realities of international power structure and the environment of this last decade of the 20th century. In his opening remarks at a press conference on June 30, 1992, held after the completion of one year in office, Narasimha Rao observed, "On the foreign policy front, India has been quite alert to the changing global scene. In the conduct of our foreign policy, Non-alignment continues to be our beacon. Its relevance has been greatly enhanced in the new context in which came to receive good and favourable response and it earned an international recognition. In 1957, even the Soviet Premier Khrushchev decided to support peaceful co-existence among all nations.

However, a big set-back to the popularity of Panchsheel occurred when China, in October 1962, openly violated this principle by committing aggression against India. India was shocked but her faith in Panchsheel was not shaken. She continued to accept it and advocate it as the principle which alone could help the nations to develop good, friendly and co-operative relations among themselves.

Between 1991-96, India added five new principles to the Panchsheel. Inaugrating a two-day seminar on Panchsheel and Global Diplomacy in New Delhi on 27 June, 1994 (marking the Four Decades of the signing of the Panchsheel Agreement between India and China in 1954), the then Prime Minister Narasimha Rao held that to the existing five principles, five more can be added. These are to be: the middle path, back to the villages, model village, technology and tradition, and a new world order. These were designed to ensure that vast segments of people were not left out by the rapid economic and technological changes. Narasimha Rao went to the extent of describing Panchsheel as a "holy doctrine". In 1997, both India and China again, affirmed full faith in Panchsheel as the principle for conducting of relations among nations at all the levels. In fact, Panchsheel has acted as an ideological foundation for Indian foreign policy.

### Foreign Policy under United Front Government (Gujaral Doctrine)

The United Front Government laid great emphasis on improvement of relations with the neighbouring countries. It put forth Gujaral doctrine under which unilateral concessions were made to the neighbouring countries with regard to travel and trade, without expecting reciprocity. Effort was made to promote free trade among the SAARC countries. Another notable feature of the Gujaral Doctrine was to eliminate the outside intervention in the region.

### Foreign Policy under BJP-led Coalition Government (NDA)

The BJP-led coalition government came in to power in 1998. It gave a new orientation to the foreign policy which is more realistic than moralist. It insists on reciprocity. Under the new policy, greater emphasis is being laid on security of the country. On this plea, India conducted explosions at Pokhran in May 1998. Indian foreign policy under Vajpayee government laid special emphasis on need to exercise nuclear option in the interest of national security. In December 1999, the BJP-led government had to cope with the crisis resulting from the hijacking of an Indian Airlines plane to Kandhar (Afghanistan) by Islamic terrorists. It had to release some terrorists for securing the release of the hijacked aircraft and the passengers. It compelled the government to give added attention to the security needs of India as well as to the necessity of meeting the menace of crossborder terrorism and international terrorism. It decided to join hands with the USA and other major powers for co-operating to fight international terrorism effectively. Throughout 2000-04, the NDA Government remained actively involved in international diplomacy, particularly for increasing co-operation with the USA, Russia, France, UK, Germany, European Union, ASEAN countries and Israel. It kept up its fight against cross-border terrorism and gave full support to the US-led war against international terrorism. India's new nuclear policy was kept intact and vigorous efforts were made to strengthen India's security as well as the nation's march towards rapid economic development through liberalization, privatization and globalization.

- To work for securing a multi-polar world.
- To develop and maintain India's military preparedness in accordance with India's security needs and status needs.
- To work for the creation of a global convention against terrorism.

- To effectively and actively participate in the UN peace-keeping operations.
- To create and operationalize a nuclear command structure and to act as a responsible nuclear nation.
- To work for making India a developed nation through rapid industrial-technological and economic development and ensure a dual role for India in the emerging world order of the 21st century.

The foreign policy of the NDA-coalition government reflected the following features:

- To continue participation in the NAM and accept its relevance in the emerging world order.
- To develop high-level co-operative relations with the USA.
- To maintain and improve relations with Russia, China, Japan, France, the UK, Germany, Israel, the European Union and ASEAN Countries.
- To secure for India, a permanent seat in the UN Security Council.
- To maintain India's new status as a nuclear weapon state, to give a proper and needed direction to India's new nuclear policy, to develop and maintain a minimum nuclear deterrent force considered essential for the security needs of India and to keep pending the issue of signing the CTBT.
- To secure the interests of the developing countries in the WTO and prevent the incorporation of discriminatory clauses in the new economic and trade regime.
- To co-operate effectively and vigorously with all other nations for meeting the menace of international terrorism.

## NEW PARADIGMS IN FOREIGN POLICY OBJECTIVES

### India-US Nuclear Deal

The bilateral relations between India and US have reached a new height after the much hyped Civilian Nuclear Deal. This deal will shoot India to one of the big leagues of world as many of the areas of the deal are central to India's national development. These include energy, agriculture, science and technology, trade, investment and high technology, health and environment. This agreement also means that the hurdles faced by India in procuring nuclear technology and fuel have been removed for good. The 123 Agreement is treated as a historic milestone in their strategic partnership by completing negotiations on the bilateral agreement for peaceful nuclear co-operation. This agreement will govern civil nuclear trade between these two countries and open the door for American and Indian firms to participate in each other's civil nuclear energy sector.

The old foes, India and USA have turned into friends in due course of time and under world's changing power equation. Over the years, the visits between the world's most powerful country's chief to one of the world's largest economy and developing power has changed the whole enigma of the bilateral relations. This has led to make India to be one of the strategic partner of USA.

India has been a member of the nuclear club for more than 30 years after it conducted its first peaceful nuclear explosion test 'Smiling Buddha' in 1974 and joined the elite club of nuclear superpowers after Pokhran Test. In the emerging power equations across the globe, India is fast acquiring the position of global superpower through all the spheres, economic, scientific, democratic, etc. for the future results of the national development.

The level of transformation in India-U.S. relations and the establishment of a global, strategic partnership between the two countries is marked by the highly successful summit meetings March 1-2, 2006 in New Delhi and July 18, 2005 in Washington D.C. between Prime Minister Manmohan Singh and President George W. Bush. The much-hyped Indo-US Nuclear Pact was the centre-piece of President George W. Bush's first visit to India and July 18 Joint Statement on nuclear co-operation. India will get US nuclear fuel and technology through this pact.

Under the deal, India has undertaken to separate its civilian and military nuclear facilities, place the former under full-scope International Atomic Energy Agency (IAEA) safeguards, take various measures to prevent export of nuclear-weapons technology, contribute to other international non-proliferation regimes as well as to continue with its declared moratorium on nuclear tests. In other words, India would comply with all obligations of Nuclear Weapons States (NWS) which are signatories to the Nuclear Non-Proliferation Treaty (NPT) that India has consistently held to be discriminatory and has thus never joined.

**Highlights of Indo-US Nuclear Deal**

Following are the key aspects of the Indo-US civil nuclear deal:

- The agreement not to hinder or interfere with India's nuclear programme for military purposes.
- US will help India negotiate with the IAEA for an India-specific fuel supply agreement.
- Washington will support New Delhi develop strategic reserves of nuclear fuel to guard against future disruption of supply.
- In case of disruption, US and India will jointly convene a group of friendly supplier countries to include nations like Russia, France and the UK to pursue such measures to restore fuel supply.
- Both the countries agree to facilitate nuclear trade between themselves in the interest of respective industries and consumers.
- India and the US agree to transfer nuclear material, non-nuclear material, equipment and components.
- Any special fissionable material transferred under the agreement shall be low enriched uranium.
- Low enriched uranium can be transferred for use as fuel in reactor experiments and in reactors for conversion or fabrication.
- The ambit of the deal include research, development, design, construction, operation, maintenance and use of nuclear reactors, reactor experiments and decommissioning.

- The US will have the right to seek return of nuclear fuel and technology but it will compensate for the costs incurred as a consequence of such removal.
- India can develop strategic reserve of nuclear fuel to guard against any disruption of supply over the lifetime of its reactors.
- Agreement provides for consultations on the circumstances, including changed security environment, before termination of the nuclear co-operation.
- Provision for one-year notice period before termination of the agreement.
- The US to engage Nuclear Suppliers Group to help India obtain full access to the international fuel market, including reliable, uninteruppted and continual access to fuel supplies from firms in several nations.
- The US will have the right to seek return of nuclear fuel and technology.
- In case of return, Washington will compensate New Delhi promptly for the "fair market value thereof" and the costs incurred as a consequence of such removal.
- Both the countries to set up a Joint Committee for implementation of the civil nuclear agreement and development of further co-operation in this field.
- The agreement grants prior consent to reprocess spent fuel.
- Sensitive nuclear technology, nuclear facilities and major critical components can be transferred after amendment to the agreement.
- India will establish a new national facility dedicated to reprocessing safeguarded nuclear material under IAEA safeguards.
- Nuclear material and equipment transferred to India by the US.
- India has agreed that 14 of its civilian nuclear reactors will be open to international safeguards.

- The fast-breeder reactor programme will not be subject to outside inspection.
- India will decide status of all future reactors—whether civilian or military.
- New civilian breeder reactors to be under IAEA safeguards.
- All civilian reactors under permanent safeguards, but in return guaranteed lifetime fuel supply.

### India's Nuclear Status, At a Glance

- India has a flourishing and largely indigenous nuclear power programme and expects to have 20,000 MWe nuclear capacity on line by 2020.
- Because India is outside the Nuclear non-proliferation treaty, due to its weapons programme, it is largely excluded from trade in nuclear plant or material, which has hampered its development of civil nuclear energy.
- Its nuclear weapons capability has arisen independently of its civil nuclear fuel cycle and uses indigenous uranium.
- Because of its relative isolation in international trade and lack of indigenous uranium, India has uniquely been developing a nuclear fuel cycle exploiting its reserves of thorium.

### Pros and Cons of the Nuke Deal

India needs nuclear energy as part of a mix to meet rising electricity requirements as its growth rate comes close to 10 per cent per annum. The energy deficit is acting as a speed-breaker to India's growth. At present, just 3 per cent of India's power requirement comes from nuclear sources. The government plans to produce 20,000 MWe of nuclear power by 2020, up from the current installed capacity of 3,700 MWe.

In order to generate more power, India needs to buy nuclear reactors and nuclear fuel from abroad. Its own programme has been a success, but if the growth of nuclear power has to be accelerated, then help from abroad is essential.

As the pre-eminent power on the global stage, the US can facilitate the purchase of nuclear reactors and technology from abroad by India. In December 2006, it passed a law (the Hyde Act) to allow for nuclear commerce with India. New Delhi, which is not a member of the NSG, is banking on the US to get the group to make an exception for India so that it can boost its civil nuclear sector.

The Nuclear Suppliers Group (NSG) is an informal grouping of 45 nations which came into existence after India conducted its first nuclear test in Pokhran in 1974. It seeks to limit the transfer of nuclear technology and fuel in the name of promoting non-proliferation.

The Indo-US agreement permits nuclear trade, transfer of nuclear material, equipment, components and related technologies as well as co-operation in nuclear fuel cycle activities between India and the US. It allows India to re-use (reprocess) spent nuclear fuel, create a reserve of nuclear fuel and provides guarantees in case there is a glitch in the implementation of the agreement. Furthermore, it recognizes that India has a military nuclear programme, something the US has never done in the past. The accord is for an initial period of 40 years and can be renewed for further periods of 10 years at a time.

India's nuclear programme had never made a distinction between its civil and military programmes. Under the accord, however, this distinction has to be made. Fourteen of the 22 (nuclear) thermal power reactors will be placed under International Atomic Energy Agency (IAEA) safeguards by 2014. As of now, only 19 per cent of India's installed thermal power capacity is under IAEA safeguards—this figure will go upto 65 per cent by 2014.

There is nothing in the draft agreement that prohibits India, in principle, from testing a nuclear device again.

India can test again, but it will come at a cost. Under American domestic law (the Hyde Act read with the Atomic Energy Act), all co-operation must come to an end in case India tests a nuclear device in the future. However, the US has promised to take into account the circumstances in which the nuclear weapon is tested. Also, there has to be a one year notice period for ending co-operation under the agreement.

The Hyde Act is domestic American law named after Congressman Henry J. Hyde—that allows for civil nuclear cooperation with India. It was passed in December 2006.

The US has granted India up front rights to reprocess spent nuclear fuel, something it has not done for China.

The civil nuclear co-operation between the US and a foreign state is enabled through Section 123 of the American Atomic Energy Act of 1954.

The Cabinet has to appropriate the 123 agreement, not Parliament. Three more steps are needed—New Delhi has to negotiate an India-specific safeguards agreement with the IAEA, get clearance from the NSG and the US Congress has to give its final approval to the 123 agreement. India-specific safeguards mean that such provisions will apply only to India. We will agree to safeguards on specified reactors only if there is an assurance for lifetime supply of nuclear fuel. India will have the right to take "corrective measures" relating to safeguards in case of supply of nuclear fuel is interrupted. Only IAEA inspectors will be able to visit the safeguarded nuclear facilities. American inspectors will not have such access.

**The ABC of Agreement 123**

- The name comes from Section 123 of the US Atomic Energy Act, under which the US has to conclude any bilateral civilian nuclear co-operation agreement.

The key features of 123:

- It gives India assured fuel supplies for its civilian nuclear reactors in return for them going under permanent safeguards.
- India can have nuclear cooperation and trade with US and others without compromising its weapons programmes. India need not sign the NPT or put its nuclear facilities under full-safeguards.
- It allows India to reprocess and recycle spent fuel.

India gets access to more and diversified sources of energy. It breaks open a regime that block India's access to high technology. After the nuclear test in 1974, doors will now be open for high-tech and dual-use tech in sectors as diverse as IT, defence, space, pharmaceuticals.

Strategic implications for India:

- India will not be a nuclear recluse
- The deal won't be offered to Pakistan
- It gets to keep its nuclear weapons.

The interests of US:

- Rise of India helps US as in the post-Cold War world, i.e. US and India on the same side.
- The deal allows India to achieve its target of 20,000 MW power by 2020. Also, its clean energy and savings on carbon emission will be big.
- US firms can partner India in high-tech ventures which they are forbidden to do at present.

The points of Opposition in the US to the Deal:

- It will undermine global non-proliferation system.
- The non-proliferation lobby feel it's too generous to India.
- That it shouldn't get the right to reprocess spent fuel.
- India will make N-weapons with its own uranium.
- It will send 'wrong signal' to Iran, North-Korea and Pakistan.

The possible downsides of the Deal:

- If India conducts an Nuclear test, the deal could fall part.
- The bar on tests would be upheld by the Nuclear Suppliers Group (NSG).

Relevance of the HYDE ACT:

- US, according to its Atomic Act, cannot have nuclear co-operation with a country that's not signed the NPT or submitted itself to safeguards. The Hyde Act gives US administration the waiver to reach a pact.

**Highlights of Manmohan's Statement**

- Civil nuclear energy co-operation agreement between two states possessing advanced nuclear technologies and having the same benefits and advantages.
- Ensures the autonomy of India's strategic programme is fully maintained.
- Ensures full civil nuclear co-operation, including technology transfer on industrial or commercial scale.
- US to support Indian efforts to develop strategic reserve of nuclear fuel to guard against any disruption of supply over the lifetime of our reactors.
- India's right to reprocess US-origin spent fuel secured upfront.
- India to establish new national reprocessing facility dedicated to reprocessing foreign nuclear material under IAEA safeguards. India and US will mutually agree on arrangements and procedure under which such reprocessing will take place.
- Agreement protects the interests of the three-stage nuclear programme as it provides for use of fissionable material in national facilities under IAEA safeguards.
- Provides for transfer of enrichment, reprocessing and heavy water production facilities to India through amendment. The US has not allowed such transfers to any other country.
- Decision to undertake nuclear test in future is India's sovereign decision.
- No change in India's position that it will accept only IAEA safeguards on civilian nuclear facilities. This will be in a phased manner, as identified in the Separation Plan and only when all international restrictions have been lifted.
- No provision that US co-operation will be subject to annual certification process.

- No consent to any provision that mandates scrutiny of India's nuclear weapons programme or unsafeguarded nuclear facilities.
- Implementation of agreement will not hinder or interfere with India's nuclear activities.
- Nothing in agreement impinges on India's strategic programme or ability to conduct advanced R&D.
- No question of compromise on independent foreign policy.
- Elaborate multi-layered consultation process included with regard to future events that may be cited as a reason by either party to seem cessation of co-operation or termination of agreement.
- US can seek cessation of co-operation only if it is prepared to take extreme step of terminating agreement.
- India's right to take corrective measures to be maintained even after termination of agreement.
- India target 20,000 MW of nuclear power generation by 2020; this can be doubled with international co-operation.
- India-specific safeguards agreement with IAEA, change in NSG guidelines to enable nuclear commerce will be the beginning of the end of the technology-denial regime against India.
- Major spin-offs for the development of industry, both public and private.

**Timeline of the Indo-US Nuclear Deal**

| | |
|---|---|
| July 18, 2005 | : Bush-Singh joint statement calls for a nuke deal between two countries |
| March 02, 2006 | : India-US ink landmark nuclear agreement |
| April 20 | : N-deal must be seen in light of growing ties: Rice |
| May 18 | : N-deal to be within July 18 framework: Rice to Indian parliamentarians |
| May 12 | : N-separation plan tabled in Parliament |

| | |
|---|---|
| June 22 | : US says it is against deal breaker changes to N-deal |
| June 23 | : India says it is committed to credible minimum deterrent |
| June 28 | : US House of Representatives' international relations committee passes Bill seeking Indo-US nuke deal implementation by an overwhelming 37-5 majority |
| June 29 | : US Senate Foreign Relations Committee marks up the bill for implementing N-deal with 16 members voting in favour and only two against it |
| July 06 | : Indians in US did their bit—Minister for Overseas Indian Affairs |
| July 15 | : Bush, Putin praise Indian non-proliferation |
| July 19 | : We will stand up for the deal we negotiated: Burns |
| July | : India won't accept new conditions in N-deal: PM |
| July 27, 2006 | : US House passes Indo-US nuclear Bill by a landslide |

**China Strategy**

The Manmohan Singh Government has shown little understanding of issues of national security. It lacks a comprehensive strategy on how to respond to China's maritime encirclement of India through its "string of pearls" policies in the Indian Ocean, extending across Thailand, Myanmar, Bangladesh, Sri Lanka, Pakistan, Maldives and Seychelles.

The Prime Minister has severely eroded the effectiveness of our counter-terrorism strategy against Pakistan through ill-advised moves and statements, such as his equating India and Pakistan as "victims of terrorism". By his ill considered and hasty decision to set up a "Joint Mechanism" on terrorism with Pakistan, without giving any deep thought to even what the terms of reference of the Group should be, he has allowed Pakistan to put us in a position where, by participating in this ludicrous "Joint Mechanism", we are tacitly accepting that terrorist violence in Jammu and Kashmir is a "freedom struggle" and not "terrorism".[1]

The Prime Minister's blunders in dealing with the issue of Pakistan-sponsored terrorism should be evident from the fact that while he empathises with General Pervez Musharraf as being a "victim of terrorism". Ms Benazir Bhutto proclaims: "Why is it that all terrorist plots in Madrid, London, Mumbai, seem to have roots in Islamabad? Pakistan's military and intelligence services have for decades used religious parties to recruit. Political Madrassas (religious schools that preach terrorism by perverting the faith of Islam) have spread by the tens of thousands." In response, Mr Pranab Mukherjee said: "While terrorism is perpetrated by non-state actors in most parts of the world, in India, militants and terrorists are also sponsored and aided by agencies across our borders."

**Imaginative Approach**

It must, however, be acknowledged that the Prime Minister has taken an imaginative approach to dealing with Pakistan on the issue of Jammu and Kashmir. By firmly proclaiming that there can be "no change in borders" Dr. Singh has now got General Musharraf to respond with a set of proposals that constitute the beginning of a practical basis for evolving a framework for resolving the Kashmir issue, over a period of years. While moving in this direction, we should insist that what we are seeking is a "permanent" and not an "interim" solution.

Statements by Dr. Singh suggesting that a withdrawal from Siachen was impending and that he would show "zero tolerance for human rights violations", without a word of praise for the dedication and restraint of our armed forces in defending our territorial integrity have only confused and demoralized our armed forces.

At the same time, the nuclear establishment has grave misgivings about the Prime Minister's commitment to the development of our nuclear deterrence and the growth of our indigenous fast breeder nuclear power programme.

During his tenure as Finance Minister, Dr. Singh was unsparing in cutting the Defence budget and being parsimonious in allocations for nuclear power. We lost the strategic edge we had in the 1980s, thereby tempting Pakistan to embark on its Kargil misadventure.

While there may have been compelling reasons for these decisions, the perception does nevertheless persist that on issues of nuclear policy Dr. Singh thinks more like fellow economist Dr. Amartya Sen, rather than those who adopt a realist approach to national security.

Even those who support the Prime Minister's efforts to expand co-operation with the US are worried about what is perceived as his readiness to accept American prescriptions on conducting relations with Pakistan. One hopes Dr. Singh will allay these concerns in the second half of his tenure as Prime Minister.

## WINDS OF CHANGE—INDIAN FOREIGN POLICY

Indian foreign policy under the Manmohan Singh-led government has made a hasty departure from the hitherto seen principles of foreign policy. Up until this government's assumption of office, Indian foreign policy had wandered aimlessly for many years. In the past, India was seen merely as a regional heavy-weight and nothing more.

However, the information technology boom, and subsequently, the stupendous levels of economic growth have brought India into the forefront of global politics once again. India is no longer a dormant power shying away from making its presence felt on the international arena. There has been a shift in Indian foreign policy and this government has been successful to a great extent in making India's opinions count.

Perhaps the most important success in India's foreign policy has been the forging of closer ties with the US. The United States' relations with India were cool at best until the culmination of the Cold War. The testing of nuclear weapons by India did not go down well with Washington either. However, with the efforts of the Vajpayee administration in its latter years and more importantly, with the Manmohan Singh-led administration in the last eighteen months, there has been a distinct change in the way the US perceives India. India is now a "civilian" nuclear power and has been included in the list of responsible nuclear weapons-possessing nations. At every opportunity, the Bush administration makes an attempt to sing praises about the two nations' relationship. The recognition of Hindi as a strategic language by Washington may be perceived as gimmick by many, but for the Indians, it is a gesture that only holds positive connotations for the future.

India's relations with Russia remain as friendly as they were years ago. This is despite the fact that India is forging closer ties with traditional rival, the US. Earlier, India maintained its distance from the US for it did not want to disappoint Russia. Today, India has begun buying weapons from the US and Russia doesn't seem to mind. Smart diplomacy in New Delhi has helped India forge closer ties with the US, while at the same time not hampering its relations with its long-time ally, Russia.

The antagonism between India and her neighbour China seems to have passed into distant memory-well...at least for the moment. Chinese Premier Hu Jintao has categorically stated that China sees India as a working partner and not as a competitor. India, for its part, has realized that this arrangement is just what suits best as India is in no position to compete with the East Asian juggernaut at present. Border issues with China were close to being resolved in Vajpayee's tenure as PM and territorial disputes are no longer the focal point of Sino-Indian talks. It has to be added, however, that the simultaneous experience of rapid economic growth in these two countries has also had a major impact on relations between them.

The impasse over Iran's nuclear programme could be India's biggest foreign policy test in the near future. Whether or not India will vote in favour of referring Iran to the Security Council, remains to be seen. India and Iran have always maintained close ties in the past and India hopes to set up a gas pipeline from Iran to India to meet its ever-growing demands for energy. Yet it cannot afford to turn its back on the US as an India-US Nuclear Cooperation Agreement is nearing completion. A "yes" vote in the IAEA would affect Indo-Iran relations, while a "no" vote could lead to a halt in the nuclear agreement with the US. India needs to make a choice that would not hamper its strategic ties with either of the two nations.

It may be worth keeping in mind that even if Iran is referred to the Security Council, nothing will come out of it as China is investing heavily in Iran's energy sector and Iranian natural gas and oil exports to China are a major contributing factor to China's economic machinery. Is there something the Indians can learn from these facts?

The separation of the civilian and military nuclear programmes seems to be the crux of the issue. How far back will India go into the programme to separate its fuel cycle? The nature of deterrence, procurement and quality of uranium and the costs and benefits attached to the deal, need further debate to shed more light on the issue.

### The Process of Decision-making

Though the foreign policy of a country is greatly influenced by the various domestic and external factors, the process of decision-making at various levels plays no less important role in its formulation. According to J. Bandyopadhyaya, the rationality or otherwise or a foreign policy depends on the nature and extent of articulate public opinion and the manner of its expression, the institutions of the political parties concerned with foreign policy, pressure groups, Parliament, the Foreign Office, the Foreign Minister and finally the Cabinet. It shall be desirable to examine the role of various institutions in the policy formulation.

**Cabinet:** Cabinet, which is expected, under Parliamentary system of government in India, to act as the highest and collective decision-making body in respect of foreign policy, has by and large failed to play this role. During the times of Nehru, the foreign policy was dominated by the Prime Minister himself. Sardar Patel, another important member of his cabinet hardly took any interest in foreign affairs. During the time of Indira Gandhi also, the foreign policy was exclusively determined by the Prime Minister and the other ministers played very little role. With the formation of the Janata Government in 1977, the

Cabinet started playing an important role in the formulation of country's foreign policy. In fact, Morarji Desai, the Prime Minister, functioned more as convener of the Cabinet rather than the undisputed leader. After the ouster of Janata Government and return of Congress to power, once again Prime Minister started playing decisive role with regard to foreign policy of the country.[2] Under Rajiv Gandhi also, the decisions with regard to foreign policy were taken by the Prime Minister in consultation with his Foreign Minister. But generally, the foreign policy of the country has been framed by the Prime Minister in consultation with the Foreign Minister and other trusted colleagues, and the cabinet as a body has not played any effective role in the determination of country's foreign policy.

**Political Parties:** India which has a multiparty system, some sort of consensus must be reached on foreign policy by different political parties. In fact, in the larger interest of the country, it is desirable that the foreign policy of the country must be based on consensus of political parties and groups. Till the emergence of Janata Party in 1977, the country witnessed a single party dominance (viz., that of Congress) and there was hardly an effective opposition in Parliament. As a result, there existed a virtual unanimity on the principles of country's foreign policy. Though in parliamentary system of government, all decisions regarding foreign policy are made by the party or parties in power, the opposition parties also play an important role in its formulation both within and outside the parliament. In fact, in a country like India party institutions play an important role.

**Party Institutions:** The role of these institutions has varied according to strength of the party in the Parliament. So long country witnessed one-party dominance, there did not exist any difference between the government and the party. The former naturally exercised decisive influence on both domestic and foreign policy. Institutions of various political parties in India have also played an important role in the decision-making process. However, four formal institutions of Congress Party existed which were expected to contribute to the formulation of the foreign policy, directly as well as indirectly. These four institutions were—the Foreign Department of the All India

Congress Committee; the Standing Committee on External Affairs of the Congress Parliamentary Party; the Congress Parliamentary Party and the Congress Parliamentary Party Executive.

**Pressure Groups:** Unlike in United States where the pressure groups play an important role in the formulation and determination of foreign policy, in India the pressure groups play only a negligible role in foreign matters. The business interest groups like the Federation of Indian Chambers of Commerce and Industry have mainly passed resolution with regard to economic policy of the country and hardly exposed views with regard to the foreign policy of the country. This was confirmed by V.K. Krishna Menon, who played an important role in the formulation of Indian policy. The early years after independence confirmed that most of the business interest groups in India do not try to influence the foreign minister in any way either with regard to the general orientation or specific aspects of foreign policy. This view was also confirmed by other foreign ministers like M.C. Chagla, Swaran Singh, etc. This was probably due to the fact that till recent years, the business associations did not have important economic interest in foreign countries. No doubt, in recent years there has been considerable increase in private Indian investment in foreign countries, specially in countries of West Asia, South-east Asia, and Africa, which has encouraged the Indian industrialists and traders to take more keen interest in the foreign economic relations.

**Ruling Elite:** The ruling elite plays an important role in the formulation of country's foreign policy. In fact, the foreign policy of a country at a given time depends on how the elite perceives and responds to the prevailing challenges in the domestic and foreign fields. The foreign policy which is ultimately evolved by the elites bears the impact of their views and personality. It is well known that the foreign policy of India bears a close imprint of Jawaharlal Nehru who occupied the office of the Prime Minister for about two decades and also acted as the Foreign Minister of the country. Nehru also sought help and advice from a number of eminent personalities like Krishna Menon, K.M. Panikkar, Dr. Radha Krishnan, Sardar

Patel, Swaran Singh, etc. who greatly contributed to the shaping of country's foreign policy. The other important personalities who exercised great influence on country's foreign policy include T.N. Kaul, D.P. Dhar, P.N. Haksar, I.K. Gujaral, G.N. Dixit, etc. It is true that Nehru played an important role in the formulation of India's foreign policy during the formative years, but he denied that he originated the foreign policy.

**Public Opinion:** In every country, the final decision with regard to the domestic and foreign policies rests with the common people. But generally, the people take keen interests only in matters relating to domestic affairs. They show interest in foreign policy only at the time of war or international crisis. Thus, the people are involved in foreign policy only in a limited way. In a country like India where the people are comparatively backward, their involvement in foreign policy matters as compared to advanced countries, is very limited. This is one account of three reasons. Firstly, on account of very high rate of illiteracy, people are not able to get the benefit of national or international press and are more often than not influenced by caste, community, religion, local and regional considerations. Secondly, in India, very meagre information on foreign policy is made available to the people through press, parliamentary debates, etc. Thirdly, the lack of modern means of communications for several decades since independence, has prevented the general public from exercising any effective influence on the formulation of foreign policy. Even the intellectuals are not consulted while formulating the foreign policy.

**Parliament:** The Parliament also exercises considerable influence on the foreign policy of the country through various Parliamentary Committees. As regards the role of the Parliament with regard to the formulation of country's foreign policy, the executive has generally tended to ignore the Parliament and often taken major policy decisions without taking the Parliament in confidence. Thus, the Estimates Committee and the Public Accounts Committee have exercised control over foreign affairs through its power of financial control over the External Affairs and other related ministries. The estimates committee in its

Report on Ministry of External Affairs submitted in 1960-61 recommended the reorganization of the Foreign Office and the missions abroad. These recommendations had an indirect impact on the formulation of foreign policy. The consultative committee of Parliament on External Affairs is another important forum where important discussions are held on the various facets of Indian foreign policy. Generally, the forum of the Committee is used by the government to offer detailed explanation about its foreign policy so that it is readily accepted by the Parliament.[3] M.C. Chagla, India's Foreign Minister under Indira Gandhi, commenting on the role of the consultative committee of Parliament for External Affairs observed that, it is "more of an agency for getting policies accepted and muting criticism than for influencing foreign policy".

It is evident from the proceeding account that sufficient attention has not been paid to the institutionalization and planning of foreign policy. Quite often, the political leaders preferred to adopt a policy of *ad hocism*. However, in the new context when the international relations have become complex and multi-dimensional, this attitude can hardly serve the interests of the country. It is desirable that adequate institutions must be created for the formulation of foreign policy along scientific lines so that the national interests can be best protected.

## CONTINUITY AND CHANGE

Foreign policy of any country is the product of a complex interplay of history, geography, past experience, present requirements, perceptions of the ruling elite of national interests and ideological consensus. It is also shaped and moulded by the domestic balance of forces, the regional balance of forces, and the international balance of forces. History and geography give continuity to foreign policy, domestic and international circumstances produce changes. Prof. Morgenthau emphasizes that national interest is the driving force behind a country's foreign policy.

The foreign policy of India has its origin in the past. In the very first session in 1885, the Congress denounced the annexation of Burma and objected to the military activity going on beyond the natural lines of defences of this country. At the meeting of the All India Congress Committee in Delhi in 1921, the National Congress passed its first general resolution on foreign policy, and openly declared that the present government (British) of India in no way represents Indian opinion. Another significant pronouncement about the foreign policy of India was made at the Haripura Session in 1938. The Resolution said: "The people of India desire to live in peace and friendship with their neighbours and with all other countries, and for this purpose wish to remove all causes of conflict between them. In order, therefore, to establish world peace on an enduring basis; imperialism and the exploitation of one people by another must end. Thus, the basis for the foreign policy of free India was ready before India actually gained freedom."

## DISTINCT FEATURES OF INDIA'S FOREIGN POLICY

Analysing all these, the following distinctive features of India's foreign policy come to the fore.

**1. Non-alignment.** India was the chief initiator of the policy of non-alignment. The policy of non-alignment means detachment from military blocs and a faith in solving all international disputes through co-operation. She adopted this policy, because she wanted to play a more dominant role for the cause of world peace. Opposing the policy of alignment, Nehru said, "By aligning ourselves with any one power, you surrender your opinion, give up the policy you would normally pursue because somebody else wants you to pursue another policy. I do not think that it would be a right policy for us to adopt. We will neither be following the policy based on our ideals inherited from our past or the one indicated by our present nor will be able easily to adopt ourselves to the new policy consequent on such alignment."

Geographical consideration also demanded that India should follow a policy of non-alignment. She has two leading communist powers on or near her border—China and Soviet Union. As a result, military alliance with the Western bloc were ruled out, because it would be viewed as an unfriendly act by the two communist powers.[4] An alliance with the Communist countries was not possible because India by her traditions could not approve the revolutionary ideology of communism.

It must be noted that non-alignment does not mean that friendly co-operation is not possible with other countries. Further, non-alignment also does not mean neutrality. Neutrality as a policy has little meaning except in times of war.

Thus, it would be wrong to designate the foreign policy of India as policy of 'neutrality' because a country which adopts policy of neutrality has no positive opinions on issues which divide the blocs. India on the other hand has spoken clearly and with conviction on the various international issues. For example, she considered the march of North Korean troops into South Korea as 'aggression', she condemned the British and French invasion of Suez as a 'naked aggression', she condemned though after much waiting, the Soviet interference in Hungary; she was very critical of US bombardment in Vietnam.

**2. Opposition to Imperialism and Colonialism.** Another feature of the India's foreign policy is that it is opposed to imperialism and colonialism. The government has consistently championed the cause of the exploited nations against the colonial and imperial powers. In a speech before the UN General Assembly on November 3, 1948, Nehru said: "We in Asia who have ourselves suffered all these evils of colonialism and of imperial domination, have committed ourselves inevitably to the freedom of every other colonial country. There are neighbouring countries of ours in Asia with whom we are intimately allied. We look to them with sympathy. We look at their struggle with sympathy. Any power, great or small, which in that way prevents the attainment of the freedom of these peoples does an ill than to world peace. Great countries like India who have passed out of that colonial stage do not conceive it possible that other countries should remain under the yoke of colonial rule."

It may be observed that India has not been merely raising slogans against colonialism and imperialism, she has actually followed this policy. For example, when the Dutch government tried to re-establish her hold over Indonesia, India convened a meeting of Foreign Ministers at New Delhi and made an appeal to the Security Council. As a result, the Independence of Indonesia was ultimately recognized. Likewise, India supported the Independence demand to Libya and opposed the moves of the South Africa to incorporate the territories of South-West Africa into her Union. She also advocated the cause to Tunisia and Algeria.

**3. Opposed to Racial Discrimination.** The Indian Government has also opposed the policy of racial discrimination, Nehru said: "We repudiate utterly the Nazi doctrine of racialism wheresoever and in whatever form it may be practised. We seek no domination over other and we claim no privileged position over other people. But we do claim equal and honourable treatment of our people wherever they may go and we cannot accept any discrimination against them." India has not only condemned the policy of racial discrimination followed towards Indians in South Africa but also supported the cause of the Negroes in the United States and the black majority in Rhodesia against the white minority. India has been a strong advocate of her policy of racial equality. It was mainly due to effort of India that UN General Assembly condemned the Union of South Africa for its policy of Apartheid.

**4. Co-operation and Coexistence.** Co-operation and coexistence has been another important principle of India's foreign policy. The idea of different systems existing side by side without clash is not new to India. This policy of coexistence is expressed in the Panchsheel or Five Principles of peaceful coexistence incorporated in the agreement between China and India of April 1954. The five principles are mutual respect for each other's territorial integrity and sovereignty; non-aggression; non-interference in each other's internal affairs; equality and mutual benefit; and peaceful coexistence.

**5. Faith in United Nations.** India has great faith in United Nations and stands for settlement of all disputes under the aegis of the UN through peaceful means. For that very reason, the Government of India took the question of Kashmir to the United Nations. The role of India in Korea and Indo-China are the outstanding examples of India's co-operation with the United

Nations. However, within the United Nations, India has refused to blindly follow either of the two power blocs and has determined her stand on the various world issues keeping in view the interests of world peace. When India summoned a conference of the Asian countries in New Delhi in January 1949, allegations were levelled against her that she was trying to ignore and bypass the United Nations. Nehru at that time made it clear that "We meet to supplement the effort of the security council, not to supplant that body, we meet in no spirit of hostility to any nation or group of nations but in an endeavour to promote peace through the extension of freedom." From time to time, India has been making available to the UN the necessary men to implement its decisions. Thus, she sent personnel for the observation group in Lebanon to ensure that there was no infiltration of personnel or supply of arms or other material across the Lebanese border. Similarly, India contributed a contingent during the Congolese conflict.[5]

**6. Bias in Favour of Asia.** Although India has been following a policy of friendship towards all the nations of the world, she has special interest in development of the closet possible ties with other Asian and African nations which share her point of view. India has not only tried sincerely to solve the problems facing the Asian countries but has also forged them together through various conferences. The beginning in this direction was made by holding conference at New Delhi in 1947 and 1949. Even the Bandung Conference of the Afro-Asian countries was held in Asia. Profs. Palmer and Perkins describe Bandung Conference as, "the most significant international conference ever held in Asia and the first conference of its kind in history". India has sometimes been accused of aiming at the leadership of South-east Asia, but she has always disclaimed any such ambition. The fact remains that India has been a leading champion of Asia's claims to a greater place in the world affairs and she has always taken an initiative in this regard.

**7. Sympathetically Disposed Towards Divided Countries.** As India had to face the bitter consequences of the partition of the country, she has always shown sympathy towards the divided countries. She opposed the partition of Palestine and suggested a Federation of the Arabs and Jews. She also opposed the division of Korea and Indo-China (Vietnam, etc.). She has also been supporting the cause of German Unification to do away with the evil efforts of its partition into East and West Germany.

**8. Ties with Commonwealth.** India has also been supporter of Commonwealth and joined it by a treaty. India joined the Commonwealth because she could get certain economic benefits by her association with this august body. Further, on the eve of her independence, India needed the shield of British navy to secure Indian ocean. But India's membership of Commonwealth has provoked lot of controversy from the very beginning. In the Indo-Pak conflict of 1965 when Great Britain sympathized with Pakistan a demand was made by many that India should quit the Commonwealth. But the government turned down this demand by pointing out that the organization was not British but mainly Afro-Asian. Majority of the members of the Commonwealth belonged to Asia and Africa.

## UNPRECEDENTED CHANGES

The world has witnessed unprecedented changes during the last decade. One could not have imagined that within hardly four decades of the World War II, the controversial Berlin wall would collapse and the Cold War would meet an inglorious end. It was also inconceivable until a few years that the iron curtain over the Eastern Europe would be lifted and that the mighty Soviet Union would disintegrate.

Besides, until a few years ago, one could not conceive of a situation where development and economics would dominate international relations and the mighty security alliances so carefully built-up over the years since World War II would lose their power and even some of them like SEATO, CENTO and Warsaw Pact would fizzle out as non-entities.

Is it not a strange irony to suggest that billions of dollars spent on research and development (R&D) of the strategic weapon system—the Strategic Defence Initiative[6] (SDI) so assiduously built-up during the Reagan years and the grand theories like zero-sum games deterrence, first strike, second strike, mutually assured destruction (MAD) are gradually becoming outdated? Similarly, is it not a fact that Third World solidarity, non-aligned movement, the new international economic order, the North-South dialogues, the South-South co-operation, are gradually losing significance? Is it also unrealistic to think that the present day international politics is gradually being hijacked by the multinational, religious fundamentalists, drug barons and more recently by the cross-country terrorists?

In addition, one could not conceive until a few decades ago that ethnic conflicts, and the sub-national movements would result in a dramatic redrawing of the political geography of the world. There is also no gain-saying the fact that the erstwhile non-issues like human rights, protection of global environment, the sustainable development and social issues like women, tribes, indigenous culture are gradually leaving their imprints on the restructuring of the agenda for international relations. No doubt linkage politics is going to arrive at its logical conclusion.

## FOREIGN POLICY UNDER JAWAHARLAL NEHRU

Right from the time of independence in 1947, when the world was ideologically divided between the two power blocs, the objectives of India's foreign policy as clearly defined by the first Prime Minister, Jawaharlal Nehru, was based on the premise of middle path which got crystallized as non-alignment.

There was obviously a clear consensus in the country for a foreign policy which revolved around an independent approach without getting entangled by either ideological or military alliances.

The major determinants for the evolution of such a foreign policy in the post-colonial phase can be identified as follows: First, India was keen to preserve its national interest by keeping away from either the Western capitalist bloc led by the United States or the socialist bloc led by the Soviet Union. Second, having emerged from the slumber of colonial exploitation, the adject poverty of the country posed a serious challenge to the evolution of a foreign policy which would substantially depend on both the blocs in order to spearhead its economic and industrial development. That's why, a mixed economy approach suited the policy planners. Third, India having emerged as a major Third World country wanted to play its role for a peaceful world order which would logically abhor violence and always support a peaceful settlement of international disputes. War was not going to be used as an instrument of its foreign policy though our foreign policy at that point of time was not passive in the sense that Nehru's India was supportive of the major UN peace-keeping role in Korea, Hungary, Congo and elsewhere. The major setback to the foreign policy came at the time of Sino-Indian border conflict in 1962 when India was ignored by both the capitalist and socialist power blocs and a humiliating defeat exposed the country's earlier claim to play a global role in view of its subcontinental size and a glorious past. In spite of such a major setback, India did play a pivotal role in spearheading the Afro-Asian movement which ultimately crystallized as a Third World Solidarity at various global forums like the UN and the Commonwealth of Nations. The emergence of the Non-aligned Movement (NAM) as also a by-product of that solidarity. During the 1950's and early 1960's, India also played an active role in the process of decolonization and the fight against apartheid—then prevalent in South Africa and Namibia.

Finally, although at the early stage, India wanted to improve its image in the immediate neighbourhood which was marked by some abbreviations here and there. For instance, the emphasis of Panchsheel in India's dealing with neighbours, especially China, is a case in point signed in 1954 by Jawaharlal Nehru and Zhou Enlai, the then Prime Minister of India and China respectively. It emphasized mutual respect for each other's integrity and severity, non-aggression, non-entrance with each other's internal affairs, equality and mutual benefits, and peaceful coexistence. But the Hindi-Chini bhai-bhai phase in the last stage of Nehru years soon gave way to mutual tensions over the MacMahon Line and it resulted in a limited war between the two countries during 1962. India's relation with another important neighbour like Pakistan remained tense during the Nehru phase and even there-after. Although India's bilateral relations with the other South Asian neighbours like Nepal, Bhutan and Sri Lanka by and large remained cordial, Nehru's spontaneous reaction to the

Royal Coup in Nepal during December 1960, brought some irritants to Indo-Nepal ties. Even the issue of according citizenship to the Tamil Plantation workers in Northern Sri Lanka created some tensions between India and the island republic. However, it was sorted out to a certain extent during the short tenure of Lal Bahadur Shastri as India's Prime Minister (June 1964 to January 1966) when the Sirimavo-Shastri Accord was signed between the two countries.

## THE CONSOLIDATION PHASE: SHASTRI TO INDIRA

When Lal Bahadur Shastri took up the stewardship of the nation, the Indian image abroad was at a low key. Nehru's dream of peaceful world order with a historic role for India remained shattered. The country was facing a belligerent neighbour (Pakistan) with overt support from some external powers (China and the US) and the Soviet Russia was at best a fence-sitter. Shastri lost no time to consolidate the Indian defence force on the one hand and mend India's broken links with immediate neighbours. India during his tenure, gave a befitting reply to a belligerent neighbour like Pakistan when during the limited war in September 1965, the Indian army almost reached the outskirts of Lahore before cease-fire could be declared under the auspices of the United Nations Security Council. The Tashkent Declaration which was brokered by the Soviet Union and signed between Field Marshal Ayub Khan and Lal Bahadur Shastri on 10 January 1966, provided for (i) restoration of normal and peaceful relations between India and Pakistan, (ii) restoration of their obligations under UN charter to settle their disputes through peaceful means, (iii) agreement to base their relations on the principle of non-interference in the internal affairs of each other, and (iv) meetings at the highest and other levels on matters of direct concern to both.

In this effort to inject a dose of positive bilateralism in India's foreign policy, Shastri signed an agreement with Sirimavo Bhandarnaike, the then Prime Minister of Ceylon (now Sri Lanka) in October 1964. Under the Agreement, out of the 7,75,000 India Tamil settlers in Sri Lanka, 3,00,000 were to be granted Sri Lankan citizenship and 3,25,000 were to be repatriated to India within a period of 15 years. The status and future of the remaining 1,50,000 Tamils was to be settled later. Any assessment of Lal Bahadur's foreign policy would require a mention of his maiden broadcast to the nation on 11 June 1964, when he said: "We all seek friendship and develop our relations with all countries irrespective of ideology or their political system.... We conceive of Afro-Asian solidarity not as an end in itself but as a means for achieving certain noble objectives.... The problem that mankind faces today is the achievement of peace and disarmament. Indeed what a realistic and down-to-earth statement which is even more relevant in the present global environment.[7]

Mrs. Indira Gandhi during her long tenure as India's Prime Minister (1966-79) and (1980-84) further consolidated India's image as a formidable leader of the emergent Third World. When she successfully hosted the seventh non-aligned summit in New Delhi in 1983, she injected a fresh blood to a sick movement. She indeed transformed the NAM as the greatest peace movement of the world. Even if she was perceived as authoritarian by a section of the Indian elite, she emerged as a true champion of anti-imperialism, world peace and the national liberation movements the world over. She was also instrumental in correcting the coloured image of India by the Western powers, especially the United States. After the liberation of Bangladesh, in which India played a catalytic role, Richard Nixon the, then US President and his Secretary of State, Henry Kissinger, considered India to be a "new Influential".

Although India was alleged to harbour a "pro-Soviet" title in her foreign policy, given the threats to India's security at that point of time—especially from the neo-imperialist Western powers backing the so-called "Islamabad-Beijing-Washington triangle", New Delhi had no other viable alternative.

At the thick of the civil war in Pakistan during 1970-71, the Indo-Soviet Treaty of Friendship, Peace and Co-operation was signed in 1971 and it remained valid for 20 years. It provided that the two countries (India and erstwhile Soviet Union) would keep in touch with each other on major international problems affecting the interests of both the parties. "They will not enter into or participate in military alliance which is directed against any one of them. They will abstain from providing assistance to any third party that emerged in armed conflict with one of them. If any of the two parties is attacked, both will hold mutual consultations in order to remove such a threat and take effective measures to ensure peace and security of the countries. Neither of the parties shall enter into alliance, secret or public, which is incompatible with the treaty.

Another major landmark of Indira Gandhi era was the signing of the Shimla Agreement. Even at her moment of glory after the dismemberment of Pakistan in 1971, she proved to the rest of the world that she would not be lacking in her initiative for peace, even with a hostile neighbour. The Shimla Agreement signed between India and Pakistan in July 1972 provides as follows: (i) Both the parties would resolve their differences by peaceful means through bilateral negotiations. Both committed themselves to peaceful coexistence, respect for each other's territorial integrity, sovereignty and non-interference in each other's internal affairs. (ii) Hostile propaganda against each other would be stopped. (iii) Meeting between the Heads of Governments and their representatives of the two countries would be convened to discuss future ways and means for the establishment of durable peace and normalization of relations. As the present Indian government is seized with the hostile propaganda and covert interference by Pakistan in the internal affairs of India, Shimla Agreement needs to be read between the lines in order to comprehend the double standards of Islamabad in its dealings with New Delhi.

## THE JANATA PARTY GOVERNMENT—MENDING FENCES WITH NEIGHBOURS

During the brief Janata party rule (1977 to 1979), there was a dramatic U-turn in India's neighbourhood diplomacy. The Morarji Desai government maintained a studied silence, when the military regime, headed by Zia-ul-Huq, after a farcical trail by the Pakistan Supreme Court, hanged the ousted premier Zulfiqar Ali Bhutto. The Janata government's indifference to such a 'judicial murder' was calculated move to improve India's links with the immediate neighbours. Such a policy is comparable to the delayed reaction of the Deva Gowda government to the merciless public hanging of former Afghanistan President, Nazibullah, by the Taliban-led rebel government in Kabul.

The Morarji government, in order to inject a dose of positive bilateralism, signed the hitherto unthinkable Salal Dam Agreement with Pakistan. It also signed an Agreement with Bangladesh for equitable sharing of Ganga waters between India and Bangladesh. Two separate agreements on trade and transit were signed with Nepal. Thus, in all sincerity, efforts were made by the then External Affairs Minister, Atal Behari Vajpayee, to improve India's ties with the South Asian neighbours. The Janata Government's efforts to normalize relations with China, did not bring enough dividends and Vajpayee's China visit was mistimed in the sense that during that period, China launched an offensive against Vietnam.

Another novel experiment during the Janata Phase was the so-called "genuine non-alignment" or a policy of equidistance between the two superpowers. But in reality, the Desai government soon realized its futility, when the Jimmy Carter government in the US refused the shipment of enriched uranium to Tarapore plant on the ground that India was non-committal to the signing of the NPT and was "insensitive to human rights violations in Kashmir".

## THE GLOBALIZATION DRIVE

The world witnessed unforeseen changes in the undercurrent of international politics since the end to 1980s, as has been discussed at the outset and accordingly leaders like Rajiv Gandhi and Narsimha Rao decided to get rid of the old dogmas. India's development strategy was radically changed. New Delhi decided to favourably respond to global market forces especially when Manmohan Singh took charge as the Finance Minister in the Rao Cabinet. Successful techniques were evolved to get rid of so-called "Hindu rate of growth". The Indian economy was deregulated to the maximum possible extent, as a result of which the rate of per capita growth, which never crossed 2 per cent figure in the past four decades, started showing an upward swing to the extent that many western observes started calling India as the future "Asian tiger". The spree for liberalization and globalization brought India closer to the major global economic powers like USA, Canada, Germany, France, UK, Italy and Japan. New Delhi could also improve its political and trade relations with China, another emergent Asian tiger. However, while developing India's close links with major global powers, India's image in the Third World and in the NAM suffered a relative decline.

## THE GUJARAL DOCTRINE

The United Front Government headed by Deva Gowda and thereafter Inder Kumar Gujaral inhered a stable economy with a comfortable rate of growth. The position of foreign exchange reserve showed over the years a considerable improvement. Inspite of some tensions among the coalition partners about the internal issues of political corruption, autonomy of the provinces, demand for new states, management of the public sector undertakings and allocation of resources between the Union and the States, the Government could achieve a broad consensus on foreign policy and security issues not only among the United Front partners, but also between the government and the opposition. It was clearly demonstrated when all the major political parties like the Congress and BJP unanimously supported the Indian Government's opposition to the so-called Comprehensive Test Ban Treaty (CTBT) at the negotiation stage in Geneva and at the time of voting against a resolution in the UN General Assembly.

This solid domestic, consensus and the economic improvement enabled the United Front Government to earn respect abroad. When the then Foreign Minister, I.K. Gujaral, visited South-East Asia in 1996, S. Jayakumar, Foreign Minister of Singapore, while welcoming Gujaral on behalf of ASEAN on 24 July said, "India stands today as a strong economy with a GNP of more than US $280 billion and an enormous potential for rapid growth in terms of GNP (India is now ranked fifth in the world). You can provide the ASEAN with vital links to the

Indian Ocean. ASEAN, on the other hand, can be India's spring board into the Asia-Pacific. It would be hard to imagine an Asia-Pacific century without India's participation." Since 1993, India is a Full Dialogue Partner (FDP) with the ASEAN on sectoral basis. Gujaral, in his replay said, "The footprints of South-East Asia are to be seen in every aspect of India's ethos." He also clearly reiterated the new Government's commitment to achieve rapid economic growth through targeted involvement of foreign capital, technology, goods and services.

### Complete Reappraisal of Our Mission

As regards India's emerging links with the major global powers like the US, Germany, France, UK, Canada, China and Japan, the United Front Government practically continued the earlier policy of mutually beneficial co-operation of crucial issues like trade, FDI and technical assistance. At the same time, the Government reserved its right to take an independent stand on global and regional security matters including nuclear non-proliferation. However at this point, several critics attacked the dismal performance of our diplomacy in a race with Japan for a non-permanent Asian seat at the UN Security Council. The very fact that New Delhi could not muster the support of more than forty member-states, showed the need for a complete reappraisal of our mission at the UN and in other global forums.

## INSTALLATION OF DEMOCRATIC AND FRIENDLY GOVERNMENTS

The above-mentioned diplomatic fiasco notwithstanding, the United Front Government will be remembered for its impressive record of improving relations with the neighbours. The United Front Government's Foreign Minister and thereafter its Prime Minister, I.K. Gujaral, achieved this through his innovative policy known as the Gujaral Doctrine. This policy was based on two basic assumptions: Firstly, India being the most powerful country in the region, should not insist on strict and immediate reciprocation from its smaller neighbours for its goodwill gestures. Secondly, Indo-Pakistan relations being a very complex, one should be regarded as a separate category and first priority be given to improving less problematic relations with neighbours like Bangladesh, Nepal and Sri Lanka. Gujaral, for example, concluded the Farakka Agreement with Bangladesh by agreeing to provide more Ganga water to Dhaka and thereby earned the goodwill of this neighbour. While the installation of democratic and friendly governments in Nepal, Bangladesh and Sri Lanka in the 1990s facilitated the task of Gujaral, first as Foreign Minister in the V.P. Singh Government and thereafter as the author of the Gujaral doctrine in the United Front Government, his contribution in improving India's ties with these countries through his tactful and farsighted approach cannot be gainsaid.

## More Continuity than Changes

### *New World Order and the Need for Foreign Policy Reorientation*

The 1990s is considered as an important decade of this century for the dramatic transformation. It has brought about all over the world. The pace of change has been far too swift for any conceptual interpretations. These changes have transcended all geographical and ideological boundaries, and have put questions to long established perceptions and theories. The Cold War that lasted for well over four decades between the two superpowers has ended and has ushered in the so-called new world order.

- The collapse of the Soviet Union that brought the end of cold war and the consequent end of in polarism
- The emergence of a uni-cum-multipolar world where there are various new centres of power, though US still has the dominant power variables at its command
- The sudden emergence of geo-economics as the primary factor governing politics among states, as apposed to geo-political or geo-strategy, and related to this globalization on a truly global scale
- Loss of maneuverability for the non-aligned bloc as a consequence of fading pre-polarism.

The changes have been so enormous that the foreign policy and security establishments around the world are stipulating on revision. India's defence and security exports are also gearing up for addressing to new problems and issues generated by the external events. There is a need to have a fresh look at our foreign policy.

New equations, new priorities of the powers that concern India, India's interface with the global economies in its liberalization efforts all have to be taken cognizance of.

The changed international political architecture has affected India economically, geo-strategically, regionally, and from the security perspective. The macro level issues which confront India are:

(a) The increasing and collective pressure by great powers on non-proliferation, arms control, and disarmament issues.

(b) The international trends generated by some countries to control and deny access to sophisticated technologies in the super of space exploration and satellite developments.

(c) To ensure projection of India's economic potential in a manner where the necessary external contributions to Indian economy will continue.

(d) Issue of more immediate concern like:
- the onslaught of world public opinion against the recent nuclear test
- managing the impact of sanctions in the wake of the Pokhran tests
- managing the persistently adversarial relationship with Pakistan
- pressure on human rights issue
- pressure on opening up of Indian economy by world bodies
- preparing India for the next century.

The years 1998-2007 marked a turning point in India's foreign policy as the BJP-led coalition Government of Atal Behari Vajpayee assumed power amidst apprehensions of a right-wing lurch in India's domestic and foreign policies. The conducting of five nuclear tests by the government in May 1998, confirmed this fear and shattered domestic consensus in foreign policy. These tests also isolated India at the international front.

A careful look at the government's policy, however, reveals more continuity than changes. This is evident from the fact that the Vajpayee Government is not only made attempts to improve India's ties with neighbours, but it even mustered courage to talk to Pakistan on the hard core issue of Kashmir, which Gujaral had avoided. At the same time, the government attempted to strengthen people-to-people contacts between the two estranged neighbours through opening up of the New Delhi-Lahore bus service and encouraging India-Pakistan cricket matches despite strong opposition from its partner, the Shiv Sena and by reducing visa restrictions. Even the nuclear tests were in fact, the culmination of several previous regimes' strenuous effort towards this end. Unfortunately, like previous governments, the Vajpayee government, too, could not melt the ice in India-Pakistan relations. Though India could frustrate Pakistani designs in Kargil, Islamabad's military rulers are engaged in anti-India activities.

The BJP-led Government's ambiguity towards the Non-aligned Movement (NAM) also reflected continuity than changes in India's foreign policy in the post-Cold War era. Like the Narasimha Rao and United Front Governments, the Vajpayee Government, too, made serious efforts to improve its ties with US led Western power block without formally jettisoning the NAM. Vajpayee and his Foreign Minister Jaswant Singh have thus displayed understanding of the imperatives of the post-Cold War world in which NAM has lost its dynamism and vitality even though its agenda still remains relevant.

## INDIA'S FOREIGN POLICY: ACHIEVEMENTS AND FAILURES

The foundations of India's foreign policy were laid during the freedom movement. It is the product of a complex interplay of history, geography, past experience, present requirements, perceptions of the ruling elite of national interests and ideological consensus. It is also shaped and moulded by the domestic balance of forces, and the regional balance of forces. History and geography give continuity to foreign policy, domestic and international circumstances produce changes. Prof. M.S. Rajan (*India's Foreign policy in the New Millennium*), Prof. Girish Mishra (*Globalization and India: Some Implications*), Prof. Rakesh Gupta (*Foreign Policy in the Last Decade*) have interpreted their views relating to future of India's foreign policy in *World Focus* (Vol. 20, Oct.-Dec. 1999). Prof. Morgenthau is of the opinion that national interest is the driving force behind a country's foreign policy. The principles of India's foreign policy have stood the test of time a belief in friendly relations with all countries of the world, the resolution of conflicts by peaceful means, the sovereign equality of all states, independence of thought and action as manifested in the principles of non-alignment and equity in the conduct of international relations.

## CHALLENGES BEFORE THE INDIA'S FOREIGN POLICY

Across the world today, there are different sensitive issues standing before our foreign policy objectives.

They are:

- terrorism is now under current
- environmental problem has vitiated the atmosphere of India's foreign policy
- human rights violation is now at stake
- state sovereignty is under siege, both domestically and externally
- confusion in arms control agreements. Collective pressure by great-powers
- volatile and uncontrollable global financial market conditionalism
- the emergence of super-national regional groupings
- cross-border criminality
- the influence of satellite television
- anarchy of the internet.

The principles and operation of India's foreign policy have been subjected to much criticism. These are:

- It has been pointed out that too much importance has been attached to idealism

- The policy of non-alignment pursued by India has been subjected to criticism
- India's membership of the commonwealth has also been a subject of much criticism. It is alleged that this has restricted the freedom of action and prevented the country from pursuing an independent foreign policy
- It is alleged that India has completely neglected the vital principle of power in the conduct of international relations and laid more emphasis on peaceful settlement of international disputes
- The foreign policy has failed to produce the desired results. India has not only failed to set the Kashmir issue resolved but also protect the people of India from policy of discrimination being pursued by South Africa.

## CENTRALITY OF INDIA IN FOREIGN POLICY OBJECTIVES

### Rise of Asian and African Nations

The Indian policymakers could rightly visualize the rise of Asian and African nations in international relations as independent sovereign states. They always viewed Indian Independence as a great sign of the rise of Asia. As such, they gave full attention to the cause of peace and unity in Asia which later on got developed into the concept of Afro-Asian unity for peace and progress. The concept of Third World unity for peace and progress emerged as a further extension of the concept of unity with newly emerged independent and developing nations. Being an Asian country, and because of the common objectives of anti-imperialism and anti-colonialism among the countries of the Third World; and also became the common need for, socio-economic development through mutual co-operation. India has always identified herself with the Third World. The Indian foreign policy has been a champion of the cause of the Third World unity and co-operation for development. In the earliest stages of the evolution of Indian foreign policy, its chief architect, Nehru realized the importance of Asia and Africa for India and *vice versa*. Pt. Nehru observed in his speech on 7th September 1946, "We are of Asia and the people of Asia are nearer and closer to us than others." In 1947 itself, India hosted the Asian Relations Conference in New Delhi. The conference passed a resolution against Dutch attack on Indonesia. It raised voice for the elimination of imperialism and for the need to secure active contacts among the Asian nations. By 1954, Indian foreign policy had started supporting the principle of unity of Asia and the settlement of Asian problems by the Asian nations, i.e. the support for the end of the superpower and outside interference in the affairs of Asia. The objective of Asian unity was prompted not by the desire of India to dominate Asia but by the desire to make Asia play its due role effectively towards the promotion of world peace.[8] Nehru categorically stated this when he observed: "We meet in no spirit of hostility to any nation or group of nations but in an endeavour to promote peace through the extension of freedom."

**Autonomy of our Decision-making**

While addressing the Shanghai Institute of International Studies on 11th January 2006, the foreign secretary of India, Mr. Shyam Saran touched almost all aspects of India's foreign policy. He observed, "India has maintained a remarkable continuity in the fundamental tenets of its policy. The core of this continuity is to ensure autonomy of our decision-making. This was and remains the essence of our adherence to the principle of non-alignment. It is also the basis of our commitment to the Panchsheel.... "Other key elements of continuity include, maintenance of friendly relations with all countries, resolution of conflicts through peaceful means, and equity in the conduct of international relations.[9] There is also a solemn commitment to pursue an independent foreign policy, promote multi-polarity in world relations and oppose unilateralism." "India is committed to strengthen multi-lateral institutions and mechanisms as this approach was deemed indispensable for meeting global challenges such as terrorism, proliferation of weapons of mass-destruction, pandemics like HIV/AIDS or avian flu and drug trafficking. It was also needed most for securing the pooling together of scientists and technological achievements and collective wisdom of peoples around the world in overcoming the scourge of poverty, disease and environmental degradation. India believes that UN Security Council must, in its composition, reflect the contemporary geo-political realities and not those of 1945. Its actions must be representative legitimate and effective and its methods of work and decision-making processes more democratic, transparent and responsive. "India with its large population, dynamic economy, long history of contribution to international peace-keeping and other regional and international causes, deserves to be a permanent member of the UN Security Council. Currently 'Look East' policy is a vital part of India's foreign policy. And India has been actively engaged in creating a bond of friendship and co-operation with East Asia that has a strong economic foundation and a co-operative paradigm of positive inter-connectedness of security interests."

### Unity of the Third World

This statement clearly summarizes the main features of Indian foreign policy in the contemporary times. Later, this concept of unity and peace in Asia was extended to cover Africa also. In April 1955, the first conference of the Afro-Asian Nations—the Bandung Conference, was held and an important step was taken to secure Afro-Asian solidarity. India played a key role in this conference. Panchsheel was adopted by the conference. The main purpose of this conference was, as Dr. Baljit Singh says, "to promote and consolidate economic, cultural and political co-operation between the nations of Asia and Africa and to pursue a common policy against imperialism and colonialism in all its manifestations". The conference heralded a new era of Afro-Asian solidarity and helped the consolidation of Afro-Asian power in the United Nations. The emergence of the concept of the Third World and its unity became possible, because of the strength and popularity of Afro-Asian solidarity movement. India belongs to the Third World. The unity of the Third World, its struggle to secure its due rights from the developed countries, and its commitment to the cause of mutual friendship and co-operation among the countries of the Third World have been the goals very dear and important to the Indian foreign policy. It stands committed to the cause of Third World unity in its struggle to achieve her rights, particularly a new international economic order based upon fair and equitable distribution of world resources between the developed and the developing countries. As a member of the G-20, India has been actively trying to project the interests and needs of the developing countries. Now, India has been quite successfully trying to secure the rights of the developing countries in the WTO.

### New Mantra 'Politics Through Economy'

As world's largest functioning democracy and as the second fastest developing economy, India has been now stepping up its economic diplomacy in international relations. Indian foreign policy has now fully accepted the new mantra 'politics through economy'. It fully upholds the new thinking that development of high-level socio-economic-cultural relations and co-operation constitutes the best means for resolution of political conflicts and disputes. India has been now getting engaged in the development of trade, economic, business and industrial relations with other key players. Indo-European Union economic relations have been now developing in a bigger way and there exists a strong possibility of Free Trade Agreement with the EU. Likewise, India has been developing her trade relations with ASEAN, countries of East Asia, particularly Japan and South Korea. India has been trying to develop high-level economic relations with regional groupings and organizations like BIMSTEC, IORARC, SCO, EAS, APEC and others. India's trade with China, Russia, Japan, ASEAN countries has been now speedily expanding. The USA also regards India as an emerging economic power. The Indo-US nuclear deal, emergence of trade in dual use technology and developing defence and strategic co-operation are decidely going to give a further push forward to Indo-US economic, trade and business co-operation and strategic relations. In fact, India's foreign policy is now trying to project India's economic potential as an IT power and knowledge power for securing the goals of India's national interest, which includes the goal of getting recognition as a great power in international relations, capable of performing a bigger role in sharing international responsibilities.

### Friendship with All Particularly with the Neighbouring Countries

The Indian foreign policy stands for friendship with all. India sincerely believes in the principle of working for friendship with all the countries on the basis of sovereign equality without any discrimination on the basis of the ideological or geographical differences. Except for the boycott of the racist regimes, the Indian foreign policy is always at work to develop friendly and co-operative relations with other countries. India has been a friend of both the communist and non-communist countries. India does not believe in permanent-enemy logic and is prepared to settle the bilateral disputes/problems through mutual efforts. Non-alignment, Panchsheel and faith in peaceful settlements of disputes are principles designed to help India in achieving its objective of securing friendship and co-operation with other nations. Particularly in respect of her neighbours, India has always been keen to develop further her friendship and co-operation. India is the biggest country of the South Asia and with the progress secured thus far in the sphere of Industrial and technological development, has the potential to be a big power, yet the Indian foreign policy has never tried to assume the role of a big brother in relation with its small neighbours. On the contrary, it has always been committed to the development of highly co-operative social, economic, political and cultural relations with her neighbours. Through the Shimla Agreement of 1971 and a number of other normalizing measures, like the agreement to have a Joint Indo-Pak Commission, Joint anti-terrorism mechanism, India has been keen to develop good neighbourly and mutually beneficial relations with Pakistan. Indian foreign policy has also been very considerate to the needs of other neighbours. Nepal, Bhutan, Myanmar, Bangladesh, Sri Lanka and Maldives. It has been developing strong trade, business and economic relations with all of these. India is fully committed to develop SAARC and to faithfully follow SAFTA.

## INDIA'S FOREIGN POLICY OF 21ST CENTURY

India's foreign policies cannot be made captive to the delusional non-alignment gladiators or India's Communist Parties who have never been known for their objectivity or to India's minority Indian Muslims vote banks where every issue is viewed in a pan-Islamic context. In today's global security environment and the international strategic realities likely to persist for the next 50 years, India neither has the luxury nor the time to find new anchors for her foreign policies from the fossilized remains of Nehruvian Non-Alignment or her "presumed power potential" not concretized so far. In the last eight years, the centre-piece of India's foreign policy has been the evolution of a strong political and strategic partnership with the United States. United States and India recognized the mutual convergences and imperatives and have been engaged in establishing a substantive bi-lateral relationship. It is the best policy of India. It has combined the twin principles of idealism and pragmatism.

Now in the 21st century, India's foreign policy is marching towards:

- sustained economic growth
- universalization of human rights
- democratic politics and social empowerment
- globalization
- environmental protection
- I-T and women's empowerment

## SUGGESTIONS: WAY OUT

- We should ensure continuity, unity and territorial integrity in India's foreign policy.
- It should maintain peace and stability as an attractive economic partner in the process of global co-operation to meet the aforementioned objective.
- The third suggestion would be to create national defence capacities to protect India's unity and territorial integrity.
- The precautionary step would involve nuclear weaponization and missile policies.
- The fifth objective would be to strengthen regional co-operation and to work for mutually beneficial equations between the South Asian and other regional groups for long-term security.
- The sixth suggestion would be to strengthen the UN, its organs and its specialized agencies.
- The seventh suggestion would be to strong enough in every respect and should attract sufficient voluntary

support from general membership of UN. India beseeching a permanent seat on the security council is not the solution.

- The eighth suggestion is that it would be to undertake the necessary organizational and institutional reforms in the ministry of external affairs on the creation of institutional mechanisms and creation of a national security council.
- Last suggestion should be a focus on dealing with macro-level problems such as population control, environment management and economic development.

## Conclusion

India's national security and economic interests dictate that India's national aspirations can best be met by formulating India's foreign policy inter-dependent with United States national interests and not in opposition to it. In the last decade of the 21st century the world is undergoing dramatic transformation. This current change in the global milieu is one of the most crucial turning points in independent India's foreign policy. India is now passing through a period that requires a careful assessment of opportunities and priorities, pending the making of a new foreign policy framework.

## NOTES

1. J.K. Baral, "The US-India Nuclear Diplomacy", *Indian Journal of American Studies* (Hyderabad), Vol. 14, No. 2, July 1984, pp. 129-44; P.S. Jayaramu, "Superpowers and the Changing International System: A Third World Perspective", *India Quarterly* (New Delhi), April-June, 1982, pp. 148-51.
2. For India's view of non-alignment, see A.P. Rana, *Imperatives of Non-alignment* (New Delhi, 1979); K.P. Mishra, "India's Nonalignment: Perspective and Tasks," in U.S. Bajpai, ed., *Nonalignment: Perspective and Prospects* (New Delhi, 1983), pp. 75-83; A.K. Damodaran, "India and Nonalignment" in K.P. Mishra, ed., *Nonalignment: Frontiers and Dynamics* (New Delhi, 1982), pp. 203-14.
3. Sarair Arain, "After the New International Economic Order: The Future of International Economic Relations" in U.S. Bajpai, ed., *Nonalignment: Perspectives and Prospects* (New Delhi, 1983), pp. 201-17.

4. I. Kende, "Twenty-five Years of Local Wars", *Journal of Peace Research,* Vol. I, pp. 5-22. Quoted in Ajami, n. 20, p. 101.
5. Vernon V. Dyke, *International Politics* (New York, 1957); Abba Eban, *The New Diplomacy* (New York, 1983); Herbert, Feis, *Foreign Aid and Foreign Policy* (New York, 1964); Joseph, Frankel, *The Making of Foreign Policy* (New York, 1963), p. 89.
6. R.L. Rothstein, *The Scientific Study of Foreign Policy* (New York, 1971), p. 8.
7. K. Subramanyam, ed., *Nuclear Myths and Realities: India's Dilemma,* Oxford Press (New Delhi, 1981), p. 9.
8. M.S. Agwani, "West Asia: Humiliation Far from Home", *World Focus* (New Delhi), January 1985, p. 9.
9. Fouad Ajami, "Third World and World Order", *Alternatives* (New Delhi), Vol. II, 1976, p. 7.